FIELDBOOK FOR CANADIAN SCOUTING

www.scouts.ca

ISBN 1-894187-00-8   Cat No. 20-667   Printed in Canada

ACKNOWLEDGMENTS

Scouts Canada would like to thank the following people, groups or organizations for their terrific help making this book possible:

The 63rd Scout Troop (Ottawa, ON), for acting as models during our photo shoot.

The Scout Shop, for supplying materials for the photo shoot.

Trailhead/Blackfeather, for supplying materials for the photo shoot.

The Canadian Recreational Canoe Association, for assistance with the Canoeing chapter.

Denis Bourque, from Environment Canada, for help with the Weather chapter.

The Canadian Red Cross, for copyright permission and assistance with the Water Safety chapter.

St. John Ambulance, for copyright permission and assistance with the First Aid chapter.

Copyright permission from:
Camping's Little Book of Wisdom
Canoeist's Little Book of Wisdom
Camping Life Magazine

From left to right:
Valerie Valieres
Glen Sauve
Amanda Hardy
Matthew Forgie
Chris Cody
Steve Sauve
Kneeling:
Billy Cody
Matthew Clark

FOREWORD

What does "the outdoors" mean to you?

It means different things to different people. For some, it's a way of life — how they make a living. For others, it's their "escape" from the world's hustle and bustle.

Awareness and appreciation for the outdoors also varies from person to person. As well, it may change throughout the year as busy schedules and other interests push "the outdoors" into a back corner of our mind. But, occasionally it's good and healthy to set aside hectic agendas and spend quality time in the outdoors. When we do, our horizons expand as we're reminded that far greater powers than ours are at work; we're but small players in a much bigger picture.

Developing a greater awareness and appreciation for the outdoors is an excellent way of developing one's own character. This relates well to Scouting programs and our Mission Statement: **To contribute to the development of young people in achieving their full physical, intellectual, social and spiritual potential as individuals, as responsible citizens and as members of their local, national and international communities through the application of our Principles and Practices.**

Scouting's Practices are a system of progressive self-education that include:

▲ A Promise and Law

▲ Learning by doing

▲ Membership in small groups

▲ Progressive and stimulating programs

▲ A commitment to the values of doing one's best, contributing to the community, respecting and caring for others, and contributing as a family member

▲ Using outdoor activities as a key learning resource.

The outdoors provides a setting and a focus for all Scouting programs. The Beaver Promise highlights this commitment well; children promise to love God and help take care of the world — a pretty simple statement with profound implications!

We are only here a short time as caretakers, but every one of us has a profound responsibility to preserve and protect Earth's resources for the prosperity and enjoyment of future generations.

INTRODUCTION

Ask youth why they joined Scouting. Most will say, "To go camping!"

From its very beginning, Scouts Canada has actively supported camping experiences among members as a regular part of our programs. This proud tradition continues today. In fact, coast to coast whenever Canadians think about camping, they think about Scouting. That's our national image!

Lord Baden-Powell (Scouting's founder) considered camping a great opportunity for leaders and youth alike. "In camp you will learn more about your boys in a few days than in many months of ordinary meetings," he said.

Scouts Canada strongly supports B.-P.'s opinion of camping and the outdoors. In fact, Scouting's policy statements reflect his thoughts: "(C)amping and outdoor activities are essential parts of the programs..." and "(E)very member has the right to the opportunity to participate in camping and outdoor activities."

To provide these opportunities, leaders require varying degrees of attitude, skills and knowledge relating to the outdoors. This book is designed as a resource for both youth and adults as they plan and prepare for exciting, outdoor adventures.

Note: Use *The Fieldbook for Canadian Scouting* with *Scouts Canada's By-law, Policies and Procedures* and the *Scouts Canada's Camping/Outdoor Activity Guide.* Be sure to follow local Scouting policies and all Canadian laws when enjoying the outdoors.

TABLE OF CONTENTS

CHAPTER ⓵

▶ Before Setting Out

Leader Note

Scouts Canada has developed *By-law, Policies and Procedures* and the *Scouts Canada Camping/Outdoor Activity Guide* to help leaders prepare and deliver their programs and activities safely. All leaders must be aware of these, and any other policies and procedures put in place by their local Scouting councils. This information is available at your local Scout Shop or council office. As well, you must know the federal or provincial laws governing outdoor activities.

Before you embark on a weekend outing to a nearby park or a month-long northern wilderness adventure, your first step involves research. Find out as much as possible about everyone's skills and abilities, and your proposed route. This increases your chances for a safe and enjoyable outing.

According to *Webster's Dictionary*, research involves "careful, systematic study and investigation in some field of knowledge." In Scouting, you'll learn about (research) the great outdoors and your own attitudes, skills and knowledge. You'll discover ways to safely introduce Scouting youth and adults to fun, challenging experiences. The information you gather will help you plan and shape excellent programs and activities that will inspire everyone to grow as individuals. The key is to have people with the right equipment at the right place at the right time.

"Research" sounds tedious, but we research different things every day without realizing it. One of the first things people do in the morning is look outside to check the weather; then we head to the kitchen where we inspect the fridge and cupboards to see what's available for breakfast.

Why do we follow this particular sequence? It helps us plan our day. It's research!

For a successful outdoor adventure, you need to conduct similar research. This helps you prepare a safe and enjoyable trip. If we forget

to check the weather forecast before heading off to school or work, and don't dress for the imminent rain, we'll probably just get wet. We may not escape as easily during an outdoor wilderness trip many kilometres from civilization. Consequences can be far more severe!

For many youths and some adults, Scouting provides their first taste of the outdoors. Experienced young people and leaders responsible for introducing "new recruits" to outdoor life should list everyone's questions and concerns — an important step in your research. Get everyone involved asking questions and providing planning input. All members will then understand the group's plans so they can prepare themselves.

Are there other benefits to involving everyone in the planning? You bet! Group planning increases everyone's interest and enthusiasm. It starts to build a team spirit for your adventure. Many people find that half the fun of a trip occurs while they research and plan.

Usually, your questions will focus on six helpful words: who, what, why, when, where, how. The scope of your questions will differ, depending on who asks them (e.g. parents, youth, group committee, local commissioner), and the kind of outing.

Here are some topics to consider:

Who?

▲ Who will go on the trip?

▲ Who will be the first aider?

▲ Who will lead the trip?

▲ Who must approve the outing?

▲ Who is coordinating the adventure?

▲ Who will carry the maps?

Where?

▲ Where will we go?

▲ Where is the nearest hospital?

▲ Where can we get the equipment we'll need?

When?

▲ When will we go?

▲ When are the leaders available? The participants?

▲ When will we return home?

What?

▲ What will we do when we get there?

▲ What knowledge and skills will we need?

▲ What clothes, footwear or equipment will we need?

▲ What will we eat?

▲ What qualifications and experience do the leaders have?

▲ What are Scouting's policies for the outing?

▲ What permits and permission will we require (e.g. fire permits, land owners' or parents' permission)?

▲ What are the skills and capabilities of the group?

▲ What experience does the group have?

▲ What is our emergency plan?

▲ What fears or reservations do the participants have (e.g. getting lost, wild animals, darkness, thunder, lightning)?

▲ What will we sleep in?

▲ Will we be accessible by phone? What is the number?

▲ What is the weather forecast?

▲ What risks or hazards are we likely to encounter?

▲ What is our risk management plan?

How?

- ▲ How will we get there?
- ▲ How far will we travel?
- ▲ How long will we stay?
- ▲ How old will the participants be?
- ▲ How much will it cost?

Why?

- ▲ Why are we going?

A Healthy Investment

When working with a new or inexperienced group, spend extra time doing research. Try dividing your group into smaller segments, giving each one different items to study. Have them report back to the entire group. Once you've completed your research, you might produce a page describing the adventure and answering the questions everyone asked. This information will help participants and their parents. You may also refer to it when you plan future adventures.

Once you've researched and experienced a trip or two, you'll build up a "file library" of great information. This will save you research time for future trips. Once your group begins to develop confidence and skill in the outdoors, you will probably find them yearning for new, more challenging adventures. At this point you've successfully "set the hook." Group members will now be keen to test themselves, their skills and their abilities.

Invest as much time as necessary in your research phase; it could make the difference between a safe, enjoyable experience, and a miserable one!

CHAPTER ②

▶ Planning Your Adventure

What Is Planning?

"To devise a scheme for doing…" — that's the definition found in *Webster's Dictionary*.

Planning involves taking all the information about your trip (gathered from research) and developing a "plan" for an outdoor adventure. It involves making decisions about where, when, why, who, what and how the adventure will happen. In this planning stage, you'll make travel arrangements, collect necessary approvals, and decide who is responsible for doing what. You'll also finalize your overall program for the trip — what will happen during the adventure. Your plan should give you all the directions necessary to ensure a safe, fun, challenging experience.

Trail Tip:
Involve the youth in the planning stages of outdoor adventures. Encourage them to develop their own check lists, risk awareness plans, etc.

Here are some important details to consider:

▲ Distance and time

▲ Safety

▲ Potential risks

▲ Risk management

▲ Risk assessment

▲ Emergency plan

▲ Contingency plan

▲ Common sense

▲ Goals/objectives

▲ Themes

▲ Tour permits

▲ Informing parents

▲ Camp costs

▲ Duty charts

▲ Checklists (things to do and needed equipment/supplies).

Distance and Time

Most people hike at approximately five km per hour. (**Note:** Difficult or unexpected terrain, like rough trails or steep hills, can cut your speed significantly.) Use your watch to measure the distance you travel: one hour for five km; 25 minutes for two km; 12 minutes for one km; and three minutes for 1/4 km. If you want to hike to a point 10 km from your home, it will take you approximately two hours of walking time. Add three rest periods of five minutes each, and your total outbound time will be about two hours, 15 minutes.

Always allow more time than you think you'll need when planning a hike.

Remember to file a trip plan with someone which identifies: where you are going, names of participants, when you expect to return, and other important details. Then, stick to your schedule, unless circumstances dictate otherwise.

(**Note:** A group can only travel as far and as fast as its slowest member is willing and able to go.)

Safety

Safety is a key issue to keep in mind when planning outdoor activities, particularly those that will take place far from emergency support services, vehicles, phones or hospitals. Before heading out on any outing, make sure

you're equipped to respond to unexpected accidents. Every group must have first aid equipment appropriate to the activity, and people who know how to use it. In fact, individuals should carry their own personal first aid kits customized to their personal needs. (This might include special medication, puffers, etc.) However, these people should share the knowledge of their special medication with the event leader and first aider.

Trail Tip:
Check survival and first aid kits to make sure medications have not expired.

Naturally, first aid kits are more useful if people know exactly how to use them. Everyone taking part in an outdoor adventure should know first aid basics — especially the leaders. A number of organizations and agencies provide excellent training. Why not enroll your entire leadership team?

Scouts Canada produces a *Camping/Outdoor Activity Guide* to help leaders plan and conduct outdoor programs.

Risk Assessment and Management

One of the most important elements of any outing plan should include assessing and managing risks. What does this involve? It simply means identifying potential risks and taking the necessary precautions to eliminate, minimize or manage the risks to ensure the group's safety.

Risk Assessment

All outings involve risks. In fact, many people find activities more appealing and challenging as the level of risk increases.

An important part of research involves identifying potential risks and hazards that you may encounter. Make a list of everything that could go wrong, and decide how you would respond to each difficulty. Drawing up this list is a great activity for your entire group. Involve everyone. Not only will the exercise underline the importance of safety, but everyone will be able to think out their own reaction before encountering the potential dangers. In fact, one of the first steps of effective risk management involves helping your group understand all aspects of the outing, including the risks.

Trail Tip:
If new to the outdoors, hook up with another group for your first few outings or hike/camp close to home until your confidence and skills are sufficient to travel further.

For starters, you'll want to know as much as possible about the route. Consider these questions.

▲ How long is the route?

▲ What is the approximate travel time?

- ▲ What skill level or capabilities are required?
- ▲ How will weather affect the adventure?
- ▲ What equipment is required?
- ▲ What obstacles may be encountered?
- ▲ Are there any other potential hazards or risks?

Because routes change over time, be sure to speak to others who have recently been to the area, hiked the trails, or paddled the river. Maps, pictures, books written about the area, and park staff are also helpful. If you're really concerned whether the area is suitable for your outing, have a leader check it out before embarking on your trip.

Risk Management *"Hope for the Best, Plan for the Worst"*

Once you have identified potential problems, decide whether group members have the attitude, skills and knowledge for the outing. Here's your goal: achieve an "acceptable" balance of safety and risk. If in doubt, *always err on the side of caution.* Cancel or postpone the trip until the group acquires the necessary skills or the concern has been removed.

After assessing the risks, your outing may appear to be beyond your group's capabilities. But you don't necessarily have to cancel it indefinitely. The adventure might be within safe reach after spending more time in preparation, training, or even by adding extra skilled adults or equipment.

Potential Risks

Railroads

Avoid hiking along railway lines and use extreme caution when crossing.

(**Note:** Many abandoned railway lines have been converted to bike paths or hiking trails. These are great for outings.)

Trail Tip:
Use common sense. Know your limitations and travel safely.

Roads

If you have to travel along a road, choose secondary roads rather than main highways. Walk in single file along the left shoulder facing oncoming traffic.

Night Hikes

Many people enjoy night hikes. Conduct these as you would a day hike, but wear light-coloured clothes or light-reflecting bands to make yourself visible. Carry a flashlight, and aim it down in front of you. Never flash it directly at a car because it might blind the driver and cause an accident.

Hitch-Hiking

B.P.&P. states: "Hitch-hiking is a form of begging and is not permitted."

Poison Ivy, Poison Oak, Poison Sumac

Poison ivy, poison oak and poison sumac can ruin any outdoor experience. Learn to recognize them, and then stay clear. If you do happen to contact one of these plants, wash the affected area with soap and water. If you dab on some rubbing alcohol, it'll soothe the itch. (See Chapter 7 for pictures and more information.)

Thunderstorms

Thunderstorms can be both frightening and dangerous. If you're caught in one, stay away from large trees that are standing in the open. Also, avoid hilltops and rock ledges; lightning often strikes these targets. You'll be fairly safe if you take cover in dense woods or groves of young trees. When walking in an open flat area, remove your pack and crouch down, making yourself as small as possible. *Never lie down on the ground in a lightning storm.* Lying on the ground makes you a "bigger" target for ground currents.

Emergency Plan

Part of risk management includes developing an emergency plan. It should answer all the "what if" questions that could occur. When you develop one, share it with all members of the trip; it's vital that participants know how to act during an emergency. Your plan should include:

▲ Scouts Canada permission slips, physical fitness forms complete with phone numbers where parents/spouses could be reached and other medical information.

EMERGENCY PLAN

An emergency plan will provide the leaders with the necessary information about the youth and the leaders and an action plan to follow in the event of an emergency:

The leadership team must have:

1) A current Physical Fitness form for each individual and leaders.

2) A Parent/Guardian Consent form for each youth. This includes a phone number where parents may be reached if necessary. Check Scouts Canada's web site at www.scouts.ca

3) Emergency phone numbers pertinent to their location for: Police, Fire, Ambulance and Poison Control.

4) Directions to the nearest hospital or health care facility.

5) At least one adult with the appropriate First Aid certification and equipment appropriate to the activity.

6) A method or plan for communications.

7) Evacuation plan.

8) Accident Reporting/Recording Procedures.

9) Leaves with responsible person at "home" the following: trip plan, map, list of names, phone numbers, start/finish points and times.

10) Emergency repair kits where appropriate. (ie for bicycles, stoves, tents, canoes etc.)

ACTION PLAN

In the event of an emergency the leaders have:

- identified potential emergencies and determined the appropriate response for each including, identifying who will take control
- developed an action plan to follow

For example, in the event of physical injuries:

The most qualified person available takes control until medical personnel arrive. This person will:

- assess nature of the accident and the extent of the injury or injuries.
- direct other leaders to call for appropriate assistance and to manage the crowd.
- treat or oversee treatment of casualty/casualties; this continues until medical personnel arrives
- document and report incident.
- evaluate the accident for future prevention.

- ▲ Phone numbers for emergency response personnel in the area you will be in.

- ▲ First aid kit, equipment, and trained staff.

- ▲ Evacuation plan including where to meet if the group gets separated.

- ▲ Communication: cell phone, radio, whistle, flare, fire, signal mirror.

- ▲ Accident report forms and procedures to follow for reporting emergencies and/or accidents and "near misses."

- ▲ Accurate route plan complete with the names of all individuals on the trip.

Contingency Plan

Don't let the words "contingency plan" scare you. All it means is "Plan B" — a strategy to follow in case you must change the original plan. Your "Plan B" might only involve setting a rain date.

Many things can happen that might increase risk thereby pushing your trip into a high danger zone. For example, the weather could change your plans as could a serious rock slide or forest fires. Try to anticipate these difficulties before going, and identify appropriate responses for each. Let everyone know what would happen in the event of a first aid emergency (for example), so all are prepared for "Plan B."

Common Sense

Don't forget to take along a healthy amount of common sense on your trip. Listen to common sense whispering in the back of your mind. It should always have the final word. Sure, it's sometimes fun to "conquer the challenge" and let your excited emotions carry you along, but these emotions can cloud judgement and get you into trouble fast in the wilderness.

Common sense rarely shouts out a warning. Tune your ear to its wisdom. Weigh its advice, and use it to guide your actions.

Goals and Objectives

Many outings have pre-determined goals or objectives, such as reaching a certain peak, testing skills while working on badges, or completing a hike over a specific distance. Outings with goals and objectives are usually more structured because they focus on completing certain tasks. Involve each group member when setting your goals;

otherwise they may be out of reach for some youths. Getting together to develop goals will build team spirit and commitment in the outing.

Often, large groups will share an overall goal, but members will set individual achievement goals. Recognize this reality before setting out so everyone has adequate time to experience the thrill of realizing their dreams.

Trail Tip:
Provide opportunities for youth to explore, experience new challenges and develop new skills. Be prepared to support their interests.

Themes

A group may wish to choose a theme around which to build the outing; this may increase the thrill and excitement. In some cases it can provide a reason for the adventure. Beavers or Cubs might choose "Fall Colours" as their theme and then try to see and find as many different coloured leaves as possible. At the end of the hike, they'll probably want to take leaves back to their meeting place for waxing and placing in a scrap book.

A "Prospector" theme might intrigue Cubs, Scouts or Venturers. It could incorporate elements of mapping, compass, hiking, mineral identification and cooking. The program links are endless.

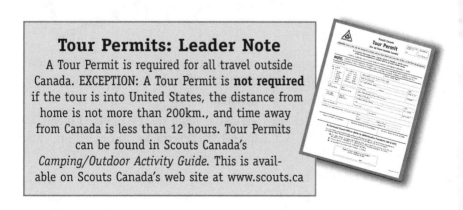

Tour Permits: Leader Note

A Tour Permit is required for all travel outside Canada. EXCEPTION: A Tour Permit is **not required** if the tour is into United States, the distance from home is not more than 200km., and time away from Canada is less than 12 hours. Tour Permits can be found in Scouts Canada's *Camping/Outdoor Activity Guide*. This is available on Scouts Canada's web site at www.scouts.ca

Informing Parents - Parental Permission

Keep parents informed about any outing, regardless of location or duration. Send a note to each youth's home containing relevant information, including:

▲ Equipment/clothing list

▲ Dates of the outing

▲ Location, mailing address of the camp and phone number

▲ Names of leaders

▲ Cost

▲ Method of travel

▲ Program highlights

Rather than a note, you many choose to invite parents to an information evening.

Forms: Important Leader Note

Leaders planning and conducting outdoor programs should consult *Scouts Canada's Camping/Outdoor Activity Guide* for accepted practices and policies, forms and applications. This also includes Scouts Canada's Physical Fitness Certificate and Parent/Guardian Consent Form. Check Scouts Canada's web site at www.scouts.ca

Camp Costs

How do you decide how much a camp will cost? It can be a tough question. Here are some guidelines that will help you estimate camp costs.

Estimated Cost of Food

Before you can calculate food costs, you'll need a planned menu. Use the "Serving Guide" (see Chapter 4) to determine your menu and quantities.

Campsite Charge

Most camps charge a fixed fee per camper per night, and require an advanced booking for group campsites. Call the camp office for details.

Rental or Equipment Purchase

A well-equipped group may not need to consider this budgetary item. If you do, then seek the best price possible.

Transportation Costs

Fuel and transportation costs can really add up quickly. Consider asking parents to provide the transportation. If you charter a bus, make sure the rental company maintains its vehicles well and provides adequate insurance.

Special Activities

Do you plan to visit an attraction or a special activity? If yes, consider the added expense. Don't forget about entrance fees and special equipment.

Crafts, Prizes and Miscellaneous Items

List all "incidentals" here, including costs for prizes, competitions, crafts, first aid supplies, and anything else.

5% - 10% Contingency

Everyone needs a safety net; a contingency fund is your safeguard. Add the first six categories and determine your contingency fund. Use this when unforeseen costs arise.

Subtract any donations and grants received, as well as proposed fundraising amounts, from your cost estimate and divide the balance by the number of expected participants. This will give you the cost per participant.

During the camp, someone should keep an expense account (including receipts) and make a report to the group committee after the event ends.

Work out a proposed fundraising schedule after you have your proposed budget. Do this as soon as possible. If you submit a yearly plan to your group committee in September, it'll give members plenty of opportunity to raise the money. How can you involve both group committee members and the youth? Popcorn sales, calendar sales, handicrafts, bake sales and Scoutrees are all effective fundraising methods.

Who Does the Chores?

It doesn't matter whether a camp is for Beavers, Cubs, Scouts, Venturers or Rovers. Expect everyone to help with housekeeping tasks, meal preparation, and kitchen duties. Assign tasks on the basis of capability; even the youngest and smallest members can do something to help. Campers are responsible for washing their own personal dishes. Do this before kitchen dishes get washed.

The sample roster below is set up for a unit of six, camping for five days. Adapt it to suit your section and your camp.

Duty Roster

Name	Sat.	Sun.	Mon.	Tues.	Wed.
	Cook	Water	Site clean-up	Free	Fire lighter
	Assist cook	Cook	Water	Site clean-up	Free
	Fire lighter	Assist cook	Cook	Water	Site clean-up
	Free	Fire lighter	Assist cook	Cook	Water
	Site clean-up	Free	Fire lighter	Assist cook	Cook
	Water	Site clean-up	Free	Fire lighter	Assist cook

What are a cook's or fire lighter's duties? Here are some ideas. (See "Teamwork" in Chapter 4.)

Cook

▲ Prepares and cooks meals.

Assistant Cook

▲ Helps the cook

▲ Before everyone eats, puts a large pot of water on the fire to heat for dishwashing

▲ Arranges dishwashing production line and prepares rinse water with bleach solution

▲ Washes, rinses and dries kitchen pots, pans and utensils used for meal preparation.

Fire Lighter

▲ Lights fires

▲ Prepares kindling and wood

- ▲ Maintenance of stoves, lanterns
- ▲ Refuels stoves and lanterns, and safely stores fuel.

Site Clean-Up

- ▲ Keeps campsite tidy
- ▲ Removes obstacles and hazards
- ▲ Ensures site is returned to its original state.

Water Person

- ▲ Gets drinking water (purify if necessary)
- ▲ Gets wash water.

Each Person

- ▲ Sweeps out tents
- ▲ Hangs sleeping bags and pyjamas on line to air in morning
- ▲ Places all sleeping bags, clothing and gear neatly in tents during afternoon.

Note: If you're cooking over wood fires, add the duties of a woodsman. Tasks include collecting, cutting and stacking wood, as well as keeping cutting tools (axe, saw) sharp and properly covered when not in use. The fire lighter would help the woodsman.

Checklists

Checklists are like grocery lists; identify everything you require and write it down. You may have a number of different lists: a "to do" list, personal equipment list, group equipment list, food list and menu, and others.

When making your lists, it's important to identify *who* is responsible for *what*. Don't forget to give them a list of the things that they are responsible for buying or organizing. (Chapter 5 has several helpful checklists.)

Use this basic checklist when you start planning your outing.

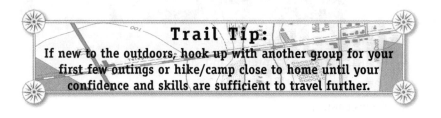

Trail Tip:
If new to the outdoors, hook up with another group for your first few outings or hike/camp close to home until your confidence and skills are sufficient to travel further.

ITEM	WHO IS RESPONSIBLE	✓
Leadership ▲ Consult Scouts Canada's *By-law, Policies and Procedures* and *Scouts Canada's Camping/Outdoor Activity Guide*.		
Administration ▲ Group committee approval ▲ Local council approval ▲ Scouts Canada camp application and safety checklist completed ▲ Notice to parents ▲ Scouts Canada Physical Fitness Certificate ▲ Tour permits ▲ Insurance ▲ Fire permit ▲ Local regulations ▲ Outing fees ▲ Contact names and numbers for parents ▲ Checklists for parents, youth, leaders ▲ Contingency plan prepared		
Transportation ▲ Arrangements completed for pickup and drop-off		
Campsite Selection ▲ Council camps ▲ Municipal, provincial/national parks ▲ Private sites		

ITEM	WHO IS RESPONSIBLE	✓
Equipment ▲ Personal ▲ Group ▲ Program resources ▲ Emergency		
Feeding ▲ Menu planning and budgeting ▲ Shopping ▲ Food preparation/ packaging ▲ Food storage ▲ Cooking		
Sanitation ▲ Drinking water ▲ Dish washing ▲ Garbage disposal ▲ Grey water ▲ Human waste		
Safety/First Aid/ Medical Attention ▲ Weather ▲ Risk management ▲ Emergency plan ▲ First aid skills and equipment		
Program ▲ Games/activities ▲ Skill training ▲ Badge training ▲ Fun or free time ▲ Program resources required		

CHAPTER ③

▶ Preparing Your Adventure

"To make ready…" — that's the definition of "preparation" found in *Webster's Dictionary*.

The preparation phase is a time of real excitement! Anticipation will start bubbling as your imagination soars. All of a sudden, you'll "see" yourself having fun in the outdoors, experiencing new adventures.

Preparation can involve many aspects. You might need to physically attune your body to the rigours of a long hike by doing a series of short hikes with a pack and your new hiking boots. Perhaps some members of your group will have to learn or improve specific skills which they'll need on the outing (e.g. compass, first aid, knots). Everyone will need to prepare food for snacks and meals, and eliminate all excess equipment.

Doing your "homework" will put you in a better position for a successful trip. Following are some helpful hints that will make your trip more pleasurable.

Outline

Prepare an outline of your outing that describes:

▲ Where you're going

▲ Details of your planned route

▲ Specific activities planned during the trip

▲ Departure and return times (specifying locations).

Draw the route on a map, indicating anticipated campsites, stops, access points, etc. Leave a copy of this map at home with an emergency contact person.

Equipment/Clothing

Have you or other group members ever contemplated an outdoor adventure as ambitious as this one? If not, you may want to bring in an experienced outdoor specialist to help demonstrate techniques and how to choose special equipment/clothing. Don't fall into the trap of thinking you need the latest (usually very expensive) high tech clothing and equipment. Find experienced adult leaders or Venturers who have discovered how to "make do" with readily available supplies. Invite parents to a meeting to find out about the trip and to ask questions. This will help when they're deciding what new equipment/clothes their youth need. Parents will have a better idea which items are a "must have," and which are a "would like to have." (See Chapter 5 for more information.)

Trail Tip:
When buying equipment, ask about warranty. Avoid products that have no warranty.

Trial Run

There's nothing as effective as a trial run to work out the "kinks" in your preparations. Plan a trial run to:

▲ Test equipment

▲ Test the group's abilities

▲ Practise old skills

▲ Develop new skills

▲ Fine-tune equipment lists.

Very quickly a trial run will reveal exactly how good each person's equipment is as well as potential weaknesses. It's much easier to find out what equipment and clothing each youth has by conducting a trial run, than by discovering it when you're in the wilderness. You will also learn how well the various members can pack and carry their load.

Trail Tip:
Put items in plastic bags or buy a rain cover for your pack to keep items dry.

For your trial run, everyone should arrive fully prepared for an overnight outing. Divide up the patrol gear and have each member add their share to their personal gear. (A youth's pack should be *no more than 25-30 percent* of their body weight.) Hike a short distance (1 km), then stop and ask everybody to unpack their gear on a ground sheet for a leader to check. When you've completed the check, read off the items on your list in the order that they should be placed in the packs. Get members to reload their packs.

Some people may have items left on their ground sheet when the list is complete. Ask them, "Is the extra weight essential for the trip, or simply a 'nice to have' luxury?" Everyone should then walk back to the meeting place with their reloaded packs. Those who are carrying extra items will have an opportunity to rethink their decision to haul the extra gear — a good reality check.

This trial run will be helpful when fine-tuning suspension systems on packs, redistributing weight, and identifying how well each person is able to manage with a loaded pack. (See Chapter 5 for more information.)

Whether planning a short afternoon outing or an overnight trip, you'll want to keep several items close at hand, either in a small fanny pack, day pack or in the top of your backpack. These may include: an extra sweater, rain gear, extra socks, quick energy food, trail mixes, a full water bottle, a small emergency/first aid kit, sunscreen, insect repellent, a map, a flashlight, whistle, pocketknife, and other essentials.

Post Trip Check

After each trip, empty your pack and gear into three piles:

1. Gear used every day.
2. Gear used a bit.
3. Gear not used.

Are there any items in the third pile you can leave behind?

Equipment Check

Before the trip, break in and test new equipment so you're sure it works properly, and you know how it works.

Check all your clothing and equipment for readiness. Here are some points to emphasize:

▲ Check lantern mantles, and replace if necessary.

▲ Refuel and test stoves and lanterns to ensure that they're in proper working order. Are the pumps well lubricated?

- ▲ Clean and waterproof your hiking boots.

- ▲ Clean water filters, and make sure they're working properly.

- ▲ Waterproof tent seams.

- ▲ Check clothing/equipment for rips and tears.

- ▲ Check the power level of flashlight batteries.

- ▲ Check your toilet paper supply. Is it in a waterproof bag?

- ▲ Sharpen knives and axes.

- ▲ Pack extra garbage bags so you're prepared to clean up litter you may find along the way.

- ▲ Make sure your emergency/first aid kit is fully stocked.

Food Preparation

You can prepare many food items prior to leaving. Doing so will reduce weight, as well as preparation and cooking time. Here are several tips:

- ▲ Remove all excess packaging, like bulky cardboard. Repackage food in resealable freezer bags or vacuum sealed bags.

- ▲ Buy at bulk food stores. It's less expensive and less wasteful.

- ▲ Does your group want to pre-cook food at home? This can save time and fuel while on the trail. (See Chapter 4)

Trail Tip:
Practise cooking and preparing meals in
the comfort of your own home.

Other Hints and Tips

▲ Decide what clothes you'll wear the next day and stuff them
along with your sleep wear inside your sleeping bag.

▲ Pack each meal separately for quick and easy access.

▲ Pack each day's meals together in one bag.

▲ Pack related items together in separate colour-coded (or labelled)
stuff sacks. For example, pack all your toiletries in one bag, and
all your seasonings and items needed for meals in another bag.

Lost in the Outdoors

Even an experienced camper can get lost, especially if the person fails
to take proper precautions. If you follow these rules, you'll reduce the
risk of getting lost.

▲ Before setting out, learn as much as possible about your route.

▲ Learn how to use a map and compass, and carry them with you.

▲ Follow your progress on your map so you always know where
you are.

▲ Watch for unusual trees, plants, rock formations and other
distinguishing landmarks as you travel. Look back to see how
these landmarks will appear on your return trip.

- Stay on existing trails when possible and within boundaries set by your leaders.

- Stick closely with your group or your "buddy."

Make sure everyone on the trip has the right attitude, skills, knowledge and equipment. Here are some additional tips that will keep you out of trouble:

- Give someone staying at home a map that shows your route, where you plan to camp each night, as well as when you're leaving and arriving back home. Stick to the plan unless conditions require that you use Plan B, your Contingency Plan.

- Dress appropriately for the weather and trail conditions. Wear a hat.

- Carry extra water, a sweater, and rain gear in a small backpack or fanny pack, even on short trips.

- Learn what steps to take if you become lost. An excellent program called "Hug a Tree and Survive" is available through your local Scout Office or RCMP detachment.

Survival Kit

Each person should carry a personal survival kit that includes:

- Waterproof matches or a lighter
- Compass
- Adhesive tape and bandages
- Medication
- Fire starter material
- Pocketknife
- Large yellow or orange garbage bag or a space blanket (for shelter and warmth)

- ▲ Whistle (pealess ones work best)
- ▲ Snack (granola bars, etc)
- ▲ Reflector/signal mirror

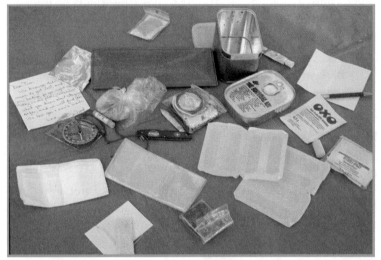

- ▲ Insect repellant
- ▲ Ointment
- ▲ Bandaids/Moleskin™
- ▲ Water purification tablets
- ▲ Bouillon cubes
- ▲ Fishing line, hooks and lures
- ▲ Duct tape
- ▲ Two to four metres of light flexible wire (for making snares or shelters)
- ▲ Pencil and paper
- ▲ Aluminum foil (two sheets, five metres long) to make cooking pot and drinking cup, or for signalling.
- ▲ An encouraging, short note from mom or dad giving instructions on what to do if lost in the woods.

Store these items carefully in a small metal container, one which could be used to cook in or gather water, if necessary.

Survival kits are fun projects for everyone. But time spent identifying how to avoid getting into situations where they might be needed is just as important.

If One Person Gets Lost

Before your group sets out, talk about what you'll do if someone gets separated from the rest. If it's a short hike, your plan may simply involve meeting back at the car; if it's a longer hike, you may decide to meet at some other agreed-upon location.

Trail Tip:
Carry a whistle. Attach it to your pack, PFD, or jacket zipper.

If you're travelling in a group and notice that one member is missing, notify the leaders at once. The group must stop immediately and try to determine when and where the person was last seen and what the person

was wearing. Next, retrace your route. It's possible that the person simply stopped to take a photograph or to look at something interesting.

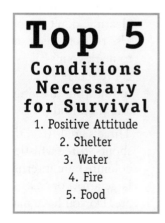

Top 5
Conditions Necessary for Survival
1. Positive Attitude
2. Shelter
3. Water
4. Fire
5. Food

When someone fails to show up within a reasonable period of time or if it's getting dark, notify local authorities immediately. Don't conduct your own search unless your group has had the proper training — one missing person is too many.

If You Get Lost

If you get lost on a wilderness trip, stay where you are and let search and rescue experts find you. As soon as people notice that you're missing, they'll start looking. The best way to help them is to stay put.

Tips to Remember

1. As soon as you recognize that you're lost, STOP! Sit down. Look around you for recognizable landmarks. Take out your map and try to locate your position. If you figure out exactly where you are, then you aren't lost. Use the map to return to your route again. If you can't decide where you are, stay put and don't panic. Wait for help.

2. Focus your thoughts. Adopt a positive attitude.

3. Keep warm and dry. Use your garbage bag (in your survival kit) as a temporary shelter to protect you from wind and rain.

4. Look around for a clearing or opening in the trees where you can make yourself visible to rescue helicopters. If you must walk around to find a clearing, don't go too far. Use twigs to make arrows to mark your trail as you go. Rescuers will be able to find your markings, and then find you.

5. Three signals (e.g. three shouts, three whistle blasts, three mirror flashes, three smoke columns) are internationally recognized distress calls. Make a large arrow or SOS sign in a clearing to indicate where you are. Do you have matches or a lighter? Build three small fires

approximately two metres apart to make three separate columns of smoke. Create lots of smoke by burning green boughs. Be careful to contain fires in fire pits to prevent them from spreading.

6. Use equipment in your survival kit to help find, gather and make the survival essentials: shelter, water and food. If you must leave your clearing in search of water or food, mark your trail so you can easily find your way back. Use water purification tablets so you'll have clean water. Don't eat strange-looking berries.

7. If you suspect rescuers won't find you before darkness closes in, build or look for a shelter. Collect enough firewood to last the night. Find a tree you can "hug" that's beside a clearing. This tree will be your friend. You'll be able to sit or lean against it, and it will give shelter from wind and rain. Make sure your tree isn't the tallest one around in case of lightning, and make sure it doesn't have dead branches that could fall in the wind.

After you've found your tree, build a bed or shelter for the night. Use large branches to build a protective framework covered with lots of boughs or leafy branches. Be sure you make a mattress of branches, too. The shelter should be just large enough for you to crawl inside and lie down, or sit leaning against a tree.

When you're ready for bed, tear a small hole in the bottom of a garbage bag large enough for you to see and breathe through. Put your hat on, zipper your clothing up, tuck in any loose ends and crawl inside your shelter. Once inside, pull the garbage bag down over your head and/or wrap yourself inside your space blanket.

8. After you build your shelter and signal fires, empty your pockets and look around you. How can you use these objects to make your forest stay better? Let your imagination loose. Try to have some fun. Why not use your key and a coin for fishing weights and lures? Make that bright-coloured wool into a fishing fly. You've got a pin or piece of wire. Great! Sharpen it on a rock and make it into a fish hook. Paper money can help start a fire.

9. Do you see or hear rescuers? Move quickly to the open area, lie on the ground to make yourself "big" for air rescuers. Wave bright-coloured clothing or blow your whistle. Do anything possible to attract attention of ground rescuers.

Debris Shelters

Anyone capable of piling up sticks, dead leaves and other bits of forest litter lying on the ground can build a debris shelter.

Did you know that a squirrel's nest is just a ball of leaves that creates an insulating dead air space? When temperatures drop, the dead air space helps to conserve body heat; in extreme heat conditions, it insulates and keeps the squirrel cooler.

If lost in the bush, you should build a debris shelter *before* the temperature drops, or the rain and wind starts blowing.

Build your debris shelter by laying a ridgepole on the ground at one end. Lean the other end on an upright stick or in a crotch of a tree. Your ridgepole must be long and high enough that you can lie down underneath on your side without touching it with either your feet or shoulders.

Next, gather armloads of various sized sticks. Start with the larger ones; lean them up against the ridgepole on both sides and down the entire length. (See diagram) Fill in the spaces with smaller sticks until you can't see through.

These sticks are important. They will act like the roof joists of your shelter.

Now, gather armloads of leaves, twigs, boughs and brush that you find on the forest floor. Avoid using living branches or bushes unless it is an emergency.

Pile enough of this material on your shelter roof so you can stick your arm into the wall without breaking through. If the wall isn't thick enough, you won't stay warm and dry.

When you've finished your shelter, make a thick (knee high) pad of soft and dry leaves inside. Pile in lots to make a kind of natural sleeping bag.

Practise building debris shelters on a regular Scout meeting night. Tie it into a "Lost in the Woods" or "Hug a Tree" survival theme. Involve a local Rover crew if possible. (Many Rovers have received special "Hug a Tree" training.) Your group can build debris shelters almost anywhere that has a bit of brush and minimal ground cover.

International Symbols

There are many international symbols that you can mark on the ground to attract aircraft. Symbols must be 15 metres long and three metres wide to be seen from the air. Carry a card with these symbols in your survival kit.

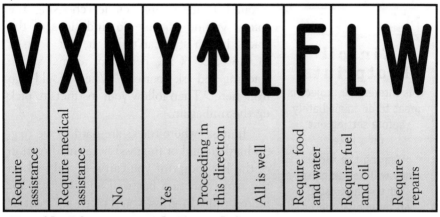

V	X	N	Y	↑	LL	F	L	W
Require assistance	Require medical assistance	No	Yes	Proceeding in this direction	All is well	Require food and water	Require fuel and oil	Require repairs

Trail Signs and Tracking

Trail marking and trail reading are both useful and interesting skills to learn. Start with simple trail signs when hiking and playing games, and then advance to reading and following the tracks of birds, animals, and humans. Can you interpret the stories they tell?

Trail signs can be made with chalk, stones, twigs or grass. When you are finished with your signs, "erase" them.

Tracking Animals

Baden-Powell said, "One of the most important things a Scout has to learn is to let nothing escape his attention. He must notice small points and signs and then make out the meaning of them."

It takes a lot of practice before a person can really start noticing everything.

Just recognizing tracks on a trail is not enough; you must also learn to tell how old they are. Much depends upon the state of the ground and recent weather.

To tell the age of tracks, look for damp ground where the sun or the wind hasn't dried up the imprint. Light rain sometimes provides an excellent clue to help you date a track. Look for places where individual

Tinfoil Footprints

This interesting project is great to do immediately before setting out on a hike.

Wearing the shoes they will be hiking in, get youths to step on individual pieces of tinfoil placed on a folded towel or a piece of carpet. This should leave an imprint of the sole or tread of the shoe. Now label each piece of tinfoil with the youth's name. If someone gets lost, you'll be able to identify that person's tracks immediately.

raindrops have fallen on the track. The rain will have eroded a part of the print.

Have you lost sight of a track? Don't give up. Simply put your handkerchief or a stick in the last print you noticed, then work around it in a large circle, choosing the softest ground possible to find signs of the track. If you still can't find it, put yourself in the place of the person or animal you're tracking and ask yourself, "Where would I go from here?" Then follow your instincts to pick up the trail again.

In areas where tracks are hard to see (e.g. on hard ground or in grass) note the direction of the last footprint you can see, and look in the same direction but well ahead of you for more prints. In grass, you'll often see bent or trodden grass blades; on hard ground, watch for scratched or moved stones. When taken together and interpreted, these small signs tell an interesting story. Watch for these stories and dramas; they're all around you.

Some Tracking Hints

Here's an old tracker's rule. Face the sun when tracking; you'll often be able to see imprint shadows that will give valuable clues. When you've found a track, 'fix' it in your mind.

After you've identified an animal track, try to put yourself into the animal's mind. Ask yourself: Why was it going in this direction? Was it in a hurry, or was it taking its time? Was there a possible attack from a predator from the ground or the air?

The ground's condition — pebbles or stones overturned, damp or dry — may give clues when the animal passed by. In winter, a light fall of damp snow provides the best tracking conditions. In very light snow the wind will soon erase tracks, so with this kind of weather condition you'll have to move quickly after the snow has stopped falling.

Trail Signs

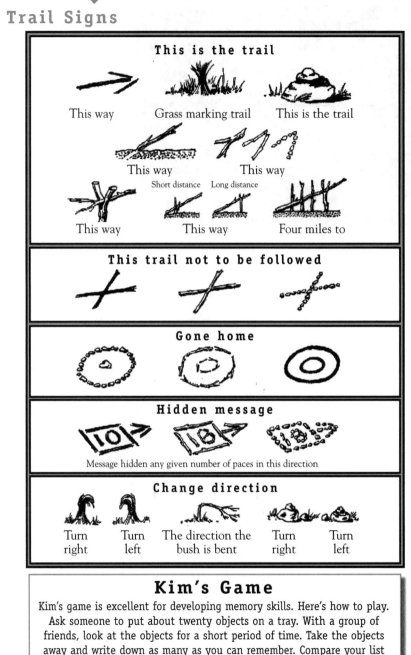

This is the trail

This way   Grass marking trail   This is the trail

This way
Short distance   Long distance

This way

This way   This way   Four miles to

This trail not to be followed

Gone home

Hidden message

Message hidden any given number of paces in this direction

Change direction

Turn right   Turn left   The direction the bush is bent   Turn right   Turn left

Kim's Game

Kim's game is excellent for developing memory skills. Here's how to play. Ask someone to put about twenty objects on a tray. With a group of friends, look at the objects for a short period of time. Take the objects away and write down as many as you can remember. Compare your list with others, and discuss how you remembered the things you did.

1) day pack
2) weekend pack
3) insulated water bottle holder
4) camp fuel with pour spout
5) propane canister
6) flashlight
7) two burner stove
8) assorted pots
9) fry pan
10) griddle
11) assorted eating utensils
12) assorted cooking utensils
13) cooler
14) single burner collapsible stove
15) single burner stove
16) fuel bottles
17) bow saw
18) two burner collapsible stove with fuel bottle

19) duct tape
20) sleeping bag
21) pillow
22) journal and pen
23) toilet paper in zip lock bag
24) lantern case
25) boots
26) water jug
27) water treatment system
28) box of wooden matches
29) topographic map
30) compass
31) jackknife in case
32) whistle
33) small axe and sheath
34) collapsible water jug
35) large expedition type internal frame pack
36) wide brimmed hat

37) nalgene bottles
38) bowl
39) mug
40) dehydrated/freeze dried food
41) therm-a-rest mattress and chair kit
42) small internal frame pack
43) sleeping bag in compression bag
44) tent in a bag
45) aluminum shock-corded tent poles
46) ensolite pad
47) polypropylene socks (wicking)
48) wool socks
49) fleece pants
50) wind pants
51) fleece shirt
52) polypropylene undershirt

CHAPTER 4

▶ Meals and Nutrition

Cooking and eating in the outdoors present exciting challenges, and when you're properly prepared, can provide a pleasant experience. Everything seems to taste better when cooked outdoors!

Fuel for Our Bodies

Fun, challenging activities burn up lots of energy (calories) that must be replaced. In this sense, your body operates much like a car. When a car is just idling, it doesn't burn great amounts of fuel, but as soon as it accelerates, fuel consumption increases. Youth 'idling' at school or at home don't require great amounts of food (fuel), but as soon as they start hiking, playing games, or exploring the outdoors, their bodies burn much more fuel.

Like food, the amount of water a person consumes must increase as physical demands rise. When someone works hard, the body loses large quantities of water. This may be obvious (perspiration) or not so obvious (vapour).

When you plan outing menus, consider the kinds of activities your group will do and the length of time members will be doing them. Are you planning an overnight activity? Then, your menu must include foods that will keep internal furnaces well stoked to get you through the night. Otherwise, nights can be cold and very long! Strenuous and physically demanding programs will naturally require more food, as will outdoor winter activities.

As well as increasing your food intake for these activities, it is important to get the right type of food at the right time. Our bodies burn calories to produce heat and energy. Some foods provide a quick, short-term burst of energy that's great for getting up and over the next hill. Other foods burn much slower providing heat and energy over longer periods of time — great for getting a hiker through a long day. Choose your menus carefully and adjust them to match activity demands. Throughout this chapter we'll discuss specific food types and the short- or long-term energy they provide.

The average Scout-aged youth will burn 1800-2400 calories during a normal day. This calorie requirement will increase to approximately 3000-4000 for a summer camp and 4000-6000 for a winter camp.

Nutrition

You'll meet basic nutritional needs if you choose items from the four groups listed in *The Canada Food Guide*. These include: grain products, fruit and vegetables, milk products, and meat and alternatives. A balanced diet selected from this Guide will ensure that you obtain proper amounts of protein, carbohydrates and fats.

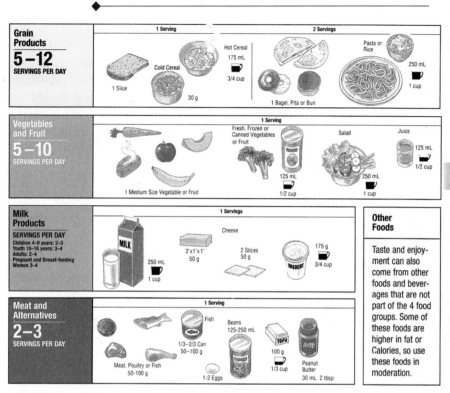

Grain Products

5–12 SERVINGS PER DAY

1 Serving
1 Slice
Cold Cereal
30 g

2 Servings
Hot Cereal
175 mL
3/4 cup
Pasta or Rice
250 mL
1 cup
1 Bagel, Pita or Bun

Vegetables and Fruit

5–10 SERVINGS PER DAY

1 Serving
1 Medium Size Vegetable or Fruit
Fresh, Frozen or Canned Vegetables or Fruit
125 mL
1/2 cup
Salad
250 mL
1 cup
Juice
125 mL
1/2 cup

Milk Products

SERVINGS PER DAY
Children 4–9 years: 2–3
Youth 10–16 years: 3–4
Adults: 2–4
Pregnant and Breast-feeding
Women 3–4

1 Servings
MILK
250 mL
1 cup
Cheese
3"x1"x1"
50 g
2 Slices
50 g
175 g
3/4 cup

Meat and Alternatives

2–3 SERVINGS PER DAY

1 Serving
Fish
Meat, Poultry or Fish
50–100 g
1/3–2/3 Can
50–100 g
1-2 Eggs
Beans
125–250 mL
Tofu
100 g
1/3 cup
Peanut Butter
30 mL 2 tbsp

Other Foods

Taste and enjoyment can also come from other foods and beverages that are not part of the 4 food groups. Some of these foods are higher in fat or Calories, so use these foods in moderation.

Different People Need Different Amounts of Food

The amount of food you need every day from the 4 food groups and other foods depends on your age, body size, activity level, whether you are male or female and if you are pregnant or breast-feeding. That's why the Food Guide gives a lower and higher number of servings for each food group. For example, young children can choose the lower number of servings, while male teenagers can go to the higher number. Most other people can choose servings somewhere in between.

Enjoy eating well, being active and feeling good about yourself. That's VITALIT

© Minister of Public Works and Government Services Canada, 1997
Cat. No. H39-252/1992E   ISBN 0-662-19648-1
No changes permitted. Reprint permission not required.

Serving Guide

This list shows suggested food quantities per person per meal during an active day. Simply multiply the specific quantities by the number of campers in your group to find the total food quantities you need. Keep in mind that older youths will eat much more than younger ones.

Vegetables (Fresh)	
Potatoes:	225 grams (g)
Lettuce:	$1/4$ head
Corn on the cob:	2 cobs
Onions:	110 g
Cauliflower:	140 g
String beans:	110 g
Stewed tomatoes:	170 g
Green peas:	110 g
Carrots:	140 g
Lima beans:	140 g
Spinach:	170 g
Cabbage:	170 g

Fruit	
Grapefruit:	$1/2$
Apple:	1
Watermelon:	90 g
Cantaloupe (medium size):	$1/2$
Orange:	1
Juice:	224 mL
Raisins:	30 g
Applesauce:	225 g

Beverages

Cocoa or chocolate per serving:	15 g
Coffee per serving:	15-30 g
Freshie or Koolaid:	1 package for 6
Tea per serving:	7-15 g

Canned Food

Applesauce, cherries, fruit cocktail:	110 g
Canned peaches:	110g
Pork and beans:	225 g
Corn, peas, carrots:	110 g
Tomatoes:	140 g

Meat

Roasts:	170 g
Baked ham:	170 g
Corned beef:	170 g
Meat loaf:	140 g
Chicken:	200-225 g
Beef stew:	170 g
Hamburger:	140 g
Bacon:	3 slices
Liver:	110 g
Fish fillets:	140 g
Wieners:	2-3
Sausages:	110 g
Pork chops:	195 g
Steak:	195 g
Cold ham:	110 g

Cereals

Dry cereal:	85 g
Oats (porridge):	70 g
Shredded wheat:	85 g ($1^1/_2$ biscuits)

Miscellaneous

Salt:	14 g
Pepper:	7 g
Bread:	2-4 slices
Milk: (powdered milk can replace whole milk for cocoa, porridge, etc.)	750 mL
Sugar:	85 g
Honey:	55 g
Butter/margarine:	85 g
Peanut butter:	85 g
Marmalade or jam:	85 g
Soup (homemade or canned):	224 mL
Soup (dehydrated):	$^1/_4$ package
Eggs:	1 or 2
Macaroni:	70 g
Syrup:	25-40 g
Ketchup:	40 g
Cheddar cheese:	30 g
Spaghetti:	85 g
Rice:	40 g
Flour for griddle cakes:	85 g
Crackers:	2 -3
Pickles:	70 g
Salad dressing:	55 g
Flour for pies:	30 g
Cream cheese:	55 g
Cookies: approximately	3 each

Carbohydrates

Carbohydrates are divided into two categories: simple and complex. Simple carbohydrates (e.g. sugars, dextrose, fructose, glucose) digest quickly and turn into energy, giving the body a quick boost. But they also rapidly burn up and may leave the body tired and needing more food. Complex carbohydrates (starches found in grains, vegetables, legumes) provide more energy over a longer period of time. They give the body needed fibre, vitamins and minerals. Whole grain breads, bagels, cereals, granola, potatoes and pastas are good examples of complex carbohydrates. These provide terrific body fuel for outings.

Because carbohydrates burn up fairly quickly, the body must consume a lot of them to maintain energy levels.

Protein

Protein helps build muscles and body tissues, and speeds the healing of injuries. Foods that contain high protein levels include meat, fish, chicken, eggs, yogurt, cheese, nuts, peanut butter, and salami. Protein uses more energy and takes longer to digest than carbohydrates, but it stays with your body longer and releases energy over a longer period of time.

Fats

Nutritionists agree that most people should reduce the amount of fats in their diet. Saturated fats especially (e.g. butter, cheese, chocolates) should be replaced by polyunsaturated fats (e.g. vegetable margarine). However, nutritionists also recognize the need for some fats in your menu, especially for winter outings.

Your body digests fats slowly. This means that fats do not provide quick energy like carbohydrates. Fats do stay with your body much longer, though. Because fats are stored in your body and release energy slowly, they are probably best suited for activities requiring high energy for long periods of time, like backpacking or active winter outings.

A supper containing some fat will release its energy slowly throughout the night and keep campers warm. If you don't need a quick start in the morning, fat in your breakfast can provide an energy base for the day. Some foods containing high fat levels include butter, nuts, cheese, and bacon.

Water

Outdoor activities require plenty of water for cooking, washing and drinking. Although you can manage without food for a surprisingly long time, this does not apply to water! Your body is more than 70 percent water. Since it uses and loses water at a great rate, you need to constantly replenish your body to prevent dehydration.

How much you require per day varies from person to person, and depends on the weather and the kinds of activities you are participating in. Most people need four to six litres per day for light activity, and up to nine for hot, high activity days.

Drink water regularly; dehydration can sneak up on you. Some warning signs include: thirst, a sticky feeling inside your mouth, low urine output, and dark coloured urine. Dehydration can cause depression, poor judgement, slowed muscle response and a host of other problems that can ruin your trip.

To prevent dehydration:

▲ Carry one or two litres of water — more if your next water source is unknown or far away.

▲ Break for snacks and drinks regularly (at least once per hour).

▲ Drink before you are thirsty.

Years ago our grandparents could simply dip their cups into a bubbling brook for a cool, refreshing drink. Times have changed. Health Canada encourages people using the outdoors to boil, chemically treat, or filter all water. In the Department's words: "Canadian wilderness waters are generally of excellent quality, but... no surface water can be considered safe for human consumption without treatment."

Take these words as a caution; don't let them scare you away from outdoor adventures.

Lightweight campers and day hikers entering the wilderness should either carry drinking water from home or have the means to treat water they use. Let's take a closer look at the reasons for these precautions.

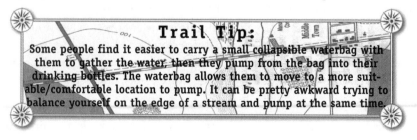

Trail Tip:
Some people find it easier to carry a small collapsible waterbag with them to gather the water, then they pump from the bag into their drinking bottles. The waterbag allows them to move to a more suitable/comfortable location to pump. It can be pretty awkward trying to balance yourself on the edge of a stream and pump at the same time.

Bacteria, viruses and protozoan cysts (minute organisms) may contaminate open water. Disease-causing organisms (pathogens) can turn a fun, relaxing trip into a pretty uncomfortable and miserable experience.

Giardia lamblia is a dangerous protozoan commonly referred to as "Beaver Fever." Beavers, as well as other animals, defecating into or near water may cause contamination. The Giardia parasite is a microscopic creature which enters the human digestive system as a cyst. Once in the stomach, the cyst releases a parasite that attaches itself to the intestinal wall. A Giardia cyst may be as large as 8-12 microns, but it can manage to fit through a hole as small as 5 microns. (One micron is one millionth of a metre or one thousandth of a millimetre.)

Giardia's symptoms include stomach cramps, diarrhea, gas and fatigue. These symptoms generally appear about one week after drinking the contaminated water.

A person needs only to drink a few cysts to contract the disease. After someone drinks contaminated water, the cyst reproduces itself, increasing in numbers until it causes sickness. At this point, the person becomes a disease carrier and continues to be, until the disease either runs its course or a doctor's prescription kills the protozoan.

Cryptosporidium or "Crypto" is another protozoan found in the wilderness. Slightly smaller than Giardia, Crypto (4-6 microns) may fit through a hole as small as 3 microns. Like Giardia, Crypto is caused by animals defecating into or near the water. Crypto's symptoms are very similar to Giardia's, but they can also include a low fever. Those who get this disease must simply let it run its course (approximately one week).

Everyone should practise good hygiene around camp, especially near food or water sources, because someone with either of these illnesses can pass it on to others.

Campers and hikers can ensure clean drinking water by using many methods, including boiling, chemicals, filters, and purifiers.

Boiling

"Heat is the oldest, safest and most effective method of purifying water," according to Health Canada. Boiling water for at least five minutes will kill bacteria, viruses and cysts. (Health Canada advises you to add *one minute* of boiling for each additional *300 metres* above sea level.) If you choose this water treatment method, be prepared to carry plenty of fuel, allow time to boil the water and let it cool. It's an excellent method for most outdoor camping, especially for base camps.

Trail Tip:
Use a wind screen and covers on your pots to make the most efficient use of your stove.

Chemicals: Chlorine and Iodine

Chlorine and iodine are the two most frequently used chemicals. Hikers can use chlorine bleach by adding it to water — two drops of bleach for every one litre of water. Shake the solution well, then let it stand for 30 minutes before drinking. Choose bleach that is not more than a few months old.

If you're using chlorine tablets, follow instructions on the container label. Make sure the tablets haven't reached their expiry date.

Iodine is also an effective water purifier. Eight to ten drops of two percent tincture of iodine or one iodine tablet will disinfect one litre of water. When using iodine crystals, follow printed instructions on the label. Keep iodine away from children. It's toxic!

Health Canada does *not* recommend anyone using iodine for more than three weeks. Don't let young children or pregnant women use this method as they are particularly sensitive to iodine.

Chemicals may leave an unpleasant taste in the water, but you can mask this by adding juice crystals, coffee or tea.

Filters

Filtering systems physically remove dirt, dust and dangerous elements by pumping water through a canister containing a fine screen. When selecting a filter, make sure it has an absolute pore size of 0.3 microns or less, and follow instructions closely to achieve maximum performance. (The absolute pore size is the largest hole in the filter which will allow water to pass through.)

Purifiers

These devices combine a filtering system with chemicals to destroy pathogens.

Water Summary

Campers can remove bacteria effectively by boiling, adding chemicals (chlorine or iodine), using purifiers or filters. Viruses can be removed by boiling, adding chemicals, or using filters with an absolute pore size of 0.3 or less.

In Canada, because our main concerns centre on bacteria and Giardia, the best methods to ensure clean water involve boiling for at least five minutes, or using filters or purifiers.

Most experienced hikers and lightweight campers carry two or more litres of water from home to get them started; then they filter the rest as they go, stopping whenever they find a suitable water source. They try to carry one or two litres of water at all times, especially when travelling in unfamiliar areas. (**Note:** Take special care to keep your water bottles and water filters clean and in proper working condition.)

As tempting as that clear, bubbling little stream may appear, don't risk drinking from it directly. Spend a few minutes to treat the water first.

"Dining Out"

The kind of food and cooking method you use when camping will vary according to the outing you've planned. A backpacking meal might consist of a simple "just add water" cup of soup, and a bagel on the side of the trail. A base camp meal might involve a gourmet turkey dinner, complete with stuffing and gravy, with a freshly baked pie for dessert, served on a perfectly-set picnic table in a dining tent.

Preparing and eating outdoor meals doesn't have to be an ordeal. It can be most satisfying. Practise your cooking skills at home, helped by parents or experienced friends. This will minimize your frustration when the closest electric stove is 50 km away.

Price and weight: these are two factors that might affect your meals and equipment. Some dehydrated meals and equipment are fairly expensive. But you can make your own dehydrated food, backpack stove, and reflector oven at home to soften the financial "pain." Weight is an ever-present concern for backpackers. Follow this rule of thumb when making a menu: two pounds of food per person per day.

"He who has the most money and most modern equipment," the saying goes, "is not necessarily the best-fed camper." Most seasoned campers can whip up some pretty amazing meals in their blackened old pots over glowing campfire coals.

If you are staying at a campground where you can drive right to the site, your group can bring pretty much whatever it wants; this might include coolers, barbecues, stoves and even heavy Dutch ovens. If your group is canoeing with few or no portages, you can load the canoes up with most of these same luxuries. Of course, backpacking means you're limited to whatever you can carry on your back.

When staying at a campground, preparing meals is fairly convenient; you may choose to prepare and eat three full meals per day. But when canoeing or lightweight camping, you may choose to prepare a good breakfast and supper with frequent snacks along the way, instead of stopping to prepare lunch. Unpacking gear and cooking can take a big "bite" from your day.

Breakfast

Most campers start their day with a good breakfast. This builds a solid energy base. Breakfast may be the most important meal of the day, especially when youth are participating in rigorous outdoor programs.

Fruit, a drink and a main course make a healthy breakfast. Breakfast may vary according to available time and equipment. It may range from an orange, a glass of juice and a bowl of granola cereal with a bagel, to a full-fledged meal of bacon, eggs, hash browns and toast with an orange and juice. Those with a flair for cooking may wish to prepare a fancy omelette complete with all the fixings. Backpackers wanting to get off to a quick start may begin their day with juice (from crystals), a bagel with peanut butter, and a bowl of hot instant porridge with dehydrated apple slices and brown sugar. If time is not an issue, they may choose to serve up a slice of ham, some powdered eggs, and cheese on an English muffin, and coffee or tea.

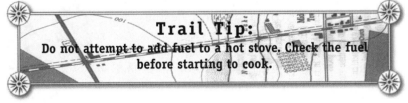

Trail Tip:
Do not attempt to add fuel to a hot stove. Check the fuel before starting to cook.

Lunch

Lunch at a standing camp might include: water, milk or juice, and grilled cheese sandwiches, soup, macaroni and cheese, hot dogs or hamburgers. Fruit makes a great dessert.

Canoeists or backpackers may extend their lunch over the whole day between breakfast and supper. They may take frequent short breaks to drink and snack on quick, high-energy foods that will carry them for the next hour, when they'll snack again. These people will keep their food in an easily accessible pocket or pouch, so they don't have to spend time unpacking gear. Quick snacks might include crackers with cheese or peanut butter, a handful of trail mix or GORP, or granola bars.

Supper

This is usually the main meal in your day. Make it relaxing and fun. Suppers should be nutritious enough to replace the energy consumed during the day, and should provide sufficient calories to keep you warm through the night.

At a standing camp, any gourmet delight is possible for supper. Favourites may include one-pot meals like spaghetti, beef stews, casseroles, or a "meat and potatoes" meal. Accompany these with a bowl of soup or a salad, and follow them up with cakes or puddings.

Wacky 'Expert Camp Tip

A potato baked in the coals for one hour makes an excellent side dish. A potato baked in the coals for three hours makes an excellent hockey puck.

Your cooking methods may vary at standing camps. They might include campfires, barbecues, reflector ovens, tinfoil pouches or even Dutch ovens.

Paddlers or hikers always appreciate a hot, filling meal after a long day. Plan for enough time to set up camp and relax a little before supper. Pasta dishes and easy-to-prepare, vacuum-sealed or dehydrated meals are favourites.

Teamwork

Cooking meals for a group of six or more people is a big job. Make sure no person is saddled with all the responsibility of gathering fuel and water, preparing food, and cleaning up. Give everyone a role; break into teams for more labour-intensive tasks.

The fuel and water team makes sure there is enough water and fuel on hand; collects and treats water; keeps supplies of tinder, kindling, firewood and charcoal protected from the weather; and starts fires in time for cooks to prepare the meals.

The cooking team gets the food supplies together; follows menus and recipes exactly; serves meals on time; puts away food; soaks cooking pots; and puts the clean-up water supply on the fire before serving meals.

The clean-up team sets up the wash and rinse water for dishwashing; cleans cooking pots and utensils; cleans up kitchen and dining areas; stores all group equipment; disposes of all garbage and trash; and puts out the fire.

Rotate your campers through each team daily so everyone has a chance to learn about each different duty. (See Duty Chart in Chapter 2)

Lightweight Meals and Dehydrating Food

After a long day on the trail or on the water, most campers prefer a good, hot meal that is quick and easy to prepare and requires little clean-up afterwards.

You may choose to buy some dehydrated meals at a local camping store to cut down on weight and space. Although these meals are usually quite good, there's nothing like preparing your own proven favourites.

If you're travelling by canoe and have a cooler, you can prepare favourite meals at home and freeze them for the trip. This process cuts down on preparation time and clean-up. You'll really appreciate your home preparation when you're tired and hungry after a strenuous day paddling.

Though limited by space and weight, overnight backpackers may decide to carry a small "lunch bag" sized cooler to hold a favourite frozen meal. A can of stew or spaghetti isn't too onerous a burden either for just one night. Remember: whatever you carry in, you must carry out.

Keep in mind that youths shouldn't carry more than 25-30% of their body weight. Pack as light as possible. Leaders may want to divide a large group into smaller groups of three or four for cooking, eating and sleeping. This helps reduce the overall weight each individual must carry.

Supermarkets sell many "lightweight foods" such as macaroni and cheese, instant soups, rice and cereals. Specialty camping stores also offer a good selection of dehydrated foods.

Have you ever made pizza in a frying pan? Use pita bread or English muffins with dehydrated tomato sauce, cheese, pepperoni or salami, and spices. Cover with tin foil and heat until the cheese is melted. Delicious!

Pre-packaged macaroni and cheese is popular with all ages. Add a small tin of ham or tuna and you've got a good meal for three or four. Instant potato scallops are also good. Once more, by adding a small tin of meat, you'll make a wholesome feast for three or four.

Single portion, frozen, boil-in-a-bag meals provide another good option — tasty, but a little on the heavy side. Keep them frozen or very cold, and use them as quickly as possible. These frozen meals are ideal for winter camping when spoilage isn't a big concern. They require no preparation, minimum exposure of bare hands, and you can eat them directly from the pouch. Here's the bonus: clean-up often consists of merely burning the pouch and washing the spoon.

Have you ever considered dehydrating your own foods at home? You can do it:

▲ In the oven

▲ By sunlight

▲ By building/purchasing your own dehydrator.

Pick up information at a library describing how to do it safely, and how to store the food properly after it has been dehydrated.

Winter
▲ Weight not a factor
▲ Boil-in-a-bag meals
▲ Dehydrated foods

Canoe
▲ Weight isn't a problem
▲ Food in coolers
▲ Fresh or canned food

Backpacking or Lightweight Camping
▲ Weight is a factor
▲ Dehydrated, lightweight foods
▲ Pre-mixed, portion adjusted meals

To make your own beef jerky, start with 450 g of lean beef. Cutting with the grain, slice it into thin strips 1/2 cm wide. Sprinkle it with salt and pepper, then place the meat on a cake rack with a cookie sheet underneath. Set the oven to its lowest temperature setting. Place the beef in the oven, leaving the oven door open 5-8 cm, and let the meat dry for approximately eight hours. When done, store it in plastic sealable bags. It's great for a nutritious snack.

Before drying meat, why not marinade it? You'll really enhance the flavour. Camping cookbooks offer many recipes for beef, pork and chicken marinades.

You may choose to make your own boil-in-a-bag meal at home. You can purchase a vacuum sealer to do this or simply use resealable freezer bags. Freeze the meal at home, and keep it frozen until required. When you're ready to use it, boil a pot of water and insert your frozen pouch. Boil the water until the meal has thawed, then re-heat.

Wacky 'Expert' Camp Tip

Old socks can be made into high fibre beef jerky. Simply smoke them over an open fire.

Make sure your pouch doesn't melt away on the bottom of the pot. Here are three tips that will help prevent this calamity:

1. Empty the contents into a pot for reheating.

2. Double bag the pouch. Allow the outer bag to remain inflated so the pouch will float.

3. Poke a stick through the top of the bag and suspend it from the top of the pot.

While quick and convenient, these meals are a bit heavy for hikers and must be kept refrigerated, limiting their use to short overnight trips.

> **Caution!** Food preparation requires proper hygiene, packaging and refrigeration.

Desserts

What better way to end your day than sitting back with a tasty dessert? Instant pudding, jello and bannock with jam are some favourites. They are lightweight and tasty in the back country.

Repackage at Home

Before setting out from home, examine the food items you have selected and identify ways to remove excess packaging. This will reduce both weight and garbage. Repackage these items in resealable freezer bags or plastic, leakproof containers. Besides making a mess in your pack, a leak could contaminate other food items. Food placed in resealable freezer bags can be fitted easily into pots and other containers — a great space saver.

To reduce weight and breakage, avoid metal and glass containers. If you repackage food items that require special directions for preparation, cut out that portion of the packaging and include it in your new package.

To make it easier to locate meals, place all breakfast items in one coloured bag, lunch items in another bag, and so on. For multi-day trips, put all meals in different coloured bags and label them accordingly.

When camping with a group, it's usually more economical to purchase food items in bulk. This makes it easy to repackage and distribute them among group members.

Trail Tip:
Collect lots of small plastic containers with tight fitting lids for storing and packing food and small items.

Cooking with Stoves

What's the most important advice when using stoves?

Read and carefully follow the instructions at all times!

Stoves come in one-, two- and three-burner models. The latter models are ideal for standing camps, while single-burner stoves are more practical for lightweight camping. Most stoves operate with some sort of pressurized fuel tank that permits the user to regulate the amount of fuel released to the burner. This controls the heat output for cooking.

Stoves are fast and efficient and have little impact on the environment. Avoid stoves that use non-recyclable, non-refillable fuel canisters. (See stove section in Chapter 5 for more details.)

Trail Tip:
Release pressure in stove tanks before packing for travel or storing.

Aluminum Foil Cooking

You don't need pots and pans to make a perfect camp meal. Simply spread some margarine on the layer of foil facing the food; this will keep it from burning to the foil. Cut your meat and vegetables into small chunks, add a little salt, pepper, and barbecue sauce, and wrap it in two layers of tin foil. Roll, fold the edges to keep steam and juices from escaping, and place the foil packages on a hot bed of coals for approximately 20 minutes. Turn the pouch over several times while it's cooking. When the food is ready, cut through the foil layers and eat directly from the pouch.

When you have finished eating, roll the foil into a small ball and pack it out with the rest of your garbage for disposal at home. (**Note:** Using aluminum foil is not as environmentally friendly as other cooking methods.)

Cooking Over Fires

There's something very special about cooking over an open fire. Perhaps it's the satisfaction of using the same methods as early settlers and explorers. Preparing meals over a campfire requires special skill and care. Before you begin cooking, you'll need quite a bit of preparation. For starters, find a suitable fire pit. Then, gather softwood kindling for lighting the fire and larger sticks of hardwood to provide good, hot cooking coals. (**Note:** Check with local authorities to see if a fire permit is required, or if fires are even permitted.)

When you have finished cooking, let your fire burn out, then pour water over the ashes to extinguish any hidden flames. By allowing the fire to completely burn out, you are eliminating chunks of unburned wood and can leave your fireplace ready for the next campers. Remember these two important rules when cooking or enjoying campfires:

1. Never leave a fire unattended.

2. Before going to bed or leaving your site, make sure your fire is completely out. Pour water over the coals and ashes until they are cool to your touch. (See Fires, Chapter 7.)

Trail Tip:
Carry matches in a waterproof container.

Modern Backpack Ovens

Lightweight campers can now enjoy freshly baked foods (including pizza and pies), even in remote areas thanks to modern backpack ovens. Manufacturers have designed some models which reflect campfire heat (reflector ovens); and others that are placed directly on a stove's burner where it captures heat in a metal box or pan covered with a heat shield. Backpack ovens allow campers to broaden their menus to include more of their favourite recipes from home.

Dutch Ovens

Although Dutch ovens are usually avoided by most lightweight campers, they are excellent for standing camps. Cooks can prepare almost any food in one of these cast iron or aluminum ovens.

When purchasing a Dutch oven, consider these points:

▲ Dutch ovens come in a variety of sizes, usually starting at 20 cm in diameter and increasing to about 45 cm.

▲ A 30 cm oven is most suitable for a group of six to eight people.

▲ Make sure your Dutch oven has at least three legs on the bottom. These will raise the bottom just enough to place hot coals underneath.

▲ The lid should have a lip around the edges to prevent coals from falling off the top, and a handle on it, to make it easier for lifting the lid when hot.

▲ The oven itself should have a heavy wire lifting handle for moving it on and off the coals.

Before using your new, cast iron Dutch oven, "season" it as you would a cast iron frying pan. Wash the oven in warm, soapy water, then coat the oven with a salt-free cooking oil. (This will seal the metal pores and prevent rust.) Now, pour a small amount of cooking oil in the bottom of the oven and place it in your home oven for one hour at medium heat. When the Dutch oven has cooled, coat it once more leaving a thin coating of oil on all surfaces. Many people repeat this final coat after each use to prevent rust.

Most people use charcoal briquets for cooking with their ovens; these are easier to handle than chunks of wood. Begin by burning the charcoal until it has changed from black to grey ash in colour. When it has reached this stage, form a bed of coals. Place the oven on this bed, and add some coals to the oven's lid. To regulate the temperature, either add or remove briquets using metal tongs and an oven mitt.

Preheat oven before placing food in it. Do this by placing coals underneath and on top of the oven for a few minutes. Experienced Dutch oven chefs place more briquets on top than underneath. This helps create the best baking heat in the air space at the top of the oven. Start with 4-6 briquets underneath and 8-10 on top. That much charcoal (taking into effect wind conditions and weather) should produce a temperature between 150°C to 200°C in a cast iron pot with a 30 cm diameter. You might want to experiment using an oven thermometer to measure the heat as you add and remove coals from the oven.

Storing Food

Protect all food from the elements (wind, rain, sun and heat), and especially from insects and animals. Camp food can be divided into three basic groups:

1. *Requires refrigeration.* (E.g. fresh milk and fresh meat) Salmonella may develop in poultry and eggs if these products aren't kept refrigerated.

2. *Must be kept cool.* Fresh vegetables, fruit, butter and processed meats (e.g. bacon, smoked ham) must be kept cool.

3. *No refrigeration.* Canned or dry foods require no refrigeration.

Blocks of ice take longer to melt than ice cubes.

Campers must keep foods in the first two groups in some form of refrigerator. Insulated coolers with ice or freezer packs are excellent for most standing camps and canoe trips without portages. Coolers are available in many sizes and shapes, ranging from a lunch bag size (suitable for a backpack), to huge ones that are suitable for large groups on multi-day outings. Coolers also offer protection from insects and animals.

Perhaps your Scouts would like to experiment by cooling food products in a cold running stream or by making an evaporation cooler. (Note: These methods are not as reliable, however, and do not provide protection from animals.)

Save plastic milk containers and 1- or 2-litre waxed cardboard juice containers with screw-off caps. When filled with water and frozen, these fit easily into coolers. After they thaw, the water can be used for drinking, or refrozen.

To keep food products cool in a stream, find a shaded section of the stream where the water runs fairly quickly. It's important to find some means to keep the items from being carried away by the current. Building a rock wall or submerging the items in a weighted pot with a rock placed above it may be your best solution. (**Note:** If you build a rock wall, make sure you put the rocks back before leaving your site.)

To make an evaporation cooler, you'll require two pails, a large piece of cheesecloth, and a length of rope to hang the pails from a branch.

Suspend both pails (one with food in it and the other filled with water) with the water pail just above the food pail. Drape a large piece of cheesecloth over both. Immerse the cheesecloth in the water pail with a rock. The water evaporates and creates a cool temperature for the food below. The hotter the day, the faster the rate of evaporation, and the cooler the temperature is beneath the cloth.

Note: Lightweight campers, and canoeists making frequent portages, should ensure their food doesn't spoil by choosing foods that don't require refrigeration.

Note: Campers must keep all foods away from animals at all times. At standing camps, this is easy. Just put coolers and other food items in the trunk of a vehicle between meals.

Bear Bagging

The best method to store food or garbage in remote areas is by suspending it from a branch or on a rope strung between two trees. Find a location at least 100 metres away from your campsite. Place food items in sealable plastic bags (to minimize odour) and then inside a strong compression bag or stuff sack. Look for a suitable branch five to six metres above the ground. Suspend the bag at least three to four metres off the ground, two metres below the branch and three metres out from the tree trunk.

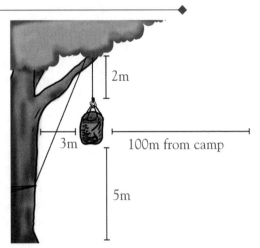

2m

3m 100m from camp

5m

When suspending the bag, tie a carabiner to one end of 16 metre long parachute cord. Throw this over the branch and fasten the carabiner to the bag. Now pull the cord, raising the bag until it is about four metres off the ground; tie off the end of the cord to a nearby tree. If you can't find a suitable branch, tie some parachute cord between two trees at least seven metres apart, and about five metres off the ground — the extra metre to allow for sag in the rope — and suspend the food bag from your "clothesline."

(**Note:** It is easier and safer to throw a weighted line over the branch than climbing the tree.)

Bears and raccoons are not the only forest food thieves. Mice and squirrels are just as determined to rob your food cache. Using thin rope or cord makes it more difficult for them to reach your food. If you suspend your food on a rope or cord threaded through an upside down, burnt-out can, smaller animals will be discouraged. Barrels with screwtops or clamp on lids are also effective against most critters.

Wacky 'Expert' Camp Tip
Get even with a bear who raids your food bag. Kick its favourite stump apart and eat all the ants!

Flies and insects are sure to hover around any campsite; you'll need to keep them away from all cooking and eating utensils, as well as food supplies. Insects may carry disease which can turn a camping trip into an ordeal. Avoid these unpleasantries by keeping your site neat and tidy. Store your food properly, wash your dishes after each meal, and dispose of all food scraps correctly. These measures will help keep flies, wasps and insects away.

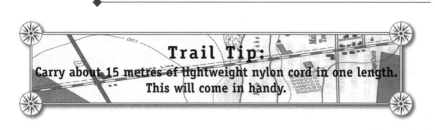

Trail Tip:
Carry about 15 metres of lightweight nylon cord in one length.
This will come in handy.

Clean-Up

The proper time to wash dishes is immediately after finishing a meal. In fact, heat the water while you eat. To prevent contamination, wash dishes at least 30 metres away from any water source. Never wash or rinse dishes in rivers, streams, or lakes. By washing dishes, pots, pans and cutlery thoroughly, you'll prevent bacteria and sickness from spreading.

At a standing camp, set up three large wash basins using dish detergent and a disinfectant in the following manner.

▲ Scrape as much "gunk" off as possible before beginning the wash cycle.

▲ Wash personal dishes before starting on the pots, pans, etc.

Basin 1: Wash thoroughly in hot water with a detergent solution until clean.

Basin 2: Rinse in clean water with a minimum temperature of 43°C.

Basin 3: Sanitize by immersion in one of the following.

Disinfectant	Strength	Temperature	Contact
Hot water	N/A	77°C	45 sec
Chlorine	100 PPM*	24°C	45 sec
Quaternary Ammonium	200 PPM*	24°C	45 sec
Iodine	25 PPM*	24°C	45 sec

*PPM= parts per million

This process isn't quite as easy in the back country because you probably won't carry three wash basins, but using pots or bowls in place of the basins will achieve the same results. If you don't have enough pots or bowls, simply wash the dishes in hot water using a biodegradable soap or detergent to remove all food particles. Dry before placing them in your pack. Remember to sterilize them in boiling water before your next meal.

Drying Dishes

Air drying is acceptable if you first shake off excess water, and if you complete the process quickly. A better method involves wiping all items dry. This will eliminate moisture and the spread of organisms. Completely dry dishes or utensils are also less attractive to flies.

Food Scraps and Waste

Put all garbage in sealed plastic garbage bags for quick removal. This is easy at standing camps, but it's also vital during lightweight camping. When planning your menu, it's important to package your food in reusable containers and in proper quantities. This practice will minimize waste.

Leftovers, garbage and food scraps must be "packed out" or burned if you have a campfire. If you dispose of or burn these scraps quickly, you can avoid attracting flies and animals. It is not acceptable to bury food scraps or garbage, since this disposal method will often attract animals to the site.

Strain your dish water to remove all food scraps. Then spread the water discreetly around the ground (preferably in mineral soils) where it won't linger in puddles and attract flies.

Never dump dish water in or near any water sources. Disposal should take place at least 30 metres from any water source and in a gravel area where it will be naturally filtered and not lay in a puddle.

CHAPTER 5

▶ Equipment

Advances in today's technology let us do things faster, safer, easier and more comfortably than ever before. This applies to outdoor equipment as well. Of course, if you want the latest technology, it comes at a significant cost.

When introducing youths and leaders to the outdoors, realize that for many, this will be a new experience; they may not have the necessary equipment. They will likely look for your advice when choosing equipment appropriate for the group's activities. Because of expense, many youths, parents and leaders will want to "make do" with equipment they already have or can borrow.

With a few exceptions, Scouting programs don't involve activities that require state-of-the-art outdoor gear. Leaders need to buy or rent appropriate equipment at the most reasonable price.

Trail Tip:
Lightweight, backpackable ovens are perfect for baking everything from breads to pizza!

Trail Tip:
Air out, clean, check and maintain your gear after each use.

Ask yourself these questions before purchasing any equipment:

▲ How often will I need or use this item?

▲ Will I use it often enough to justify the purchase?

▲ Is it something that I can borrow or rent at least until I decide if I like it or not?

▲ Under what conditions will I use this item?

▲ What type of camping will I be doing? Car camping? Canoe trips? Backpacking? Winter ski/snowshoe trips?

▲ Will I require lightweight compressible items for backpacking, or can I get by with heavier, bulkier items for standing camps?

▲ Do I just need equipment for summer use or for all year?

▲ How much can I afford to spend?

Before buying, remember the expression: "You get what you pay for." Look for reputable stores with knowledgeable sales staff, good product warranties, and quality materials and construction. Talk to other campers to find out what products work well for them and to determine what equipment you need. The comfort and quality of your trip depends on many factors; some you can influence, some you can't. This is why it is so important to have as many things in your favour as possible, especially equipment. Good equipment will help ensure a safe, healthy outdoor experience.

Sleeping Bags

A good sleeping bag: it's one of the first things a new camper needs.

Understanding what a sleeping bag is designed to do will help when you go looking for a new one. A sleeping bag will *not* make you warm. It simply provides insulation that *captures the heat* generated by your body. That's important to know. It is also important to know that under certain circumstances up to 60 percent of your body heat may be lost through your head. If you plan to camp all year round (or at least three seasons), get a sleeping bag equipped with a hood for cold weather camping.

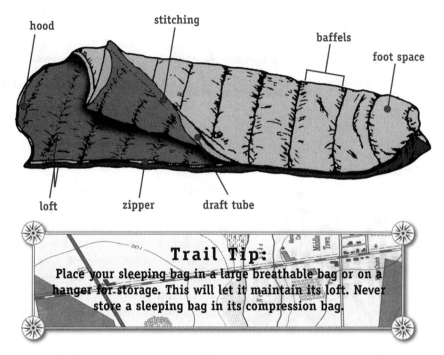

hood
stitching
baffels
foot space
loft
zipper
draft tube

Trail Tip:
Place your sleeping bag in a large breathable bag or on a hanger for storage. This will let it maintain its loft. Never store a sleeping bag in its compression bag.

Heat Loss: The Facts

Our bodies lose heat in five ways:

▲ Radiation

▲ Convection

▲ Conduction

▲ Evaporation

▲ Respiration.

Radiation

When heat passes from one object to another without warming the air space between, radiation has occurred. (Example: the sun's rays warm the earth and then the heat absorbed by the earth warms surrounding air.) Radiation is the reason it's important to cover your head with a hat and/or a hood when in a sleeping bag during a winter camping trip.

Convection

Most heat escapes from a body by convection when air or water passes over or close to the body and carries its heat away. The amount of heat lost increases as the amount of air or water movement increases. Large sleeping bags that allow lots of air movement will be cooler in summer and much harder to keep warm in winter. We protect ourselves against heat loss from convection by surrounding our bodies with insulating materials and a windproof outer barrier.

Conduction

Conduction occurs when heat transfers from one surface to another by direct contact. When you sit down on a cold rock for a break, you'll soon have a cold bottom — an example of conduction. If you lay your sleeping bag directly on the ground without putting enough insulation underneath, you can expect to lose heat from conduction.

Water chill occurs when your body loses heat from direct contact with cold water. Because water is a great heat conductor, wet clothes will draw heat from your body much faster than dry clothes. Keep a layer of clothes next to your body that can wick moisture away from your skin, rather than absorb it.

Evaporation

The body naturally produces perspiration to keep skin moist. Perspiration also helps regulate body temperature. As our activity level increases, so does the amount of perspiration that our bodies produce. Evaporation occurs when perspiration converts to vapour by using heat from our body. Campers can help their bodies regulate the heat by adding or removing layers of clothing according to their activity level.

Respiration

When you inhale cold winter air and exhale warm air from your lungs, you lose a significant amount of internal heat. In cold weather, wear a scarf over your face to help preheat the air you are inhaling. When sleeping, it is important to keep your mouth and nose out of your sleeping bag to prevent moisture from your breath making the sleeping bag damp.

Shapes and Sizes of Sleeping Bags

Sleeping bags come in three common shapes: rectangular, mummy, and barrel. Some manufacturers modify these to provide more interior space by making them longer or shorter.

Buying a sleeping bag is like buying a pair of jeans; fit and comfort is everything. You wouldn't buy jeans without trying them on, and you shouldn't buy a sleeping bag without "trying it on." Take the bag out of its compression bag, shake it out, and climb in. Make sure the bag fits properly. Does it allow enough room for you to move around in without leaving too much extra space to heat?

Rectangular Bags

Most sleeping bags are rectangular. They are the simplest and least expensive design to produce. Rectangular bags have the same width from the top to bottom, and provide lots of room for tossing and turning. The largest of the three styles, they are relatively heavy and bulky, and don't hold in heat as well as other designs. Although these factors generally restrict their usage to canoeing, car camping, and short backpacking trips, rectangular bags are acceptable for most summer camping trips.

Planning an early spring or late fall camp, but don't want to buy a cold weather sleeping bag? You might rent or borrow one. (See Winter Camping chapter for more ideas.) If your rectangular bag doesn't have a hood, wear a good hat or hooded sweater to bed on cold nights. Also, try closing off the top of the bag as much as possible to keep heat in.

Mummy Bags

Mummy-shaped bags are very good, especially for cold weather camping. Because they are close fitting all along the body and generally include a hood (complete with a drawstring to draw the hood in close), they are the most efficient at providing insulation.

Mummy designs are narrow at the feet, wider at the hips, chest and shoulders, and then taper in at the top. When campers draw the hood in close, just their mouths and noses are exposed. This keeps breath moisture out of the sleeping bag. Because of its shape, most campers generally sleep on their backs with toes pointing upward.

Mummy style bags require less material to make and generally use lightweight, highly compressible insulating materials. This construction results in a light, compact and efficient bag for backpacking and lightweight camping. Some extra features mummy bags incorporate for comfort and heat retention include a box-shaped foot (which allows extra foot room), a draw string at the shoulders (to prevent drafts from going down into the bag), and an adjustable shaped hood.

Barrel Bags

Barrel sleeping bags (sometimes called "modified mummy" bags) represent a compromise between rectangular and mummy bags. These are narrow at the feet, wide through the body, and tapered at the shoulders. Many include a hood.

These sleeping bags are designed for people who find mummies too confining. Although the bags allow some room to move inside, they provide good heat retention — though not as much as mummy bags.

Shells

The shell, or outer layer, of your sleeping bag must be tough enough to resist tears and rips. It should also repel moisture and be able to "breathe."

Good quality bags have nylon taffeta or rip-stop nylon shells — easily recognizable by all the little squares in the fabric. Better yet is a windproof, waterproof, breathable fabric shell, such as Gore-Tex™.

Avoid sleeping bags with cotton shells. They're heavy and bulky, don't stand up well to frequent use, will absorb huge quantities of water, and take forever to dry.

Insulation Materials

Despite attempts to duplicate the natural properties of down (the fluffy under-plumage of waterfowl), science has only come close. Manufactured synthetic fibres retain more warmth when wet and are less expensive than down, but down still provides the best warmth-for-weight, compressibility and resilience of all insulating fibres. As well, the industry still uses down as the standard against which new synthetic insulating fibres are measured.

Loft

"Loft" refers to the thickness of a sleeping bag once it's fluffed up. A good quality sleeping bag will retain its loft for many years. (Down keeps its loft much better than synthetic materials.)

Down

Down for sleeping bags comes from ducks and geese. (Goose down is best.) It is available in many different grades and is measured by its "fill power" — the volume filled by one ounce. The more space a given amount of down can fill, the more loft (thickness) and warmth it provides. Although the industry standard is 550 cubic inches per ounce, many manufacturers "overfill" their sleeping bags up to a maximum 750.

What are the drawbacks of down?

It is very expensive (though it will outlast synthetics by many years), and, if it ever gets wet, it loses almost all of its insulating value. It also takes a very long time to dry. To overcome these drawbacks, some manufacturers produce down sleeping bags with a Gore-Tex™ outer shell. This compromise works well, but it drives the price up even higher.

(**Note:** If you suffer from hay fever and feather allergies, avoid down bags.)

Synthetic Insulation

Scientists have produced a range of affordable alternatives to down. These synthetic fills retain some of their insulating value even when wet, and they are generally less expensive than down. Following are some of the most common synthetic insulation:

Quallofil™

This insulation consists of short, non-continuous, synthetic fibres, each smaller than a human hair. Fibres contain four microscopic tubes that trap air and provide more loft. Sleeping bags made with Quallofil™ are usually bulkier and heavier than those made from other synthetics.

Hollofil™

Synthetic and hollow, these fibres are about five cm long and must be sewn onto a backing material to prevent them from bunching up. Because Hollofil™ traps more air per ounce than Quallofil™, it provides better insulation. But the backing material makes Hollofil™ heavier and bulkier than most synthetics.

Polarguard HV™

Continuous-filament, hollow, synthetic fibres interwoven into sheets or batts, Polarguard™ will not shift or settle when used in sleeping bags. It maintains its loft longer than most synthetics but is fairly heavy and bulky.

Thinsulite™

This material is exactly what it sounds like: thin insulation. Thin layers of short strands of polyester and polypropylene fibres trap air to increase its insulation properties. Thinsulite™ isn't as bulky and doesn't produce the same loft as other fibres, yet it provides similar insulation qualities.

Lite Loft™

This material, by using synthetic microfibres many times smaller than other synthetics, traps more air and provides better insulation in less space. This makes Lite Loft™ great for lightweight camping.

Primaloft™

Sometimes referred to as "synthetic down", Primaloft™ retains heat even better than down. Primaloft™ retains heat and resists moisture absorption better than most other synthetics as well. It is extremely lightweight and compressible.

Construction

Insulation materials are only effective when contained within a bag. The insulation must not be able to shift, settle or bunch up, causing hollow (cold) spots. Most manufacturers use baffles to keep insulating materials in place.

Some synthetic insulation bags have a "sewn through" construction method with the inner and outer linings sewn together; the insulation lies

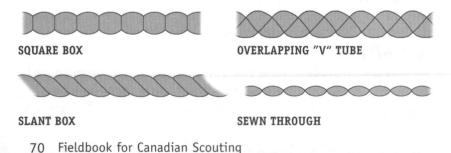

SQUARE BOX   OVERLAPPING "V" TUBE

SLANT BOX   SEWN THROUGH

between. Because this causes cold spots along the seams where insulation is compressed, it's the least desirable construction method.

The "double quilted" method is more effective. Each seam is protected by an offset layer of insulation. This is done by sewing two quilts together; the quilted portion of the top covers the seams of the lower one.

The "overlapping V tube" is similar; seams are covered by an overlapping layer of insulation.

Some synthetics come in sheets and don't need baffles to hold them in place. They are simply stitched around the edges.

Down sleeping bags use several methods to keep insulation in place. The "slant box" uses slanted baffles, while the "square box" uses a series of vertical baffles sewn between the inner and outer shell.

Other methods also exist, but most use some form of offset layering.

Don't overlook the stitching when buying a sleeping bag. Seams should be straight with extra reinforcing at ends and in high stress areas. Good sleeping bags will have three to five stitches per centimetre. You shouldn't be able to lift the thread with your fingers.

The inner liner of a sleeping bag must be cut smaller than the outer shell. This prevents the liner from contacting the shell (other than in areas compressed by the body) and creating cold spots. This is referred to as "differential cut."

Zippers

Look for nylon coil zippers rather than ones with large, metal teeth. Metal zippers sometimes freeze in winter and allow more drafts into the bag. They'll also transfer cold from the outside more readily than nylon zippers.

Manufacturer's Suggested Ratings

Most sleeping bags have a tag indicating their suggested temperature rating. Use this as *a general guide only*. Each manufacturer sets its own rating criteria as there is no industry standard. A standard would be almost impossible to establish as there are so many variables, including the camper's metabolism and weight, and the conditions in which the bags are used. The rating guide is useful when comparing different models from the same manufacturer, but it is not reliable when comparing one manufacturer against another.

Toasty Sleeping Bag Secrets

Look for these features in a good sleeping bag.

▲ A compression bag is better than a stuff sack.

▲ An insulated draft tube or zipper baffle sewn along the full length of the zipper will keep out drafts.

▲ Look for a Velcro™ tab at the top of the zipper. It will help keep the zipper from opening as you shift around.

▲ All zippers should be able to move in two directions. This feature allows you to open the bottom of the bag for ventilation.

▲ A draft collar that can be drawn close around your neck and shoulders will keep heat from escaping.

▲ An enlarged foot area (common referred to as a "boxed foot") allows more foot room.

▲ Some manufacturers include a small zippered pocket. This is useful for small items, tissues, etc. Put a pair of ear plugs inside; you can find snoring tent mates whatever the campers' ages.

▲ A bag offering a choice of right or left hand zippers lets you join two compatible bags together.

Using and Caring for New Sleeping Bags

Follow these tips on using and caring for your new sleeping bag:

▲ Carefully read and follow washing and cleaning instructions. When it says, "Do not put in dryer," DON'T!

▲ Keep the inside of your bag clean by making an inner liner for your sleeping bag. Make it from an old sheet.

▲ Don't roll your sleeping bag up after a camping trip. This places extra stress on the seams and forces its insulation to one end. Gently stuff the bag into your compression sack (starting with the feet end to allow air to escape), and then snug up the compression straps.

▲ Stuff your sleeping bag inside a waterproof bag before setting out on any trip.

▲ Be sure to air out your sleeping bag as often as possible while camping. This practice will remove moisture. Air out the bag again at home before storing it.

▲ Store your sleeping bags in a dry area where they can lie or hang in a fully lofted state.

Other Factors Guaranteeing a Warm Sleep

A good sleeping bag will help you stay warm at night, but don't overlook these factors:

▲ Before going to sleep, change out of the clothes you wore all day. This is very important. Clothes get damp from work or play; the dampness will draw heat from your body.

▲ Do not drink coffee, tea, hot chocolate, or soda pop before going to bed. You'll only have to make a trip to the outhouse — never fun on cold evenings.

▲ Don't go to bed hungry. If your body doesn't have enough "fuel" to keep it going all night, chances are you'll get cold.

▲ Eat nutritious meals during the day, especially for supper.

▲ A wind resistant shelter (e.g. tent) will help you stay warm.

▲ Sleep on a good, thick insulated mattress.

Before Buying a Sleeping Bag

A good manufacturer will guarantee its products for life against all manufacturing defects. Here are some questions to ask sales staff:

▲ What different brands are available?

▲ How long has your store been in business?

▲ What guarantee comes with the bag?

▲ Does the store have a repair department?

Many Scout Shops carry a good selection of camping supplies and equipment. Talk to their knowledgeable staff.

The Magic of Sleeping Pads

"Why am I still cold even though I'm bundled into an excellent sleeping bag?!"

Have you ever asked this question?

Perhaps, the answer lies beneath you. Tests show that an amazing amount of heat is lost downwards through conduction. To ensure a warm, comfortable sleep, buy a sleeping pad or mattress. Many brands and designs are available.

Air Mattress

Air mattresses are the most common and oldest form of camping mattress. They are simply long, rectangular, hollow chambers filled with air. Most are made from plastic, vinyl or rubberized cloth. Although air mattresses may be acceptable for summer car camping, their weight and bulk are unacceptable for lightweight camping. What's more, their large air chambers provide very poor insulation in colder weather.

Closed-Cell Foam Pads

Evazote™ and Ensolite™ are two leading names in closed-cell foam pads. They are very economical and provide reasonable comfort and insulation. These pads are blown-foam sheets that consist of thousands of tiny air bubbles. Waterproof closed-cell pads come in various qualities, thicknesses, lengths and colours. They are very lightweight and remain pliable even in very cold temperatures. Their one major drawback is bulk. When strapped to a backpack, they tend to get snagged on twigs and branches, which tear off pieces of the mattress. To prevent this, put your pad in some sort of stuff sack or wrap it in a ground sheet.

Self-Inflating Air Mattress

These are the most comfortable sleeping pads, and naturally the most expensive. Self-inflating air mattresses are open-celled foam pads totally encased in a nylon airtight shell, with an air valve. When the valve is open, air will enter and fill the open-cell foam. Once the mattress is as thick as you wish, close the valve and lie down. To deflate, open the valve and roll the mattress beginning at the end opposite the valve. This

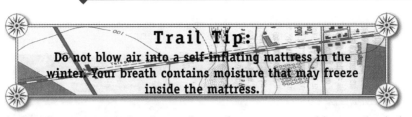

Trail Tip:
Do not blow air into a self-inflating mattress in the winter. Your breath contains moisture that may freeze inside the mattress.

forces the air out and reduces the pad to an acceptable size for lightweight camping. Once the pad is fully compressed, close the valve and fasten the straps.

When collapsed and rolled, this mattress is smaller than most other foam pads. Some even fold in half making them small enough to fit inside a pack.

Self-inflating air mattresses come in a variety of widths, thicknesses and lengths. They are a little on the heavy side (about twice the weight of the closed-cell pad), but provide twice the insulation and are very comfortable.

Some mattresses offer an optional chair kit. This is simply a cover that slips over the mattress allowing it to be folded in two. Plastic or metal stays and two straps hold it in position, transforming it into a very comfortable camp chair.

Tents: Your House in the Outdoors

Choosing the best tent for your money helps ensure comfort, safety and an enjoyable camping experience. This is especially important when camping with youth. This may be their first camping experience and you want to make sure it's a good one. Poor or inferior tents can lead to a wet, miserable, cold first outing which may turn youths off camping completely.

Let's try to narrow down the wide range of tents available. Ask yourself these questions:

▲ How often will the tent be used?

▲ Do you need a three- or four-season tent?

▲ How many people will sleep in it?

▲ What kind of camping will you be doing? Backpacking, cycling, canoeing or car camping?

Because most Scout groups focus on three-season camping, let's look at factors to consider before buying this type of tent.

Fabrics

Although cotton and canvas tents are still available, most tents sold today are made from various grades of nylon. These are the fabrics of choice. Why? They're strong, lightweight, quick-drying, and durable. Cotton and canvas tents are much heavier — suitable for car camping but not backpacking — and they take much longer to dry because they absorb water and condensation.

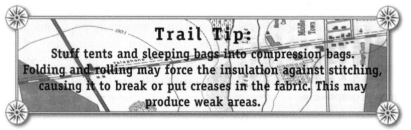

Trail Tip:
Stuff tents and sleeping bags into compression bags. Folding and rolling may force the insulation against stitching, causing it to break or put creases in the fabric. This may produce weak areas.

Features

Many new lightweight tents have two doors. They provide easier access for occupants and also permit better air flow ventilation when windows and doors are open. A second door makes it convenient for attaching vestibules at one or both entrances.

Vestibules serve as front and back porches where you can store equipment and footwear so they are protected from the elements.

Other nice features found on better quality tents include mesh pockets (for storing flashlights, eyeglasses, etc.), tie-back loops (for doors and windows), and loops hanging from the ceiling (to fasten a mesh storage shelf "gear loft" or flashlight).

Trail Tip:
Choose a tent with a full coverage rain fly.

To provide superior shelter from the elements, new lightweight nylon tents have two walls/roofs: an inner one made from breathable mesh panels that provide ventilation, and a coated, waterproof, outer one called a "fly." The inner roof also allows condensation from your body to pass through into the air space between the two layers where it is carried away by the air flowing through this space. Ventilation: that's the key to preventing condensation build-up. Most tents have two-way zippers on their doors and windows so they can be opened to increase ventilation.

The fly should extend down the walls to ground level for the best protection. Avoid tents with a fly that only covers a small portion of the roof. In the middle of a torrential downpour many kilometres from civilization, you want lots of fly coverage to keep you dry. (**Note:** Some manufactures are producing single-wall tents made from waterproof, breathable fabrics such as Gore-Tex™.)

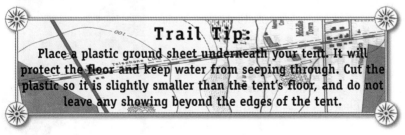

Trail Tip:
Place a plastic ground sheet underneath your tent. It will protect the floor and keep water from seeping through. Cut the plastic so it is slightly smaller than the tent's floor, and do not leave any showing beyond the edges of the tent.

Your tent floor should be made from coated nylon (making it waterproof). Good tent floors are made from a single piece of material with no seams, though larger tents will require two pieces with seams "taped" to make them waterproof. Floors should extend about 15 cm up the walls of the tent to prevent water which may splash up on the tent sides from seeping through.

Trail Tip:
Seal all seams on tents every year. You may even wish to do your pack.

All tents have seams. Manufacturers use two common methods for joining tent material together. Seams that are "bound" use one layer of material folded over the two to be joined. These are then stitched through all layers. "Lap felled seams" take the different layers to be joined, fold them over, and then stitch them together, thereby providing a flatter, stronger seam.

All seams will have long lines of needle holes. These must be water-proofed. Some manufacturers will "tape" the seams with a strip of coated fabric; some manufactures will provide a bottle of seam sealer so the buyer can waterproof the seams.

Heavy duty nylon coil zippers are another sure sign of quality.

You'll find another high quality "flag" when you inspect the screening mesh used in doors and windows. Better quality tents use a fine mesh screen to keep out "no-see-ums." Less expensive models use a poorer screen with larger openings.

Tent Poles

In the past, tent poles were made from long, heavy, rigid lengths of aluminum. Today, to reduce weight and space, poles are made from lightweight, hollow, tempered aluminum, or fibreglass cut in short lengths. These can bend to match new tent shapes and designs. Elastic cords running through the middle of the short poles join them together into one long pole. To break these "shock-corded" poles down to fit into a backpack, just pull the sections apart at the joints. Be wary of less expensive, fibreglass poles. They sometimes split or splinter at inopportune times. Some manufacturers are now using Magnum Helix™ glass/epoxy for poles. This is stronger and lighter than aluminum or fibreglass.

Tent Designs

Tents range in size from one-person ("single hoop") designs to family-size ("multi-room") tents that sleep 8-10 people. Manufacturers will usually identify their tents by the number of people they will accommodate, i.e. 2 man, 6 man, etc. Use this as a guide only. For extra space and comfort choose a tent that is rated for more people than you expect to actually sleep in it.

"A" Frame Tents

Shock-corded aluminum poles form the shape of an "A" at each end. A ridge pole joins the two "A" frames. The tent body hangs from the frame while the fly covers the entire frame and extends down both sides to ground level.

These tents feature a rectangular floor, and come in two-, four-, and six-person models. They are easy to set up, but provide limited headroom due to the tapered, steep sides.

Modified "A" Frame

Modified "A" frame tents lie lower at one end than the other. This reduction in size and weight makes the design more suitable for lightweight camping. But it also reduces inside space.

Dome Tents

A very common tent design, dome tents usually have three sets of shock-corded poles that curve over the roof. These thread through sleeves or clip to the body of the tent to stretch the sides out making almost vertical walls and plenty of interior headroom. With only three sections of poles, dome tents are usually taller than most others, but lack structural strength and are not as sturdy in strong winds unless guyed with ropes and pegs. Strong winds tend to make the tall sides collapse inward.

Geodesic Domes

These domes add one or more sets of poles (aluminum in better quality models) increasing the number of sides from six (in a three-poled dome) to eight or more. This creates an extremely strong, wind resistant shelter with lots of interior space.

Semi-Geodesic Domes

These wedge-shaped tents (high at the door end and tapered to the ground at the other end) use three poles: one hoop that crosses from side to side at the tall end, and two poles running from front to back crossing over each other along the way. Semi-geodesic dome tents are usually very lightweight and provide lots of headroom at the high end. They're great for lightweight camping.

Modified Dome

Instead of having six or more sides (like the standard dome), these tents usually have a rectangular or square floor shape with two or three sets of poles. While featuring lower profiles, these tents still provide ample interior space and are much sturdier in high winds than regular dome tents.

Although dome tents are generally regarded as "free-standing," like all other tents they must be pegged down. An advantage of free-standing tents is that you can pick them up (when empty) and move them around. When breaking camp, you can turn it onto its side facing the morning sun to dry the floor.

Tunnel Tents

Two- and three-pole tunnel tents have a series of parallel hoops. These feature the best space-to-weight ratio of all tent designs and provide plenty of interior space.

Single Hoop Tents

These are the smallest and lightest tents available. They have one hoop going from side to side or end to end, providing just enough room for one person or two "close" friends. Some of these tents weigh less than two kilograms.

Family Tents

Only suitable for standing camps, family tents are quite heavy but provide lots of interior space. Some even have two or three rooms — each tall enough for an adult to stand up in.

Maintenance

These simple rules will help protect your tent and extend its life:

▲ Always remove your shoes or boots before entering a tent. This practice will keep sand and gravel out and prevent hooks on your boots from snagging the floor or the screening.

▲ Never cook in or near your tent.

▲ Remove wet clothes in the vestibule and hang them outside to dry. Outside drying will prevent moisture and condensation build-up inside the tent.

▲ Keep insect repellents containing DEET away from the tent.

▲ Pack poles and pegs inside a separate stuff sack to prevent rips and tears.

▲ Carefully read and follow manufacturer's directions for cleaning, waterproofing and storage.

▲ Before packing, always make sure your tent is clean and dry. If you must pack a damp tent, hang it up to dry as soon as possible.

▲ If you use your tent frequently, waterproof all seams at least once a year.

▲ Pitch your tent well away from your fire pit. Sparks can destroy a tent.

▲ Don't "shake" shock-corded poles into place. Doing so may cause nicks and burrs in the ends of the poles, which may tear or snag tent material.

▲ Manufacturers suggest, wherever possible, to pitch tents in shaded areas and avoid leaving them up for prolonged periods where they will be exposed to direct sunlight.

Dining Shelters and Tarps

When camping on rainy days, dining shelters and tarps can provide welcomed comfort. They're not only good for cooking under, but they provide a gathering point between activities.

For a standing camp, you can purchase large roomy shelters complete with screened-in windows that will keep out hungry mosquitoes and other unwanted insects. These shelters are usually large enough to accommodate a standard sized picnic table. Dining shelters at camp can also serve as craft or game centres during poor weather, and provide shelter from the hot sun.

Tarps or flies can substitute for a dining tent. When they are made from lightweight nylon, they are light enough for canoe and backpacking trips. If buying a tarp or fly, watch for the same construction features as found in tents (see above). These can be easily strung between two trees to provide a "lean to" type shelter to accommodate campers.

Hot Tips About Stoves

After a long active day at camp or on the trail, it's great to "fire up" the stove and prepare a nice hot meal.

Type of Use

Will you use your stove primarily in warmer weather at standing camps, or do you plan to use it all year round? Whether buying a stove for backpacking or car camping, there are a number of models and a variety of fuels to choose from.

Single-Burner Stoves

An ideal, lightweight, single-burner stove will have these characteristics:

▲ High heat efficiency

▲ Sturdy, lightweight (preferably collapsible) construction

- ▲ Simple assembly and operation
- ▲ Windscreen
- ▲ High stability (not tippy).

The stove should have legs that extend beyond the body for support, and the cooking surface should be large enough to safely hold a pot twice the diameter of the stove's top. The heat adjustment must be safe and easy to operate. The heat adjustment must allow a user to set it for everything from a slow simmer to a full boil.

Your stove should hold at least 1/3 litre of fuel. The stove should be capable of burning for at least one hour at a high setting on a single tank of fuel. Many single burner stoves have fuel tanks or canisters that attach to the stove directly or with a hose. With this in mind, manufacturers produce tank canisters in various sizes to meet the campers' needs.

The stove should be designed so you can do routine maintenance in the field. Buy a repair kit and read the instructions so you'll be fully prepared. Before leaving home, learn how to maintain your stove. It's no fun getting stuck out in the wilderness with an inoperable stove.

Trail Tip:
Do not completely fill stove fuel tanks. Allow room for air to pressurize tanks.

If a stove is truly four-seasonal, it must be capable of working well in cold weather. Most four-season stoves burn naphtha gas. A pump helps to pressurize the tank to keep the fuel burning at a high output. Because naphtha gas burns in a vapour state, you might have to prime it with a paste before it will light in very cold weather.

Some stoves require priming all the time. They release a small amount of fuel into a small bowl below the burner for pre-heating the fuel lines and vaporizing the fuel.

A windscreen that fits around the burner is another great feature for windy days. It makes using the stove easier to light and operate, and more efficient in adverse weather conditions.

A carrying bag is a nice feature to help protect the stove while you're travelling. You can fit some of the smaller, collapsible models inside a pot for travelling — really convenient!

Stoves with pumps and generators are often a bit heavier than pressurized canister types, but they'll maintain pressure and heat output well. (Some pressurized canister stoves tend to lose pressure and heat output as the fuel is consumed.)

Two- and Three-Burner Stoves

Stoves with two or three burners are fairly bulky and heavy but are ideal for car camping and standing camps. The extra burner (or burners) makes it more convenient to prepare elaborate meals that demand more than one pot cooking at a time.

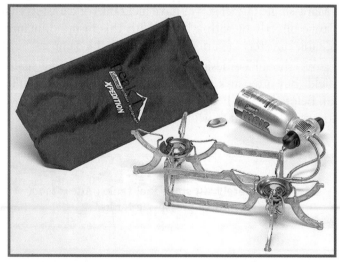

Fuel Types

Propane and naphtha (white gas) are the two best fuels for larger camp stoves with two or three burners. Both fuels are readily available at camping or hardware stores and many gas stations.

Propane is pehaps easier to use as you don't need to pressurize the tank; simply fasten the hose or tank to the stove, turn it on and light it. Propane comes in a sealed and pressurized fuel tank in a variety  of sizes; larger tanks (2 kg and higher) are refillable, but smaller disposable ones are not. These larger tanks are great for long-standing camps but are fairly heavy. The smaller ones are still quite bulky and heavy — not great for backpacking. If you want younger campers to use the stove primarily at standing camps, propane may be more convenient because it's so easy. Be sure to take special precautions when transporting fuel tanks by car. Check for regulations where they are sold.

Naphtha is also very easy to use, although you'll have to refill and pressurize the tank more often than propane. Naphtha comes in liquid form but must be vaporized for burning, which is why the fuel has to be pressurized. Once you light the burner, the heat warms the fuel line causing the naphtha in the line to expand into a vapour state. The tank is pressurized with a built-in pump which forces air into the tank. When preparing meals that require lots of cooking, this pressure will decrease, making it necessary to pump the tank again to increase the pressure. (It is most convenient to fill and pressurize the tank before cooking, rather than running out part way through.)

Trail Tip:
Fill your stove and lantern fuel tanks at home and test before setting out.

Take care when filling the tank; it's sometimes easy to spill fuel. Always use a proper funnel, especially in winter when the fuel is super cool — naphtha gas does not freeze at the same temperature as water — and can damage your skin if it makes contact. Naphtha burns hotter and will boil liquids faster than propane in any weather, which is why it's generally the fuel of choice for year-round campers and backpackers.

A propane/butane mix (blended fuel) is also available. Some manufacturers make lightweight, one- and two-burner collapsible stoves that burn this fuel. It comes in pressurized, disposable canisters or cartridges. Disposable, recyclable canisters are acceptable for short "one-canister" trips, but for extended trips, you'll have to carry more canisters and pack out the empties.

Butane

Pure butane in canisters is easy to operate and has good flame control, but it does not burn as hot as other fuels.

Multi-Fuel Stoves

A number of manufacturers produce stoves that burn a range of fuels including auto gas and kerosene. These are designed for people travelling in remote areas where white gas may not be readily available.

Serviceability and Construction

Every stove will eventually require servicing. Look for a stove you can easily maintain in the field with a minimum of tools. Make sure spare parts are also available at the store.

Look carefully at the stove's general construction. It should have a well made outer case, with no sharp edges. Is there a secure means for keeping the lid closed during transportation? Will it be easy to clean? (Some stoves have parts that are difficult or impossible to remove for cleaning or have recesses where food and dirt may gather and be difficult to remove.)

"Lighten Up" With Lanterns

Just like stoves, there are many lantern models on the market. Be sure to choose one that uses the same fuel as your stove, thereby avoiding having to carry two different types of fuels.

Though most lanterns are large and heavy, making them most suitable for standing camps, some manufacturers produce smaller versions that are excellent for backpacking.

Propane lanterns can be hooked up in tandem with a propane stove so they feed off a single large tank. Naphtha lanterns operate the same as the stoves, with pressurized tanks which require occasional pumping, but are easy to regulate.

Candle lanterns provide a suitable alternative to the larger, gas models described above. However, due to their size they only provide light over a relatively small area. These are great for lightweight camping trips.

Safety Tips for Stoves and Lanterns

Before operating any stove or lantern read the directions carefully and perhaps have the salesperson demonstrate how to use it properly.

Before lighting a stove/lantern, check that all attachments are secure, that the cap on the fuel tank is tightly fastened and that everything is turned off.

▲ To keep your stove safe from accidental tipping, set it up on a flat, level surface away from high traffic areas.

▲ Never refuel or use your stove or lantern inside your tent.

▲ Refuel a safe distance from other burning stoves, lanterns and open flames.

▲ Before travelling, release pressure in fuel tanks. Doing so may prevent an explosion or fuel leak.

- ▲ Airlines require tanks to be empty and washed thoroughly before allowing them on board.

- ▲ Keep your stove and lantern clean and well maintained at all times.

- ▲ When lighting a stove (or lantern), keep your face and body well back from the burner (globe) to prevent burns in the event of a "flare up."

- ▲ Select fuel bottles designed specifically for carrying liquid fuels. These will be made from aluminum and have a tight, leak-proof seal to prevent accidental leaks. Look for fuel bottles that have the ability to add a pour spout; these make pouring fuel much safer and easier. Fuel bottles/canisters come in a variety of different sizes. Select the appropriate size for the length of your trip.

Pots and Pans

Most pots and pans designed for camping and backpacking are generally made from either aluminum or stainless steel, though lightweight titanium products are now also available. Some pots even have "no-stick" coatings which make cooking and cleaning easier.

Usually aluminum is less expensive and lighter than stainless steel. However, aluminum scratches, pits and dents easily, which makes it difficult to clean.

Stainless steel pots and pans are a bit heavier but are much stronger and easier to clean.

Naturally, pots and pans come in a variety of sizes suitable for all needs. You can buy them separately or as part of a set. When purchasing cook-wear, look for these features:

▲ Pots that "nest" inside each other.

▲ Good, snug fitting lids.

▲ Separate pot grippers for lifting.

▲ Well-rounded pot corners for easy cleaning.

▲ Stuff sacks.

Some pots come with lids that double as frying pans. Knowing that pot lids will likely be needed to cover pots, most experienced campers buy a lightweight, no-stick, coated, frying pan with a collapsible handle.

Take special care to keep pots and pans clean after each use and before storage.

Utensils

Cooking and eating utensils (like pots) are made from a number of different materials. These include plastic, metal, wood and lexan (a relatively new product). Because lexan is lightweight and unbreakable, many campers have traded in their bent and twisted metal sets for new lexan plates, bowls, mugs and cutlery.

Campers need knives, forks, spoons, larger serving spoons, tongs and a flipper. Lightweight campers, concerned about weight, often choose to make do with a lexan bowl, soup spoon, and a pocketknife.

Keep all utensils clean and in good repair. A utensils pouch or bag will keep them from getting lost. Mesh dunk bags are great for storing dishes and utensils and can be hung from a branch to "air dry" the contents.

Of course, the utensils you take should reflect the meals planned and the desires of the cook.

Backpacks: Home on Your Back

Why is it that regardless how big a backpack you buy, it always gets filled to capacity?

If you start with an overnight trip and a huge pack, you're tempted to fill the huge space with "nice to have items" simply because you have the space. But, if you start with a smaller pack for the same trip, you'll be a little more careful when selecting items.

The trick is to select one pack that has the capacity to accommodate the necessary items for the types of trips you plan to go on and fits well when fully loaded. Many stores have stuff sacks filled with various weights so you can "load up" a pack. This will help you get an accurate "feel" for the pack when it's loaded.

Finding the right pack for a Cub or Scout is an even greater challenge than for adults. The youth will need basically the same gear as the adult but may not have the physical strength or size to carry the load. Keep in mind the general rule of thumb that backpackers should be able to carry 25-30% of their body weight.

When fitting a youth with a pack, the first concerns should be comfort and fit. Capacity is your next consideration. Because most packs let you tie sleeping bags or pads onto the back without endangering the hiker, capacity is less important than comfort.

Hikers have two styles of packs to choose from:

▲ Packs with an external frame have a clearly-visible frame on the outside of the pack.

▲ Packs with an internal frame have a built-in frame that is not visible from the outside.

Choosing between an external or an internal frame pack is strictly a matter of preference; both have strong points. Your choice may be limited by availability.

External Frame Packs

External frame packs are best suited for carrying heavy loads on well-established, wide open trails. An aluminum (or other high tech alloy) frame distributes the load weight onto the wearer's hips. The pack's bag and suspension system hang from the frame using metal pins called clevis pins. Good quality external frame packs will provide lots of adjustment points for the wearer.

Check the construction of the frame. Various methods, ranging from heli-arc welding to nuts and bolts with machined couplings, are used to connect the different pieces of frame. Test the strength of the frame by putting the bottom end of one of the side members on the floor; now, gently lean on the top of the opposite side member. Carefully increase the pressure until you have an idea of the weight it will bear. This exercise is similar to taking a fully loaded pack off your back and setting it on the ground but having it land on one corner only.

External frame packs carry the load higher on the hiker's body. This setup permits the wearer to stand straighter while walking. However, because the load is positioned higher, it may tend to sway and produce a feeling of top heaviness.

Caution! When hiking on trails with low overhanging branches, the wearer must be careful not to snag the pack on a branch, as this type of pack usually extends above the wearer's head.

External frame packs usually have two large compartments for separating gear. The top compartment should have an extension collar with a draw string to allow for some expansion. It should also have a storm flap that covers the top compartment completely. This flap extends down the front of the pack for extra protection.

When loading an external frame pack, place the heaviest items at the top closest to your back, medium weight items just below the heavy ones, and lightweight items and sleeping bags at the bottom. Putting heavy items low in the pack will cause you to lean forward and place more strain on your body.

External frame packs usually provide space below the pack's bag to tie on a tent or a sleeping bag, although some packs may have a built-in

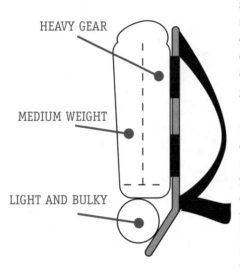

HEAVY GEAR

MEDIUM WEIGHT

LIGHT AND BULKY

sleeping bag compartment. They also usually have a number of outside pockets which make it quick and easy to reach snacks, emergency kits, or cameras — a great convenience.

External frame packs, by holding the pack away from the wearer's back, provide space for air to move through and prevent hikers from having their backs pressed close to the pack. (**Note:** Clevis pins have been known to work loose and fall off. Wrap duct tape over them and/or carry a few spares just in case.)

Trail Tip:
Do not carry fuel bottles or detergents in your food bag.

Internal Frame Packs

Internal frame packs are best suited for hiking and climbing on uneven narrow trails or for cross-country skiing.

Internal frame packs are worn much closer to the body than external packs. A hiker carries the pack and its weight lower on the back which provides a lower, more stable centre of gravity. Because of the numerous pack adjustments available, hikers frequently say that they feel as if their body and the pack have become one unit, particularly when travelling on uneven terrain.

An internal frame pack has a frame concealed within its design. Most of these packs use two parallel aluminum stays that run the length of the pack and can be removed and custom-fitted to meet the curve of the wearer's back. Some manufacturers combine the stays with a plastic "frame sheet." This approach provides more stiffness and keeps objects in the pack from poking into the hiker's back.

Internal frame packs provide some lash points but usually have few outside pockets. They hold most gear inside where it won't snag on trees. This streamlined pack also fits in canoes, airplanes and car trunks easily.

Internal frame packs are usually loaded in one of three ways:

1. *Top loading:* everything goes into one huge compartment from the top of the pack.

2. *Front loading:* a hiker can lay the pack on its back to load it through a zippered opening.

3. *Combination front and top loading.*

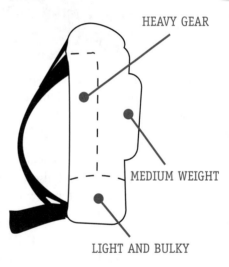

HEAVY GEAR

MEDIUM WEIGHT

LIGHT AND BULKY

Number 3 is the most common style, allowing the top compartment to be accessed through the top and having a zip-out divider shelf that separates the top compartment from a lower sleeping bag compartment.

When loading an internal frame pack, for best mobility place heavier items close to your back in the centre or lower portion of the pack.

Suspension Systems

This is the method used to fasten the pack (internal or external) to the hiker's back. A properly fitted pack will transfer up to 80 percent of the load to the hips which are much stronger than shoulder and back muscles.

A backpack should be fully adjustable to fit your body and include padded shoulder straps and back support, in addition to a well padded hip belt shaped to fit around the wearer's hips. It should also include adjustable

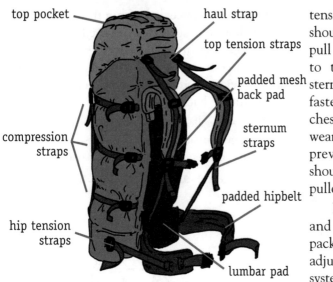

top pocket

haul strap

top tension straps

tension straps at the shoulders and hips to pull the pack closer to the body and a sternum strap which fastens across the chest. This method of wearing the pack will prevent the hiker's shoulders from being pulled back.

padded mesh back pad

sternum straps

compression straps

padded hipbelt

Both external and internal frame packs now have great adjustable suspension systems. In fact, some manufacturers offer designs specifically sized for youth and women in addition to the short, medium and tall models designed to correspond with the length of the wearer's torso.

hip tension straps

lumbar pad

Compression Straps

Buy a pack with compression straps running from side to side across the front of the pack, and also from the top front edge to the back edge. These straps, when tightened, will compress your gear into a smaller bundle and keep equipment and clothes from shifting around.

Backpack Construction

Good quality backpacks are usually made from cordura nylon and nylon packcloth. Both are durable, though cordura stands up better during rough use. A backpack should have a waterproof coating on the inside to keep your gear dry. However, it's very difficult to completely waterproof a backpack with all the stitching and needle holes in the material. Most backpackers carry a waterproof pack cover for extra protection.

Check the stitching to make sure it is reinforced in high stress areas, particularly where compression and suspension straps are fastened to the pack. Check the zippers as well. They should be the heavy duty nylon coil type.

Buying a Backpack

Once you've found a reputable store with knowledgeable staff, try on different packs until you find the most comfortable one for you. Use the chart below; it will give you a general idea how large a pack you need. (Figures are approximates.)

Overnight (1-2 days): 3000 cubic inches or 50 litres
Weekends (2-4 days): 4000 cubic inches or 70 litres
Longer trips (5+ days): 5000 cubic inches or 80 litres
Expeditions (10+ days): 6500 cubic inches or 100 litres

Tuning the Pack

▲ Loosen all straps on the pack.

▲ Load the pack with the items you need, and secure it in place with compression straps.

▲ Put the pack on and fasten the hip belt.

▲ Make sure shoulder straps are in the proper place. If they are too high, remove the pack and adjust the shoulder strap height on the back of the pack. On internal frame packs, it may be a ladder-like affair. If it is, adjust the straps up or down to fit. Another style involves a track that runs up the centre of the pack. If it is that type, loosen the screw, adjust accordingly, then tighten again. On external frame packs, you may have to remove the metal pins holding the pack to move the straps up or down for proper fitting.

▲ Try the pack on again and fasten the sternum strap. Adjust it up or down as needed.

- ▲ Now adjust tension straps at the hips and shoulders. These will pull the pack closer to the back.

- ▲ When you've reached this stage, go for a walk around the block or inside the store. Tighten or loosen the straps until you are comfortable.

- ▲ If you can't get comfortable with this pack, try another one and another until you find a comfortable fit.

Putting on the Pack

How do you get a pack on your back when out in the wilderness?

Lift it onto a stump or an area of raised ground, slip one shoulder through the shoulder strap, then lift with your legs as you slip the other shoulder into place. If you're in a flat area, squat down on one knee and lift your pack onto your raised thigh. Slip your shoulder through the straps. Lift again with your legs and swing your pack into position on your back, sliding your other shoulder into place as you go.

Adventure Clothes

The clothing you choose for outdoor activities must serve many different functions. It must protect you from abrasions, from exposure to sun, wind and rain, and from insects. Clothes must allow you to regulate your body temperature according to your needs and the temperature. It must provide insulation for retaining body heat during cold weather and allow evaporation of perspiration during heavy exercise or in hot weather. Clothing is also used to carry and store some of your equipment, such as pocketknives, first aid kits, trail snacks and wallets.

In addition, long-lasting outdoor activity clothing should be lightweight, low in bulk, highly compressible, quick-drying, durable and affordable.

Layering Clothes

The most effective way to keep a body warm and dry while participating in outdoor activities is to dress in layers. Layering your clothing lets you add or remove layers as required. For example, if you wore a heavy winter parka over regular street clothes when you were building a quinzhee, your internal temperature would soon soar. If you opened the parka, you'd be too cold. However, layering clothes would allow you to remove a layer or two while working hard, then put them back on, when finished, to keep you warm. Keeping the torso well protected and insulated is crucial. Legs still require insulation and protection, although less than the torso.

Garments manufactured for today's outdoor industry are generally designed to serve one of three functions:

▲ Wick (move moisture away from skin)

▲ Insulate

▲ Provide a protective outer shell.

Inner Layer (Wicking)

 Start with a thin, synthetic, wicking material close to your skin. This layer will remove perspiration and keep the skin dry. It's important that this inner layer does not absorb and retain moisture. If it does, you may feel warm during heavy exercise, but, when the activity stops, moisture will quickly cool and leave you feeling cold and clammy.

Middle Layer (Insulating)

 This layer (or layers) should trap dead air and provide insulation. The layer must also be capable of dealing with the moisture passed through the first (wicking) layer. It should either wick it away or absorb it without losing insulating abilities. This middle layer should be easily vented to allow excess perspiration to escape. Loose fitting, open collar designs complete with expandable cuffs and "pit zips" (underarm zippers) allow you to open the garment up so better air movement can remove moisture.

It's usually better to wear several insulation layers. They let you regulate your body temperature more accurately, and permit you to add or remove layers when needed. Insulated vests also help keep the torso warm. Not having sleeves, vests offer good underarm ventilation and lots of free arm movement. Vests and fleece garments also make good outer layers in fair weather, especially if treated with waterproofing or windproofing chemicals for more inclement weather. Some insulating fabrics include wool, down, pile, fleece, Thinsulate™, Hollofil™ and Polarguard™.

Outer Layer (Shell)

The outer layer performs many functions. It must protect you from the elements (sun, wind, rain, snow) and be durable enough to protect against and withstand abrasion. It must also allow the moisture to pass through, or provide lots of ventilation to allow moisture to escape.

Many outer shells are made from windproof, waterproof, breathable materials such as Gore-Tex™. The materials are coated or laminated with a microporous membrane consisting of millions of microscopic holes that permit vapour to move through from the inside but the holes are too small to allow rain through from the outside.

The outer layer is generally a rain shell or parka-style coat. It should cover the torso and extend below the hips so that when the wearer bends over, the parka doesn't raise above the belt line. Nylon is probably the most commonly used fibre for these garments because of its good strength, wearing ability and resistance to wind and rain. Sleeves should allow complete arm movement and not slide up the arm during activity. At the wrist there should be some method of closing off the sleeve — usually a Velcro™ strap with a bellows cuff. Make sure collars are big enough so you can turn them up to protect the back of your neck. A raised collar will reduce heat loss from the body via the "chimney effect."

Front closures should feature heavyweight, nylon, two-way zippers with storm flaps and snaps to keep out wind, rain and snow. Most outer shells include a hood. Some hoods roll up into the collar while some are detachable; others simply hang from the collar. Many hoods also have a peak and adjustable strings to draw the hood in close to protect the face.

Outer layers should include plenty of pockets for carrying handy items and snacks.

Pants

The same wicking materials used on the upper body are used for the legs. Polypropylene or fleece pants, when covered by a windproof, waterproof outer shell, work well even on cold winter days. Avoid cotton (commonly used in sweat pants and jeans) when possible. It absorbs moisture quickly, becomes very heavy, and takes a long time to dry. Nylon wind pants provide good protection from the wind, some water resistance on damp days, and excellent durability.

Loose-fitting, quick-drying nylon shorts are comfortable in warm weather, and for males can double as a swim suit, but they offer little protection from insects, trail brush and other low-lying obstacles along a trail. When selecting pants or shorts, pick loose-fitting ones that let you walk and climb easily.

Fibres and Fabrics

Two types of fibres are used in clothing: natural and synthetic (man made). Natural fibres include wool, cotton and silk. The most common synthetic fibres include nylon, polypropylene, acrylic and polyester.

Natural Fibres

Wool

Wool, one of the oldest fibres known, provides excellent insulation by trapping body heat. The many small hairs on each fibre provide the insulation. These trap minute pockets of air in the fabric and reduce the flow of heat from the body. However, perspiration can escape through evaporation.

Because wool's small hairs don't mat down when the material absorbs moisture, it retains much of its insulating characteristic when wet. This natural fibre can absorb up to 35 percent of its own weight in moisture before it begins to feel wet and cold. Since wool can absorb so much moisture, it takes much longer to dry than other materials.

These same tiny hairs which provide such good insulation may prove very uncomfortable for some wearers when worn next to the skin. Wool is not as strong as some other fibres and wears out quicker, especially in high wear areas, such as collars, cuffs and elbows. These two characteristics (itchiness and wear) make wool less suitable when compared to newer materials that provide similar insulating abilities and do not absorb any moisture. To increase wool's durability and to make it less "itchy," some manufacturers combine wool with other fabrics such as polypropylene.

Cotton

Cotton is comfortable when worn next to the skin, fairly abrasion-resistant, but takes a long time to dry.

When dry, cotton provides some insulation by trapping air. However, when cotton gets wet, all insulating characteristics disappear as the fine fibres collapse. Cotton absorbs a lot of water. This is very useful in hot weather because the damp cotton fibres allow water to evaporate, producing a cooling effect. Once it has absorbed moisture (perspiration) from the skin, cotton will begin to draw heat from your body. It is for these reasons that many people avoid cotton during cold weather outings.

Silk

Silk is a hollow fibre that provides a good space for dead, dry air. The fibre has many excellent insulating characteristics which are not affected by moisture. Why? Silk can absorb up to 30 percent of its own weight in moisture before it feels damp.

Silk is a smooth fibre that is very comfortable when worn next to the skin. It doesn't irritate the skin and is moderately resistant to abrasion. Silk is a fairly good fibre for outdoor clothing except for its high cost. Therefore, it's used primarily for smaller clothing items like gloves, socks and underwear.

Synthetic Fibres

Nylon

This fibre is very strong, lightweight, and does not absorb much water. It can be woven into a very tight fabric which offers good wind protection and fairly good rain protection when coated. Nylon fabrics may discolour when exposed to sunshine, but most clothing in regular use will wear out before discolouration becomes a problem. Because of its high strength, low weight and low cost, nylon is very popular with outdoor enthusiasts.

Polyesters and Acrylics

These fibres are very similar to nylon except they absorb even less moisture. Pile and fleece (two relatively new synthetics on the market) are typically made from polyester. These materials insulate very well, wick moisture away quickly, are lightweight and extremely durable. They're manufactured in different weights, making them excellent for wearing next to the skin in the wicking layer, or as an insulating middle layer.

Polypropylene

Polypropylene, while similar to the other synthetic materials, offers a few major advantages. It is much stronger and more resistant to wear and abrasion. Very lightweight and thin, it is excellent for lightweight camping. It doesn't absorb any water and readily wicks perspiration from the skin, thereby reducing heat loss from the body. This characteristic makes it desirable for cold weather activities when an individual may be frequently alternating between times of excessive exertion (with lots of perspiration and heat) and times of low or no exertion when less body heat is produced. However, polypropylene does require frequent washing to keep it functioning properly, and prevent it from retaining body odours.

Insulation Fibres

Insulation materials most commonly used in outdoor wear include down and an assortment of synthetics like Hollofil™, Polarguard™, Dacron II™, Quallofil™, Thinsulate™, Liteloft™, Primaloft™, and Microloft™.

Down (from geese or ducks) still provides the greatest amount of insulation for the weight. It's also the softest of all insulation materials. However, it has two drawbacks: it is very expensive, and it absorbs and retains moisture. This moisture, which may come from perspiration or rain, may cause the down to mat together, losing its insulating ability. Down also dries very slowly and must be done very carefully to ensure that it returns to its original fluffiness.

Synthetic insulation fibres are much less expensive, weigh only slightly more, and do not absorb or retain as much or any moisture. Their lower cost, good insulating characteristics and fast drying abilities make them ideal for use in outdoor clothing and sleeping bags. (See section in this chapter dealing with sleeping bags.)

Blended Fibres and Fabrics

These are a mixture of different fibres and fabrics which, when combined, produce a new superior material (often including synthetic and natural fibres). This combination gives the new fabric greater resistance to abrasion.

Head Wear

It's important to wear something on your head during most outdoor activities: in the summer to protect against insects and exposure to the sun, and in colder months to regulate heat loss. The body acts like a chimney; heat rises to the top — your head.

In hot weather, campers should wear a hat with a wide brim to protect the face, ears and neck from sun exposure. Not only will a hat help remove the heat, but it will also absorb perspiration. Cotton hats work well as they absorb a lot of moisture which in turn conducts heat away from your head. The increased surface area of the hat increases the evaporation process which gets rid of the moisture and cools the head below.

In cold weather, choose something that will prevent heat loss. Wool or fleece hats that cover your forehead, ears and the back of your neck work well. A winter hat with a peak will provide shade protection for eyes on very bright days. A wearer can use a hat to regulate body temperature by pushing it back to expose the forehead or by removing it for short periods of time during strenuous exercise.

Scarves and Bandanas

Scarves and bandanas help keep your throat and neck warm in winter or cool in summer if dipped in water before wearing. If necessary, you may even tie them up over your head and ears. For younger children, neck warmers may be a better option, since they don't leave loose ends dangling.

Hand Wear

Wear gloves and/or mitts during cold winter days. They'll keep your hands warm and dry. Mitts are warmer since the heat produced by the fingers is equally shared. In a glove, each finger must produce its own heat. However, gloves are more convenient than mitts when you're trying to handle or operate equipment that requires dexterity.

Once again, the layering technique works quite effectively for the hands. Try wearing light gloves inside mitts when you're walking or not needing your hands for detailed work. If you need to work a camera or adjust a pack, take off the outer mitts and just wear your gloves. Fingers will generate more heat when they are active, but inside the gloves they'll still have some protection and insulation from the cold.

Wool mitts and gloves provide excellent insulation value but take longer to dry when they get wet. Also they tend to wear out quicker than synthetic materials. When covered with waterproof outer mitts, wool or fleece liners work well.

Synthetics, such as nylon and acrylic, are much stronger and dry quickly but do not offer as much insulation. Leather offers good strength, some insulation and good resistance to moisture but, once wet, it takes a long time to dry. One-piece insulated gloves and mitts also work well but don't allow for very good dexterity. Manufacturers use down, Hollofil™, Dacron II™ and other new synthetics in mitts where greater bulk can be tolerated in exchange for warmth. Thinsulate™ is often used in gloves because of its high insulation value and thin material.

Effective Rain Wear

If you spend time in the outdoors, be prepared for rain. Getting wet in a warm summer shower may not pose a problem — a refreshing pleasure — but if you get wet in cold weather, it can be not only unpleasant but dangerous.

Highly active people must find something to keep the rain out while letting perspiration escape from the body — a difficult, combined task. Plastic coated, vinyl, and rubberized products keep the rain out but don't breathe at all. They trap all perspiration inside. During a warm rain shower, your clothing may become soaked with perspiration almost as much as if you stood out in the rain without any rain gear. Manufacturers have expended much effort to design clothing with ventilation panels under the arms and across the back to reduce this problem. Such clothing generally works for less strenuous activities.

Tightly woven wool breathes quite well and sheds a lot of rain, but eventually it soaks up water and gets heavy. At this stage, it will still provide some insulation but will take a long time to dry.

Manufacturers have developed new products which are windproof, waterproof and breathable. To achieve this, they laminate a membrane to another more sturdy material, typically nylon. These laminates contain millions of microscopic pores which will allow water vapour (but not larger water droplets) to pass through, thus making it waterproof and breathable. Gore-Tex™ is perhaps the best known product. Other water treatment products are also available that manufacturers claim are equally good.

Rainsuits (whether made from Gore-Tex™, plastic or vinyl) are typically available in two-pieces: pants and jacket. Jackets should have storm flaps to cover the zippers and pockets and a hood with a peak. The garment should extend below your hips. Pant cuffs should be long enough to cover the tops of your boots, while jacket cuffs need to cover the tops of your hands. This means water will not drop off the edges into boots or gloves.

Ponchos

Ponchos offer yet another option. They provide good protection to the upper part of the body and ventilate quite well because of large openings along the sides. However, ponchos may be very awkward to work in, and they catch a lot of wind. Loose, billowing ponchos and an open fire are not a good combination. Use special precautions.

Ponchos also make good groundsheets or shelter flies.

Clothing Construction

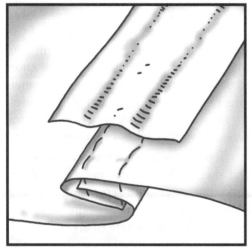

It's often easy to judge the quality and durability of a piece of clothing by looking at the quality of the materials and the way the garment is made.

Seams tell a great story. Make sure they're flat and stitched well. On waterproof shells, seams should be taped with a waterproof tape or you'll have to treat them with waterproofing solution yourself. Make sure all corners and high stress areas have some sort of reinforcement.

Zippers

Zippers on outdoor clothing are usually the heavy duty, nylon, toothed type. These are very strong, durable and will not rust. All zippers must be protected by storm flaps to keep out the weather. Two-way zippers on the front of the garment are very convenient, and are found on high quality garments.

Pockets

Pockets should be made of a strong material to stand up to outdoor wear and tear. Regular pockets (slash pockets) are fine for warming hands, but they aren't useful for carrying objects.

Jacket pockets should have zippers and storm flaps. These will protect them from the elements and keep objects inside. Large square pockets (patch pockets), especially those designed to expand (cargo pockets), are very useful for carrying equipment.

Foot Care

For a successful hike, your feet must stay dry and comfortable. Feet are, after all, the means by which you reach your destination. Keep them clean by washing every day with warm water and soap. Dry them carefully, and dust them with foot powder, especially between the toes. When they need it, trim your toenails straight across. Try to walk a little farther and run a little faster each day to toughen up your tender feet. If you feel a "hot spot" developing, stop immediately and cover the area with Moleskin™, Second Skin™ or other blister treatment products. This prevents the hot spot from developing into a blister.

Footwear

Boots

Blisters and sore feet are common injuries suffered by hikers and backpackers. These ailments are usually caused by improper or poorly fitting footwear. Hiking boots and shoes are carefully designed to provide:

▲ Support for your foot and ankle.

▲ Protection for your foot against cuts and scrapes from rocks and trail obstacles.

▲ Cushioning for the soles of your feet.

▲ Traction and grip on rough trails.

Select boots that fit properly and meet your needs.

If you plan on doing day hikes with a light day pack, a lightweight hiking shoe or boot will probably "fit" your needs. If your outdoor activities include backpacking over rough trails, you may want a stiffer, all-leather, middleweight, waterproof boot.

Lightweight and middleweight boots are usually made with nylon and suede or all-leather uppers. Nylon/suede uppers provide good ventilation but are usually not waterproof unless they have a waterproof liner. Leather uppers tend to last longer, and provide better support and protection. They are also more waterproof. Many products can keep your feet dry in wet weather.

Some manufacturers produce boots with an inner sock or membrane (Gore-Tex™) that makes the boot waterproof; others produce waterproof socks that hikers may wear to keep feet dry inside any footwear. Still other manufacturers sell sprays and pastes that, when applied to boots, make them waterproof. Each requires proper cleaning and maintenance to keep them performing at high levels. Read and follow directions carefully.

Many companies now produce hiking shoes and boots with removable insoles. These allow a person to adjust the comfort and fit of the boot by exchanging the insole with a thicker or thinner model.

The outer sole must be soft and flexible enough to provide cushioning and comfort, yet hard enough to wear well. Outer soles are available in two layers: a softer layer for cushioning closest to the foot, laminated to a harder, better wearing layer to grip the trail. Some manufacturers have even considered the environmental impact of deep tread soles and offer soles designed specifically to meet this concern.

Important Features

Here's what to look for when buying hiking boots:

▲ Padded "scree collar" around the ankle for added protection. It will keep out small stones and twigs.

▲ Stiff heel counter to keep heel firmly in place.

▲ Good tread for gripping rough ground.

▲ An easy lacing system: "D rings" on the lower boot, and speed hooks or pulleys at the top.

▲ A sewn-in gusset to keep out water and other debris.

▲ Good midsole for shock absorption.

▲ Light weight.

▲ A good combination of waterproofing and breathability, and most important, a good fit.

Years ago, new boots were so stiff and solid that they often required a lengthy "break-in" period before they were flexible and comfortable enough for the trail. Those days are gone. Manufacturers now claim that you can wear boots right away without any "break-in" period. But... it's still advisable to wear new boots for several days before embarking on a major hike — just to make sure they fit properly.

Follow the manufacturers' guidelines for cleaning and waterproofing new boots. Many will also make or provide special waterproofing products for their boots. After waterproofing the boots, wear them a few times allowing creases to form, then waterproof along the creases.

Get a Proper Fit

Many large hiking stores have a foot-measuring device (called a Brannock Device) which determines the precise length, width and arch of your foot. Ask for this device.

Bring your hiking socks with you to the store and wear them with each pair of boots you try on. Don't rush when buying hiking boots. Schedule plenty of time. Try on different models and walk around until you find the best fit. Because your feet swell during the day, start trying on boots later in the afternoon.

Because most people have one foot slightly larger than the other, make sure you try on both boots. Find a boot that is most comfortable on your larger foot. The boot should fit snugly, yet not be too tight. After putting on your hiking socks and placing your feet in the unlaced boots, you should be able to slide the foot forward just enough to insert one finger between the heel and back of the boot. Now move the foot to the back, and lace the boot up snugly. Toes should wiggle freely, but gently touch the inner surfaces of the boot. When the boot is laced up, your heel should not be able to move more than half a centimetre in any direction. Too much movement will increase friction between your foot and the boot and may result in blisters.

Many outdoor stores have ramps built for customers to test boots. Try walking down the incline. Your feet should move forward a little, but not enough for toes to touch the end of the boot.

Socks

The layering technique can also be applied to your footwear. Active feet produce a lot of perspiration. If allowed to accumulate, this moisture may cause blisters or cold feet. Good socks should move the perspiration away from the foot and provide insulation.

Experienced backpackers use a wicking sock made of polypropylene closest to the foot and a heavier wool sock over that. However, some

Trail Tip:
Whenever you use items from your first aid or survival kits, make note so you'll remember to replace these items when you get home.

manufacturers now produce socks that combine a wicking material with an insulating one. Try an assortment of socks and use the ones that suit you best.

Socks are very important in hiking. Put on a clean pair everyday. They should fit well and be in good condition.

Sample Checklist for Summer Weekend Camping Trip

Personal Gear
Wear These or Keep In Pockets

- ▲ Wide brim hat
- ▲ Lip balm
- ▲ Sunglasses
- ▲ Pocketknife
- ▲ Whistle
- ▲ Tissues
- ▲ Matches in waterproof container
- ▲ Appropriate footwear (waterproof, lightweight hiking boots)
- ▲ Wallet with medical card
- ▲ Bandana

Keep In Pockets of Pack or Pants

- ▲ Map and compass
- ▲ Water bottle
- ▲ Snack (good old raisins and peanuts: GORP)
- ▲ Sunscreen
- ▲ Flashlight
- ▲ Rain gear
- ▲ First aid/survival kit
- ▲ Equipment repair kit
- ▲ Insect repellent

Inside Pack (External or Internal)

- ▲ Mattress*
- ▲ Sleeping bag in waterproof compression bag*
- ▲ Pajamas stuffed inside sleeping bag

* may be lashed on outside of external frame pack

Clothes Bag

- ▲ Long sleeved shirt
- ▲ T-shirts
- ▲ Long pants
- ▲ Hiking shorts
- ▲ Sweater
- ▲ Socks
- ▲ Underwear
- ▲ Windproof jacket

Personal Kit

- ▲ Hand towel, face cloth
- ▲ Biodegradable soap and container
- ▲ Comb, mirror
- ▲ Tooth brush and tooth paste
- ▲ Deodorant
- ▲ Toilet paper
- ▲ Moist towelettes
- ▲ Tissues
- ▲ Sanitary napkins
- ▲ Medication

Personal Eating Kit

- ▲ Knife, fork, spoon
- ▲ Plate, bowl, mug or
- ▲ Large bowl, mug and a spoon (if travelling light)

Washing Kit

- ▲ Three collapsible wash basins
- ▲ Biodegradable soap
- ▲ Javex or other disinfectant
- ▲ Wash cloth or mop
- ▲ Drying cloths
- ▲ Pot scrubber
- ▲ Mesh bag for hang-drying on warm, breezy days.

Patrol Gear

- ▲ Tent and ground sheet
- ▲ Saw/axe
- ▲ Kitchen utensil kit (spatula, can/bottle opener, tongs, large spoon, potato peeler, egg flipper)
- ▲ Oven mitts
- ▲ Measuring cup
- ▲ Small food canisters
- ▲ Salt/pepper/spices
- ▲ Garbage bags
- ▲ Pots complete with lids (1 small, 1 medium, 1 large)
- ▲ Frying pan
- ▲ Stove
- ▲ Lantern
- ▲ Fuel
- ▲ Water container
- ▲ Water treatment system
- ▲ Cooler
- ▲ Coffee/tea pot
- ▲ Equipment repair kit
- ▲ 60 metres nylon cord
- ▲ Pail
- ▲ Table cloth
- ▲ Tarp for shelter or covering gear
- ▲ Plastic trowel and resealable freezer bags
- ▲ Paper towels

Optional Items (Personal & Group)

- ▲ Sneakers
- ▲ Binoculars
- ▲ Camera & film
- ▲ Log book/journal and pencil
- ▲ *Fieldbook for Canadian Scouting*
- ▲ Backpack oven or Reflector oven

- ▲ Watch
- ▲ Candle lantern
- ▲ Griddle
- ▲ Batteries
- ▲ Pocket tool
- ▲ Bug net
- ▲ Bug jacket
- ▲ Bathing suit
- ▲ Fishing gear
- ▲ Fishing license (may be required by law)
- ▲ Fire permits (if required)

Note: Two factors that will determine the amount and choice of equipment you take on a camping trip are: (1) the distance that the equipment must be carried (backpacking vs. car camping vs. canoeing), and (2) the size and strength of the individual carrying the equipment.

Note: For lightweight camping, you may find it is more efficient if you break into smaller groups of three or four youths. Then, divide the patrol gear accordingly: one carries the tent, one carries the food, one carries the stove, etc.

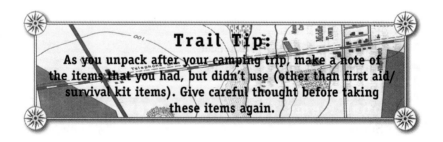

Trail Tip:

As you unpack after your camping trip, make a note of the items that you had, but didn't use (other than first aid/survival kit items). Give careful thought before taking these items again.

Add These Items for Canoe Trips

- ▲ Canoes
- ▲ Paddles
- ▲ Personal Floatation Devices (PFDs) or lifejackets
- ▲ Painters
- ▲ Whistles
- ▲ Bailers
- ▲ Extra rope for lining
- ▲ Throw/rescue bag
- ▲ Sponges
- ▲ Kneeling pads

Sample Menus at Standing Camp

Breakfast

- ▲ Milk
- ▲ Juice
- ▲ Ham slices
- ▲ Eggs
- ▲ Cheese slices
- ▲ Mayonnaise
- ▲ English muffins
- ▲ Oranges

Lunch

- ▲ Grilled cheese sandwiches
- ▲ Kraft™ dinner
- ▲ Juice
- ▲ Apples

Supper

- ▲ Spaghetti
- ▲ Garlic bread
- ▲ Juice/milk
- ▲ Fruit cups
- ▲ Cake

Backpacking or Lightweight Camping

Breakfast

- ▲ Porridge
- ▲ Bagels
- ▲ Peanut butter
- ▲ Juice crystals

Lunch

- ▲ Pita bread
- ▲ Peanut butter
- ▲ Cheese
- ▲ Juice crystals
- ▲ Apples
- ▲ Granola bars

Supper

- ▲ Boil-in-a-bag meal
- ▲ Dehydrated meals
- ▲ Kraft™ dinner and a tin of tuna/chicken
- ▲ Juice crystals

Trail Tip:
If you are a light sleeper, easily disturbed by snoring tent mates, bring along some ear plugs.

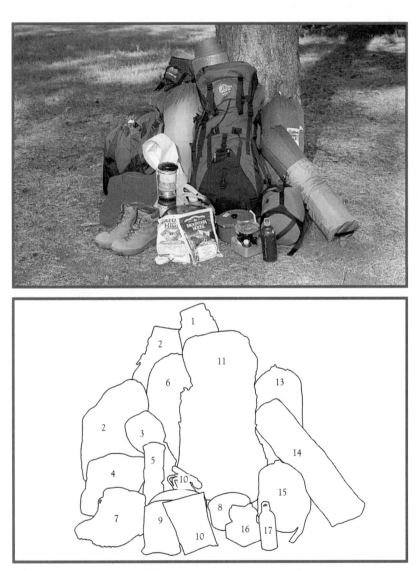

1) ensolite pad
2) day pack
3) yellow rain gear
4) fleece sweater
5) lantern
6) sleeping bag
7) boots
8) pots
9) food
10) water purification system
11) large internal frame pack
12) assorted backpacking foods
13) tent
14) therm-a-rest mattress
15) sleeping bag in compression bag
16) single burner stove in case
17) fuel bottle

My Personal Equipment List

CHAPTER 6

▶ Tools

Many tools are available that can make your camping experience easier and more comfortable. These tools include pocketknives, sheath knives, axes, saws, shovels and, most recently, multi-purpose or mini tools. To use and maintain these tools safely requires a certain amount of training, skill and respect. Where and when you choose to camp will also help you decide what tools you need.

Before cutting or digging anywhere, ask yourself, "Is this absolutely necessary?" If it isn't, don't do it. Find out what cutting or digging rules apply in your area. If you're on private land, ask the owner for permission.

(**Note:** Most national and provincial parks don't allow any trenching, digging, cutting or limbing.)

As lightweight, "no trace" camping skills gain wider acceptance, fewer people are using axes, saws, shovels and sheath knives. In most cases — especially for backpacking — pocketknives and/or multipurpose tools are all most people need.

Ask an experienced outdoorsman to help you choose tools that suit your needs. This person can show you how to use and maintain them too. With practice, you'll soon develop your own skills.

Pocketknives

More people use pocketknives than any other tool in the outdoors. A pocketknife is much more than just a cutting blade; it's a mini tool kit. Most pocketknives have one or two cutting blades, a can opener, bottle opener, screwdriver, tweezers and toothpicks. Larger models are heavier and more cumbersome, but they might include scissors, saws, files, different kinds of screwdrivers, cork screws, and more.

Your knife is a valuable tool. Take good care of it.

▲ Wipe the blade clean after using it.

▲ Keep it dry and sharp.

▲ Don't use it on things that will dull or break it.

▲ Keep it off the ground. Moisture and dirt may cause damage.

▲ Keep it away from fire and extreme heat. Heat draws the temper from the steel and makes the edge soft.

▲ Oil joints and springs as required.

▲ Keep a folding knife folded when not in use.

▲ Don't fool around with a knife. Throwing one into the ground, into tables or into trees is not only very dangerous but hard on both the knife and your surroundings.

▲ When cutting, grip the handle firmly and cut away from your body.

Sharpening Your Knife

A sharp knife is safer, more efficient, and easier to control than a dull one. A dull blade that has to be forced through wood can slip out of control and cause an accident.

Sharpen your knife with a proper sharpening stone. Many different types and grades are available. For a badly nicked blade, begin with a coarse stone. As you remove the nicks, switch to a finer stone. To do this, lay the blade on the stone. Raise the back of the blade slightly (to about a 15 degree angle) and stroke the full length of the edge from the hilt to the point across the stone towards you in a circular motion. To sharpen the other side, turn the blade over and repeat the process, this time moving the blade away from you. Alternate from side to side until the blade is sharp; then wipe the blade clean.

Sheath Knife

While small sheath knives may be useful (particularly for meal preparation), larger models tend to be heavy, awkward to carry, and unnecessary for most camp chores.

Multi-Purpose Tools

Relatively new on the market, these tools preform all the same functions as pocketknives, but they also fold open into pliers — useful for making equipment repairs. They're usually larger, heavier and more expensive than pocketknives. Only you can decide if they're worth the extra cost and weight.

Axes

With the current shift to using stoves for cooking, many people find that they do not use axes at all. You can usually break the firewood you need for cooking a quick meal with your hands and feet. However, if you're building a fire to last several hours or if the wood is wet, you may need an axe.

Axes come in a variety of sizes and weights, but for most camp duties, an axe with a 1 to 1.5 kg head and a short handle length (50-60 cm) is sufficient. Avoid buying an axe with a painted handle. You want to be able to inspect the wood's grain to check if it is straight from end to end and free of knots, cracks or splits.

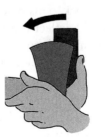

Dull axes (like dull knives) are more dangerous than sharp ones. Though you can remove rough edges and nicks with a flat mill file, it is best to sharpen your axe with a good sharpening stone. Avoid high speed grinding wheels. They tend to heat up the metal, thereby reducing its temper and its ability to hold a sharp edge.

To sharpen or hone an axe, hold the head of the axe in one hand, with the blade pointing up and the handle pointing out and away from you. Run the sharpening stone along the edge with a circular motion, from one end of the edge to the other. Then, turn the axe around with the handle now pointing at you and hone the other side in the same way. Continue alternating sides until the axe is sharp.

Axe Safety

1. Keep your axe sharp enough to really "bite" (not "chew") into wood.

2. Keep the handle tight. If it loosens, drive the wedge in deeper.

3. When not using it, keep your axe in a sheath. If you must carry it around camp, hold the handle near the sheathed head with the edge down and away from your body. During a hike, lash it sheathed to the side of your pack.

4. When swinging an axe, make sure the area is clear of obstacles and people. Stay away from low branches and roofs.

5. When passing an axe to someone else, do so with the sheath on, handle first and the head down and edge out. Make sure the other person has a good hold of the handle before you let go. (**Note:** Living trees should only be cut in emergencies.)

Using Your Axe

Brute force isn't necessary when using an axe. Its sharp cutting edge and the weight of the head do the work. Before starting to chop or split, get yourself a chopping block. This block will keep your axe from hitting the ground where a rock could deflect it into your leg or foot. Keeping a balanced stance when chopping and splitting is crucial. Extend your arms so the axe blade touches the wood. When you swing, simply extend your arms in a controlled manner.

For splitting, lift the axe just high enough for smooth wrist and forearm motion. Aim the axe blade by looking at the point where you want to hit, and then swing the axe down in a controlled drop.

For chopping, use the "contact method." Here's how: Keep the axe and the wood you want to cut in contact with each other throughout the splitting. Bring both down against the chopping block at the same time. If you're cutting a larger branch or log, use a V-shaped cut. Make the top of the "V" as wide as the thickness of the branch.

To cut off branches, start from the bottom and work upwards, cutting from the underside. If you cut into the crotch, springy branches will make you work much harder.

Splitting and chopping is tiring work; take rests when you need them.

Hatchets

Hatchets are compact, but they can be dangerous. Since they're usually held in one hand, you have less control during the swing. If the head misses its target, it may injure the user. Therefore, most outdoor experts suggest you get into a kneeling position when using a hatchet.

Saws

A folding camp saw or bow saw is often quicker, safer, lighter and easier to use than an axe. Many campers prefer it over an axe or hatchet.

Always saw with steady strokes. When starting a cut, make a notch in the wood to keep the saw blade from jumping around. Use a blade guard when you're not using the saw, and always carry the saw by the handle to prevent the blade from getting bent. After using the saw, wipe the blade clean. Keeping the blade lightly oiled with all purpose oil will not only prevent rust, but it will help keep the saw's cutting edge sharp.

Shovels

Decades ago, campers used shovels for digging trenches around tents or holes for latrines or garbage. Because these practices are no longer acceptable, campers don't need a shovel.

If you need to dig a hole for human waste, a small plastic trowel will do the job and pack nicely inside your pack when you're finished. Keep it wrapped in a plastic bag.

Safety

Always store tools in a secure place. Never leave them lying around the campsite where someone might trip over them.

CHAPTER 7

▶ The Great Outdoors

Congratulations! You're at the trailhead and ready to roll. Whether you are heading out for an afternoon or a week, there are still a couple of things to consider.

Group Travelling

Before everyone runs wildly into the woods, gather group members together to do some stretches and to remind them of the rules. Here are some to consider:

Rules

▲ No passing the designated "lead" person.

▲ No falling behind the "sweep" or last person.

▲ Only stop for breaks at agreed-upon times and locations.

▲ No racing or running.

▲ No littering.

▲ No yelling.

Make sure all members understand and agree with the rules before setting out. Talk briefly about possible hazards along the route and appropriate safety measures. Why not have everyone "buddy up" — an older youth with a younger one?

All group members should know who the first aider is and where they can find a first aid kit. The kit should be easily identified and accessible. (*Tip:* Fanny pack first aid kits are great. They're easily worn, and because most are bright red, they easily identify the first aider.)

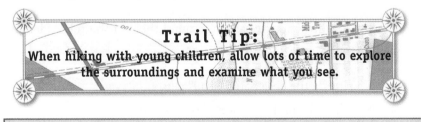

Trail Tip:
When hiking with young children, allow lots of time to explore the surroundings and examine what you see.

A group can only travel as fast and as far as its slowest member.

Stretches

Stretching gently before starting out down a hiking trail or a day of canoeing will loosen up muscles and help prevent many injuries.

Vertical stretch with
fingers interlaced

Neck stretches and
shoulder shrug

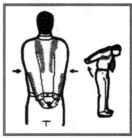

Backward shoulder
rotation with extension

Overhead shoulder stretch

Chest stretch

Upper shoulder stretch

Shoulder blade stretch

Single leg stretch

Backward trunk stretch

Lateral stretch with
shoulder stretch

Full trunk rotation

Trunk rotation
with lateral bend

Quadriceps stretch

Calf stretch

Hamstring stretch
variation

Heading Out

An experienced hiker sets an even pace (about 5 km/h), walking with a
relaxed stride. When hiking, lean forward from the hips. With your head up
swing your arms easily and breathe deeply. When carrying a pack, make you
stride as long as comfortably possible. Lean forward with a slight stoop to caus
the pack to push you forward. Keep your arms relaxed.

Hiking after dark presents new risks. Take shorter steps and be alert. Us
flashlights and allow extra space between hikers to prevent a branch from
snapping into someone's face.

Trail Tip:
If you feel a "hot spot" developing on your foot, stop and treat
it. A number of products will help, including Second Skin™ or
Mole Skin™. Even duct tape will work in a pinch.

Hiking or paddling takes effort and burns lots of energy. Drink and munch on snacks as you travel, or at least at every break.

If you're a leader, it's important to carefully monitor your group throughout the trip. Move up and down the line talking to each individual. Offer words of encouragement and support. Take time to point out interesting features along the trail. Keep spirits high by talking, singing, telling stories and interpreting your surroundings.

Watch for signs of fatigue, sore feet, sunburn, frostbite, dehydration, hypothermia, or general discontent. As soon as you notice problems, stop and deal with them.

Trail Tip:
Step around, rather than over, obstacles on the trail.

Stop regularly at pre-determined times or locations to enjoy a drink and snack, and to share moments gazing at a beautiful scene. Limit your break stops to five minutes. If you stop for longer periods, leg muscles may stiffen and you may have difficulties limbering them up again. Make sure your rest is a real one. Lie down on the ground with your legs up against a stump or rock. After five minutes, get back on the trail again.

Not everyone moves at the same pace. Your group should move only as fast as its slowest member. Many groups let their fastest members set the pace. This may cause problems especially if they wait just long enough to allow slower members to catch up, then leave again. This gives faster members a break, but not slower members. Make sure everyone gets a good break. This is important! Faster hikers should wait for the slower ones to finish their break before starting out again.

Hiking in a large group where the skills and abilities of the hikers vary to a large degree can be a frustrating experience for everyone. When this situation occurs it may be necessary to split the group, provided you have enough leaders to form two or more groups. If you form more than one group, agree on a final destination and meeting points.

Minimum Impact Camping

You won't be the only people enjoying the outdoors. Others will use your campsite days or weeks after you leave. It's very important to show respect for these outdoor enthusiasts by leaving the trails and campsites in the same (or better) condition that you found them. Use group campsites whenever possible, and encourage your members to keep their voices low to avoid disturbing other campers, as well as wildlife.

It's getting more difficult to travel far enough into the back country to leave all trace of people behind. Ever-growing numbers of people are trying to "get away from it all" by escaping into wilderness areas. Their impact is clearly visible. Trees and vegetation are damaged by thoughtless campers, and even animals are behaving differently as they become conditioned to receiving handouts and food scraps left behind by irresponsible campers. Yet, people are more sensitive about what they consider "environmental impact." Some now talk about visual as well as noise impacts. Trying to lower noise levels and reduce environmental impact, many parks regulate the number of campers per site and separate group campsites from single tent spots. Manufacturers are helping out by producing products in a variety of natural colours that blend in with the environment, rather than clash with it.

Trail Tip:
Do not wash or bath directly in a river, lake or stream.

As our wilderness diminishes, we must be even more careful how we use it, to preserve what remains. The World Bureau for Scouting has developed an excellent Personal Environmental Code. It states:

▲ I will respect all living things, for each is a link in the web that supports life on Earth.

▲ I will take from nature only what can be replaced, so no species will disappear.

▲ I will never pollute the air, soil or water.

▲ I will not buy products of endangered animals, plants or forests.

▲ I will keep my neighbourhood clean and will respect the environment wherever I go.

▲ I will call attention to cases of pollution and any other abuse of nature.

▲ I will not waste fuel or energy supplies.

▲ I will set an example of good conservation conduct, and show others why it's important for everyone to do so.

▲ I will celebrate the beauty and wonder of nature all of my life.

Why don't you adopt the World Bureau's Code or create one yourself? Help change attitudes.

Trail Tip:
Use biodegradable soaps and shampoos.

Scouting believes that responsible citizenship imposes upon each of us an increasing obligation to live in harmony with nature. In part, this means we must learn to use and not abuse, to enjoy and not destroy the natural beauty of our environment on outings. Leaders and youth in all sections must learn (and teach each other) outdoor skills which reflect this philosophy.

Here are some practical ways we can begin:

▲ Pack out all garbage, and pick up garbage left behind by other campers.

- ▲ Leave no trace; "take only pictures," leave only footprints.

- ▲ Hike along existing trails whenever possible.

- ▲ Don't wash dishes (or bathe) directly in lakes, rivers, streams or ponds.

- ▲ Use biodegradable soaps and shampoos.

- ▲ Don't feed or harass wildlife.

- ▲ Use stoves, where possible, instead of an open fire.

- ▲ Respect the rights of fellow campers. Keep voices low and leave radios and tape players at home.

- ▲ Don't cut down any living plants or trees.

- ▲ Buy or repackage food into burnable or reusable containers.

- ▲ If you have a large group, divide into several smaller parties and camp on different sites at least 100 metres apart to lessen environmental impact.

- ▲ Don't dig trenches around tents, and don't dig holes for grease pits.

Use existing washrooms/outhouses, when possible. Where they don't exist, move well off the trail — at least 45 metres away from water sources. Dig a small cat-hole (a hole for body wastes) 15 to 20 cm deep. Squat, and drop all your waste into the hole. Then, cover the waste with dirt, returning the site to its original state. The hole will contain the waste and prevent it from passing on disease-causing organisms into water sources or to other humans or animals. (For more information, see the human waste section later in this chapter.)

If you need to urinate, move well off the trail, once again taking care to stay away from water sources. If possible, urinate on rocks or sandy soil to allow the liquid to evaporate.

Trail Tip:
Check overhead for dead or loose branches before setting up your tent.

As you hike along, spend some time discussing "environmental impact" with group members. Perhaps they can identify positive measures they can take to improve areas near their homes. Have they considered adopting a stream, trail, park or campsite? If they conduct regular clean-ups, it will help preserve natural areas for future hikers and campers.

Selecting a Campsite

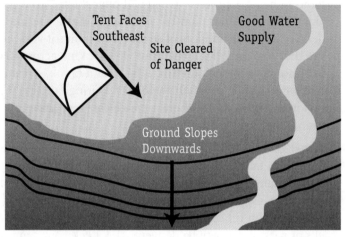

When you use established campsites, fire pits and outhouses, you limit the environmental impact to one area. Many federal, provincial and municipal parks welcome group camping and have developed areas for such use. They may even take reservations. When you arrive at the park, you'll have to register with park authorities and pay a user fee. Before using private property, make sure you ask the landowner for permission. Many landowners don't mind people camping on their property as long as someone is courteous enough to ask. They may, however, restrict campfires.

What's the "ideal campsite"? There are many different criteria. A good campsite is "discovered" not "developed." This means it's acceptable to move rocks and broken branches from the area to set up your tent, but not to cut branches and trees, dig holes and trenches, drive nails into trees or to do anything else that damages the site.

Before deciding on a campsite, consider the following:

1. Well-Drained Ground. Pick a high, dry spot where light breezes blow and where water will drain away quickly. Try to pitch your tent on an elevated area of level ground. Surrounding ground

should slope down and away from your tent. Gravelly soil covered with grass is excellent; it offers great drainage. Keep away from damp, muddy areas. If it rains, these will develop into puddles.

2. Favourable Exposure. Face your tent southeast so it will get the early morning sun, but don't forget about a shady spot to avoid afternoon heat. A protected area will offer shelter from high winds. During warmer months, you might want a site that provides a cool breeze and lots of shade. It's a bonus if you can find a site that also provides a beautiful view looking across a lake or up at a snow-capped mountain. If it's near a brook, stream or other water source, so much the better. During bug season, look for an exposed site where a breeze can keep away unwanted insects.

3. Safety. Don't camp directly under large, dead trees because of the danger from falling branches and lightning. Avoid areas with tall grass and damp, swampy areas. Mosquitoes and black flies love this habitat, especially during spring. Be careful of gullies (sudden flash floods can fill them quickly) and overhanging cliffs (falling rocks or rock slides may be dangerous). Check your campsite for poison ivy, poison oak and poison sumac. Make sure your site offers a good location for you to hang your food bag ("bear bag"). It should be at least four metres off the ground, three metres from the closest trunk, and two metres down from the lowest branch.

4. Good Drinking Water. Identifying a suitable source will help to ensure that the water you treat will be drinkable. Fast-moving rivers or streams or deep lakes are best. Take the water from as deep down as possible so you don't clog your water filter with floating surface material.

Trail Tip:
Carry a small lighter, as well as matches.

If tested water is not available, treat it yourself. Many options are available, including bringing water from home, adding chemicals, using a filter or purifier, or boiling the water for at least five minutes. (See Chapter 4 for more information.)

5. Good Fuel Supply. Many parks and wilderness areas restrict campfires to designated areas only; locating firewood on heavily used sites may be difficult. Before leaving home, find out if any rules apply regarding fires, permits and gathering firewood. Fire bans or other restrictions may mean you have to do all cooking on camp or backpack stoves. Plan for this possibility.

6. Home, Sweet Home. Treat your campsite as you would your own home. Keep it clean, tidy and undamaged. Leave it as you found it, or better.

7. Comfort. Before pitching your tent, remove rocks, dead branches and other debris from the ground. Avoid large roots and anything else that may be uncomfortable to sleep on, or that may damage your tent floor.

8. Impact. If you must camp on a new site, spread your campers out to minimize impact and to permit the area to recover more quickly.

Wacky 'Expert' Camp Tip

When using a public campground, place a tuba on your picnic table. This will keep the campsites on either side vacant.

Campsite Rating Scale

Use this chart to help find a good campsite. A score of 65 is good.

FEATURE	RATING				
	Poor (2)	Fair (4)	Good (6)	Excellent (8)	Ideal (10)
Water supply	Long carry, open source	Short steep carry, open source	Medium carry, well, spring	Short carry, well, spring	On site, clear cold spring, well
Swimming	Deep stream	Safe depth, stream	Lake (safe depth), clear	Lake (safe depth), clear, beach	Lake (safe depth), clear sand beach, graded slope, unconta- minated
Soil	Clay	Rocky or loose gravel	Gravelly	Packed sand, gravel under	Firm sandy, fertile soil, gravel under- neath
Ground cover	Weeds	Grain stubble	Hay crop	Leaf mold	Well grassed
Drainage	Low (may flood)	Drains slowly	Drains two ways	Drains three ways	Drains all ways
Tree growth	Shrubs	Saplings	20-30 year, 2nd growth	30-60 year, 2nd growth	Forest, primeval
Fuel (wood or alternatives)	Downed softwood	Downed softwood	Standing dead softwood	Standing dead hardwood & dry pine branches	Opportunity to cut hardwood - pine stumps
Topography	Steep	Flat	12% slope	5-8% slope	Gentle slope
Pests	Mosquitoes, insects	Mosquitoes, insects	Controllable flies	Few if anything	None
Public	Curious	Picnickers	Tolerant neighbours	Friendly	None
Activity area	Open area dotted with trees (ground cover, weeds and gravel)	Large open area, slopes (sandy with weeds and grass)	Large area, gentle slopes, sandy soil with sparse grass cover	Large area, gentle slopes, grass covered and small area for campfire	Large area, level, grass covered, ringed by trees and small area for campfire

SCORING - Poor=2 Fair=4 Good=6 Excellent=8 Ideal=10

Site Maintenance

Before leaving a campsite, do a quick "walk around." Make sure you've picked up all your gear, the cooking and eating area is clean and tidy, your fire is out and cold, and you have retrieved any items that you may have hung from a branch to dry.

Campfires

Check with local authorities to see if you need a fire permit, and how to obtain it.

Fire Pits

Keep campfires small, and use existing fire pits wherever possible. Gather dead wood only; don't peel bark from trees. Make sure your campfire is extinguished and cold before moving on.

Follow the "leave no trace" rule if you must build a campfire in a new site. Here's how. Find enough sand or gravel to build a base at least 7-9 cm deep and about 60 cm in diameter for your fire. Then scatter the sand and gravel after the fire has completely burned out and been extinguished with water. If sand and gravel are not available, locate a grassy area where you can carefully cut out a small section of sod, or remove the decomposing materials on the forest floor (e.g. twigs, leaves, etc.). Dig a shallow pit down to the mineral soils or gravel. Be careful not to build your fire on roots. Now, build your fire in the hole. Afterwards, when your fire has completely burned out and you've extinguished all ashes with water, replace the sod and soil.

Never build your fire directly on the forest floor, exposed rocks, roots, or near low hanging branches or trees. If you must build on a rock, find one that's large and flat enough to contain your fire. Turn it over after the fire to hide the blackened scar.

Trail Tip:
When cooking over an open fire, rub dish detergent on the outside of the pots before cooking. This makes clean-up easier.

Building the Fire

With your fire pit ready, gather enough "tinder" (small twigs, pieces of bark and dead leaves) to start the fire. "Kindling" (twigs a little bit larger than tinder) goes on next. It will ignite the larger pieces of wood which will eventually burn down into coals and provide the best heat for cooking. Collect all these materials before striking the match. If you don't, you may find that you are out gathering more wood as the fire burns down and your meal remains uncooked.

Teepee Fire Lay

This method gets its name because it looks like the framework of an aboriginal's summer home, the teepee. It is one of the easiest and quickest ways to build a fire and is particularly good for boiling or frying. Here's how to lay the fire:

1. Place a handful of tinder on the ground.

2. Push a stick into the ground on a slant over the tinder.

3. Lean a circle of kindling sticks across the standing stick with their tips together and with an opening toward the wind.

4. Crouching down in front of the teepee with your back to the wind, strike a match. Let it burn into a real flame, then touch it to the tinder close to the ground.

5. When the kindling is burning well, feed the flames with thin pieces of wood, then with thicker pieces.

6. Continue feeding the flames until the fire has reached the size you want.

Crisscross Fire Lay

This is the fire to lay when you need a bed of coals for cooking or baking.

1. Place two pieces of wood (as thick as your wrist and about 30 cm long) on the ground parallel to one another. They should be about 30 cm apart. Place tinder between them.

2. Lay a number of thin kindling sticks on top of this base, leaving a space between each stick.

3. Continue building the sticks up until it has about eight cross layers. Increase the thickness of the wood from layer to layer, always leaving space between the pieces. This spacing will allow the flames and the draft to move upward.

4. Light the tinder near the ground on the windward side.

When properly laid, the crisscross fire will flare up into a blaze and will eventually turn into a bed of glowing embers.

Ceremonial Fires

You need a different type of fire in the evening when you sit around singing songs, telling stories and enjoying skits. A log cabin style of fire is perfect.

1. Place two logs (5 cm diameter) on the ground as a base, then put two others crosswise.

2. Next, lay a whole row of heavy sticks and add layer after layer to a height of half a metre.

3. Place tinder on the upper layer, and light.

Fire Clean-Up

Once you've finished cooking, burn any burnable garbage. When you burn tin cans and foil pouches to remove food odours, remember to retrieve the remains and pack them out.

As the fire burns down, heap any chunks of burning wood that remain into a pile so they are completely consumed by the flames, leaving only ashes to dispose of when your fire has finished.

When the fire has burned itself out, sprinkle water over the ashes, stirring them occasionally to ensure that they are completely extinguished.

If you've developed a new campfire site, you're now ready to scatter the ashes and replace the sod or decomposing material from the forest floor, returning the site to its original condition.

Sanitation/Waste Disposal

Washing dishes and personal hygiene are extremely important when on the trail. Make sure your soaps are phosphate-free and biodegradable. Wash at least 45 metres away from open water sources to prevent contamination.

Never pour waste water directly into any water source. Instead, sprinkle it over rocky soil or pour it into a cat-hole 15-20 cm deep as far away from the trail and as far from any stream or lake as possible. Here's an even better solution: pour waste water (especially if it contains food particles) into your fire pit so the particles can be burned at your evening campfire.

WITH WATER

1. Sprinkle with backs of fingers

2. Spread sticks and coals

3. Sprinkle again. Do not leave it until coals are cool enough to put your hands on.

WITHOUT WATER

1. Spread sticks and coals

2. Scrape burning embers from large logs and sticks

1. Cover all with dirt

2. Check and be sure the fire is dead out.

Human Waste
Solids

Be sure you use any toilet facilities a campground provides. When no toilets are available, the action you take to dispose of human waste solids will vary according to the time of year, the number of people in your group, and what the ground is like. Naturally, you want the waste to

Trail Tip:
Wet naps or baby wipes are great for quick wash-ups.

decompose as quickly as possible, but not contaminate any water source, or be discovered by other campers.

For individuals or a small group, dig a small cat-hole no more than 20 cm deep and at least 45 metres from open water. (This is where solid wastes will decompose most quickly.) Health Canada suggests that toilet paper can be burned in your campfire. If you are in an area where fires are not permitted or you have chosen not to have a campfire, bury rather than burn toilet paper. Then, mix soil with the waste before covering with loose earth. Try to return the site to its natural state by covering with sticks and leaves. It's also thoughtful to mark the site (possibly with two crossed sticks). This marker will prevent other campers from using the same spot. Burn or pack out sanitary napkins in sealable plastic bags. (Triple bag these if you're packing them out.)

For larger groups, dig a long trench about 30 cm deep. Encourage campers to start at one end and gradually move down the trench, covering their waste after each use. To avoid disturbing someone using the latrine, place the toilet paper in a plastic bag and hang it from a tree just out of sight of the trench. If the toilet paper is missing, the latrine is in use.

Trail Tip:
Carry toilet paper in a zip-loc bag.

In winter, because it's usually impossible to dig cat-holes, place all solid waste and toilet paper into plastic bags for packing out and disposal at home. If the snow cover is very deep or the ground is frozen, dig a hole in the snow, line it with a plastic bag, collect excrement, seal the bag, double bag it, allow it to freeze if temperatures permit, then pack it out.

Make sure you dig cat-holes above the high water mark and away from natural drainage systems.

Liquid

Urinate at least 45 metres away from open water sources and well off the trail. If possible, urinate on rocks or sandy soil to allow for evaporation.

Trouble with Critters

Trail Tip:
Wear light coloured clothes, bug nets, and insect repellant during bug season.

Losing your food bag to some crafty critters can ruin your camping trip. Mice, squirrels, raccoons and bears are the usual culprits. Irresponsible campers who feed wild animals or who don't properly clean and remove food scraps from their site aren't helping the animals. They can create unpleasant — even dangerous — situations for future campers.

Food that wild animals eat is much different from that which humans eat. Their digestive systems are not like ours, and human food can make them sick. What's more, animals that have become conditioned to easy meals might not be able to survive during winter months when few (if any) campers are present.

In high-use outdoor areas, some animals have become so dependant on food handouts that they've lost their natural fear of man. The consequences can be quite tragic. Several years ago, *Reader's Digest Magazine* published a true story about a road construction worker up north. One day he was eating his lunch when he noticed a grizzly bear watching him.

He threw the bear part of his lunch, and the bear ate it. Over the next several days, this scene repeated itself. One day, another man who didn't know the routine replaced the original construction worker. Lunch time came, and the bear appeared looking for his "share." When the worker didn't share his lunch, the bear attacked and killed him.

Campers and picnickers must take special precautions to protect their food; doing so will also protect the animals as well. If you're at a standing camp or picnicking with your vehicle nearby, store your food in the car between meals. Wash dishes carefully, removing all food scraps for disposal in the garbage. NEVER take food into tents. Clean up all spills quickly, and put food scraps in the garbage or burn them in the fire. Many parks have installed "critter proof" garbage containers. Coolers with tight-fitting, clamp down lids are usually secure. Use these for keeping things cold as well as for safely storing other food items.

If an animal does visit your campsite, avoid getting too close and startling it. Remember: it is a wild animal, and you are on its "turf." Usually, just speaking to the animal in a normal voice will scare it off. If this doesn't work, try banging on a pot or yelling.

Bears

Take great care if the animal visiting your campsite is a bear. In most cases the bear will move away quickly once it is aware of your presence, unless it's provoked or protecting a cub.

If the bear has *not* noticed you, back away slowly, retracing your steps until you are out of range. If the bear has noticed you, try backing away slowly, talking to it as you go to let it know that you are not a threat, and that you are leaving. Do not stare into its eyes or act aggressively; it may perceive this as a threat, and attack. If the bear follows, don't run (you can't out-run a bear). Throw something on the ground (not food) to distract it, then move quickly away or try making lots of noise by banging objects together and waving them about.

When all else fails, look for a tall tree to climb. Black bears can climb, but may choose to stay on the ground. Grizzles (theoretically) can't climb, although they can reach quite high when standing on their hind legs. If you're not sure whether you're facing a grizzly or a black bear, remember this old woodsman's tale: If chased by a bear, simply climb a tree. Black bears will chase you up the tree, while a grizzly will simply knock the tree down.

If a grizzly bear does attack, drop to the ground, play dead, lifting your legs up to your chest and clasping your hands over the back of your neck. If a black bear attacks, *don't play dead*. Make yourself big, and shout to frighten it. Fight with whatever you can find.

Your best strategy is to avoid attracting bears in the first place. Make lots of noise as you travel through bear country: sing songs, fasten bells to your pack or boots, or talk loudly as you go. Minimize food odours, and (once more) never take food into your tent.

"Bear Bag" It!

Wilderness campers probably won't have coolers unless they're on a canoe trip. If this is true in your case, keep all food and garbage separate from the rest of your gear and hang it from a tree or from a line strung between two trees. This is called "bear bagging." (See Chapter 4 for more information.)

Poisonous Plants

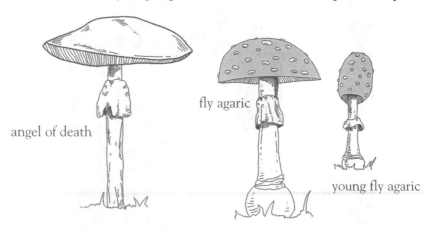

Not everything in the great outdoors is safe to touch or eat. Avoid plants that you can't identify positively.

Poison ivy, poison oak and poison sumac are found in many parts of Canada.

Poison ivy and poison oak have three shiny, toothed or lobed leaves. They grow in vines or shrubs. These plants may have white or slightly green berries. Poison sumac grows as a small shrub with a grouping of seven to eleven leaves on each stem. Usually, you'll find it in sandy beach areas around the Great Lakes, but it may also grow in wet, swampy areas as well.

These plants secrete a chemical on the leaves. If this rubs off on bare skin, the victim will likely develop a skin irritation in the form of a rash filled with tiny blisters. The rash usually develops within 24 to 48 hours of contacting the plant.

If someone in your group comes into contact with a poisonous plant:

poison ivy

poison oak

angel of death

fly agaric

young fly agaric

- ▲ Remove the plant oil by thoroughly washing the skin with soap and water.

- ▲ Wipe the area with alcohol.

- ▲ Once the rash has developed, apply calamine lotion.

- ▲ Take antihistamines to lessen the itching.

- ▲ Do not use sunburn pain relievers. These may further irritate the affected area.

- ▲ Carefully remove clothing that has touched the plant, and wash it thoroughly.

Outdoor Activities

Many activities will increase youth awareness and appreciation of nature. Scouting handbooks describe specific badge requirements that your members can work on. Don't forget to ask youths what they want to explore. Ask a resource person to help if you need special expertise. Here are some ideas:

Trail Tip:
Allow extra time for travelling, cooking and setting up camp in the winter. Remember: You have less daylight.

1. Identify plants, animals, birds and insects. After identifying as many of each as possible, discuss how they fit into food "webs." What would happen if a particular plant, animal, bird, insect or animal was removed from the web?

2. Identify different trees. How do we use them?

3. Rope off a small area and examine life in that space.

4. Find the "homes" of different animals, birds and insects; discuss their "lifestyles."

5. Animals require food, water and shelter to survive. Discuss how we can affect one or all of these, and what can happen to the animals if humans don't use care.

6. Ask each person to find a private spot in which to sit, listen and observe for 15 minutes. Later, discuss what each learned.

7. Stay up late to look at the stars and identify different constellations.

Journals/Logs

If you keep a journal or log of each outdoor trip, you'll capture priceless Scouting memories. A journal or log will also help you evaluate the experience afterwards so you can improve on the enjoyment next time.

Choose a pencil and a small, pocket-sized notebook that won't take up too much space. Seal these in a convenient, resealable freezer bag. Start your journal by recording general trip information:

▲ Where you are going?

▲ How long will you be out?

▲ Who is travelling with you?

▲ What's the nature of the trip (e.g. hiking, canoeing)?

▲ What dates do you plan to be away?

▲ What interesting weather details might you encounter?

▲ What food and equipment are you taking? Anything unusual?

▲ Have you set special goals or objectives?

▲ Before setting out, do you have any personal thoughts or feelings you wish to record? Concern? Exhilaration? Excitement?

Make mental notes as you travel. Have you seen something *extra* special, or have you learned a new skill? Take several minutes to make a sketch or describe what you've learned while it's fresh in your mind.

Your entry may involve:

▲ Simple point form notes to "jog" your memory.

▲ A letter to yourself describing (in detail) the process you followed to complete a task.

▲ A map of your route.

It's important to write clearly enough and with sufficient detail that you'll understand your notes at home.

Try to follow a similar format each day. Include details like: the weather, your time of departure, special sights, experiences, meals, problems encountered, successes, special achievements, thoughts and feelings, new ideas, rest points, route features, and anything else you want to remember. After you return home, add photos.

How often have you returned from a trip and simply put your journal away without "processing" the experience? Review your notes. Journals and logs serve as excellent memory-makers. They're also an outstanding resource when you evaluate a trip or experience. Looking through your journals or logs will provide many practical camping tips and ideas. Most important, a journal will rekindle your memories of great campfires and terrific conversations with close friends. In the comfort of an easy chair, you'll hear again the soft, bubbling sound trailing behind as you guide your canoe through a mist-enshrouded lake. Aahhh. Sheer joy!

Trail Tip:
When camping, make a list of items that you forgot to bring.

Before Leaving Your Camp

After you've cleaned up and are ready to leave a park or camp area, gather together as a group for several minutes to evaluate the trip. What gems of knowledge have you learned?

Don't forget to let the park authorities or landowner know you're leaving and that you've accounted for everybody.

Scouting's programs focus on developing youths and adults. Usually, this training takes place outside. Let's respect and care for the natural resources and instill these values in youth and leaders.

In B.-P.'s words: "Leave nothing but your thanks."

CHAPTER 8

▶ Winter Camping

Winter camping offers plenty of unique challenges that make it an exciting addition to summer outdoor experiences. Winter camping means coping with new challenges, such as building shelters, and keeping warm and dry. You and your group will have to be much more than "fair weather campers."

Camping in cold weather requires more careful preparations than summer camping. Some mistakes made in other seasons may cause only minor inconveniences; the same errors in winter may spell

disaster. But, winter camping has many attractions. (For example, you don't need bug repellent!) You can try out many different winter activities like skiing, snowshoeing, and tobogganing.

Before leaving on your first winter camping trip, consider these thoughts.

1. You'll need bigger, bulkier and heavier clothes and equipment than those used during summer trips. This means your pack must be large enough to hold everything. The extra weight of winter

gear increases the load significantly. This may cause concerns, especially when working with youth where the extra load may put them over the maximum weight they are able to carry. The extra size and bulk of clothing and gear will also restrict your freedom of movement and increase the amount of time and energy required to complete a task or reach your destination. Don't let this stop you. Group members can pull their gear behind them on a sled or toboggan.

2. The number of daylight hours is reduced, limiting time for travel, camp set-up and meal preparation. Adjust your trip schedule to fit available daylight hours.

Trail Tip:

In winter, turn water bottles upside down and bury them in the snow. The snow will insulate the liquid and slow the freezing process. If your water bottles do freeze, the cold will freeze the surface first, but you will still be able to open the cap.

3. Hiking in the snow (especially deep snow), can be slow and tiring with or without gear. If enough snow covers the ground, you may choose to travel on cross-country skis or snowshoes. Developing skill in these areas will require time and practice.

4. Life at camp will be easier if you choose meals requiring little or no preparation. They should be hot, nutritious and require minimum clean-up. Refrigeration is rarely a problem during winter camps; however, some food that you don't want frozen may unexpectedly freeze.

5. Finding drinking water and firewood may be more time-consuming than in summer. Allow extra time for these tasks.

As you plan your trip, consider each of these above factors in detail. Set reasonable distances to travel each day; they must be appropriate to the skills of your group members.

Some youths will make the transition from summer to winter camping more easily than others. Expect this. Allow lots of extra time to prepare for winter outings. You may find it necessary to acquire some special training or skills before setting out. This helps everyone have a safe and enjoyable experience.

Travelling distances in winter should be much shorter than for a summer hike or camp. Take a practice hike using fully loaded toboggans to gain an idea of everyone's abilities. Be careful not to over-exert yourself. Adjust your clothing to keep perspiration from getting your clothes damp.

Where to Go

Is winter camping a tradition with your group? You may already have a preferred winter camping spot. Otherwise, you may want to hike to a favourite summer haunt or go to your group's summer camp. Remember, the trail will look much different in winter. Many familiar landmarks will be covered with snow. You will encounter leafless trees, open woods, and frozen swamps and lakes. Drifting snow gives everything a new shape, and makes it easier to track winter birds and animals.

If it's your first winter camp, thoughtfully select a suitable campsite appropriate to the skills, knowledge, and experience of the group. Most people, when first camping in winter, choose short trips close to home. They may even prefer a site with a cabin or building for back-up.

Weather

Pay careful attention to weather reports when you prepare for a winter camp. Special reports for skiers provide useful information on snow conditions. Monitor wind chill factors, and adjust your activities accordingly.

What to Wear

Staying warm and dry: that's the secret to fun winter camping. Wear layers of loose-fitting clothing that allow moisture to move quickly *away* from your body, yet still protect you from the elements (wind, snow and rain).

Clothing doesn't *make* you warm. It only keeps you warm by trapping heat generated by your body. If you wear *layers of clothing* (two light sweaters instead of a bulky one, two pairs of socks instead of one heavy pair, etc.), air trapped in spaces between the layers will insulate almost as well as the clothing itself. This helps keep the heat in.

Space between layers also allows normal perspiration to move away from your body. Peel off clothing layers if you start perspiring heavily from exertion on the trail, setting up camp or playing games. When you stop strenuous activities and start cooling down, add the layers back on to keep warm. If your clothes get damp from perspiration, their insulating property is reduced or lost entirely; you'll quickly feel cold.

For winter camping, it's important to understand how bodies keep warm. We must maintain a delicate temperature balance — quite a challenge given the possible weather conditions and the demands we place upon our bodies. Because our bodies must maintain a core temperature of 37°C (98.6°F), winter campers must eat foods with the necessary nutrients and calories. These "fuel" our bodies. Proper dress also helps maintain this delicate body temperature.

When your body temperature begins to drop, your brain reacts by reducing the flow of heat (through the blood) to the extremities (hands, feet, arms and legs). This process helps preserve the core temperature. That's why we experience cold hands and feet. It also explains the old saying, "If your feet are cold, put on a hat." If you simply added extra socks, you'd be treating the symptom but not necessarily the problem.

When your body generates too much heat, it must find a way to cool down and maintain its core body temperature. It sends heat once again through the blood to the extremities, and begins to shed excess heat through perspiration.

On any outing, it's important to dress properly for the activity. You can regulate your body temperature by allowing excess heat to escape through loosened collars and sleeves or by exposing areas where your blood flows close to the surface (neck, armpits and head). Some coats and jackets now include "pit zips" — zippers under the arms to allow better ventilation.

Use your head to regulate body temperature. As you begin to heat up, expose some (or all) of your forehead, and remove your scarf to expose your neck. Tests show that as much as 60 percent of body heat is lost through your head. Before taking off your hat entirely, remove a layer of insulation or open up other clothing to allow better ventilation. While on the trail, removing layers may be awkward, especially if you have to pack away the removed clothes. Try fastening them to the outside of your pack or tucking them under your pack hood for quick access later on. Conversely, when your body begins to cool down again, cover up these areas you've exposed.

Layering Principles

Clothing should achieve three results if you hope to be comfortable in winter weather:

▲ Wicking (moving moisture away from the body)

▲ Insulation (trapping air)

▲ Wind/water protection.
   (See Chapter 5 for an extensive discussion on layering.)

Footwear

When hiking without snowshoes or skis, the temperature, weather and the nature of the terrain will dictate your footwear. Winter boots should be large enough to be worn comfortably over *two* pairs of socks: a lightweight polypropylene pair and a heavier wool pair. If your boots are too small or the laces are tied too tight, circulation may be restricted and

your feet may get cold. Choose waterproof, winter boots that come well up your calf. Look for boots with a drawstring at the top; these will keep snow out. Many models even have removable liners so you can carry a spare. If your boots don't have a drawstring or don't come up fairly high on your calf, a pair of waterproof gaitors will do the job.

Socks

Wear two pairs of socks. A light polypropylene pair for wicking under a heavier wool pair. They should be smooth-fitting without being too tight. There should be no holes or hard spots where the socks have been mended. Socks should be long enough to pull them well up on the calf.

Pants

Wool, or insulated snow pants worn as an outer layer, or pile/fleece pants worn under a windproof/waterproof shell, will keep your legs warm. Flap or zippered pockets are handy for keeping valuables in and snow out.

Tops

Over your long underwear, wear a woolen, fleece or pile shirt and/or sweater and/or insulated vest, then your outer shell.

Mitts

Mitts are generally warmer than gloves because fingers come in direct contact with each other, passing warmth from one to another. A pair of knitted wool mittens or mitt liners inside water repellent over-mittens work well. Gloves separate each finger, providing better dexterity. It's handy to have a pair close by for doing camp chores and preparing meals.

Headgear

A wool, fleece or polypropylene tuque that can be pulled down over the ears makes an excellent first layer, while a hood makes a great second layer. In extremely cold temperatures or when the wind chill factor is high, you may decide to add a neck warmer or a scarf.

Pointers to Remember

▲ Your clothing should be loose-fitting, not binding, and have closures at ankles, wrists, and neck.

▲ Ventilate before you sweat. Change damp articles of clothing such as insoles, socks, and mitts.

▲ Use a wind protection layer.

▲ Use your head to regulate heat; uncover to cool, cover to warm.

▲ Exercise and good diet will help keep you warm.

What to Take

Here is a basic personal kit for a winter camper. You'll need a larger than usual pack to carry the bulky clothing and equipment required for winter camping. Don't forget to leave room for your share of the patrol gear and food.

Clothes

▲ Underwear (long johns and top)

▲ Three pairs of socks (wool/polypropylene)

▲ Appropriate winter footwear

▲ Extra boot liners

▲ Fleece, pile or wool shirt/sweater

▲ Insulated vest (down or synthetic)

▲ Pants (wool, ski type or fleece with windproof/waterproof shell)

▲ Extra sweater and pants

▲ Windproof/waterproof and breathable outer shell (parka style)

▲ Polypropylene or lightweight wool gloves, with heavier wool or insulated mitts with waterproof shell

▲ Extra mitts

▲ Wool, fleece or polypropylene tuque, scarf and neck warmer.

Things to Pack

▲ Winter sleeping bag(s)

▲ Pyjamas (lightweight polypropylene underwear, long johns and top, or lightweight fleece pants and top will work fine)

▲ Mattress (Ensolite™, Airolite™ or self-inflating mattresses, Therm-A-Rest™ work well)

▲ Ground sheet (reflector type)

▲ Extra bed socks

▲ Tuque (a dry one, not the one you wore all day).

Eating Kit

▲ Knife, fork, spoon, plate, bowl and mug

▲ Or travel light with a big mug and a spoon

▲ Plastic, not metal dishes and utensils. (Cold metal may stick to skin.)

Toilet Kit

▲ Towel, soap and container, comb and mirror, toothbrush, tooth paste or baking soda, toilet paper and tissues

▲ Wet naps or baby wipes come in handy as well.

Trail Tip:
Carry fuel in properly designed containers.

Miscellaneous

- ▲ Notebook and pencil
- ▲ Pocketknife
- ▲ Sunglasses
- ▲ Emergency kit
- ▲ Personal sewing kit
- ▲ Matches in waterproof container
- ▲ Lighter
- ▲ Candle and flashlight
- ▲ Extra batteries (keep them warm; batteries die in the cold)
- ▲ First aid kit
- ▲ Map and compass
- ▲ Whistle (pealess).

Patrol Equipment

Here is a list of basic patrol items you may need for winter camping. Adjust it for longer trips and larger groups.

- ▲ Tents (if they are your choice for shelter) and ground sheets
- ▲ Lightweight snow shovel (for building snow shelters, fire pits, etc.)
- ▲ Axe and/or saw
- ▲ Kitchen utensil kit
- ▲ Tarp

- ▲ Sled or toboggan
- ▲ One dish cloth, two dish towels
- ▲ Collapsible water container
- ▲ One wash basin
- ▲ One patrol cook kit with small, medium, and large pots with lids, and frying pan
- ▲ One-burner stove
- ▲ Fuel container
- ▲ 60 metres of cord
- ▲ Candles and/or lantern
- ▲ Clothing and tent repair kit
- ▲ Coffee or tea pot.

How to Get There

Many factors affect travel plans: where you're going, how much time you have, weather conditions, snow conditions, and the number of people in your party. A one-day expedition is quickly and easily organized, but an overnight or weekend hike calls for more detailed planning. Include everyone in the trip planning process, and pay particular attention to the youths' attitude, skills, knowledge, and abilities, as well as the availability of equipment.

Choose your campsite well before dark. During winter, it takes much longer to make a comfortable camp than at other times of the year.

Before any outing, be sure to get approval from parents, the group committee, your local council and landowners. Leave a trip plan with someone reliable. It should list: all camper's names, time of departure, route you will follow, your destination, campsites you plan to use, and the time you plan to return. If possible, include a map of your route so people will know precisely where to search if your group doesn't return on schedule.

Winter travel may require snowshoes or cross-country skis. If this is the case, a toboggan or sled is excellent for holding group and individual equipment, while each person carries a small pack containing their trail necessities: thermos of hot drink, trail mix, second pair of mitts, a first aid/survival kit, etc.

Travel at a speed that matches the skills and abilities of the group. A five-minute stop every half hour makes for a pleasant trip. It allows group members to catch their breath, to cool off (prevent sweating), and to have a drink. Regular stops also help keep your group together. To ensure that everyone gets at least a five-minute break, wait until everyone has caught up before taking the break.

During all trail stops, use a buddy system to check for white spots on cheeks (frostbite) and to make sure everyone is present. Don't sit in the snow during a break; this may cause snow to melt on clothing. Sit on a toboggan, a log or rocks if necessary. Before moving on, leaders should do a "head count."

Want to avoid eye stress, headaches and snowblindness? Wear polarized sunglasses — even during cloudy weather.

Check the weather forecast before setting out, including the long-range forecast. This will help you make final adjustments to ensure group safety. If poor weather pushes the risk level beyond the skills and abilities of the group or makes travel unsafe, cancel your trip and reschedule for another date.

The temperature (including wind chill factor) is an important concern. (See chart below.) As the wind chill factor increases, take extra care to protect your body by reducing the amount of exposed skin.

Wind Chill Chart

ESTIMATED WINDSPEED (km/h)	Outside Temperature									
Calm	10	4	-1	-7	-12	-18	-23	-29	-34	-40
8	9	3	-3	-9	-14	-21	-26	-32	-38	-44
16	4	-2	-9	-16	-23	-29	-36	-43	-50	-57
24	2	-6	-13	-21	-28	-36	-43	-50	-58	-65
32	0	-8	-16	-23	-31	-39	-47	-55	-63	-71
40	-1	-9	-18	-26	-34	-42	-51	-59	-67	-76
48	-2	-11	-19	-28	-36	-44	-53	-62	-70	-78
56	-3	-12	-20	-29	-37	-46	-55	-63	-72	-81
64*	-3	-12	-21	-29	-38	-47	-57	-65	-73	-82

Little Danger (to properly clothed person)	Increasing Danger	Great Danger

Danger of Freezing Exposed Flesh

Wind speeds over 64 km/h have little additional effect

Use This Chart To Determine Your Course Of Action

1. If your calculations put you in the "Little Danger" area, travel is possible with normal precautions.

2. If your calculations put you in the "Increasing Danger" area, consider staying put. Travel only in emergency conditions, and check for frostbite frequently.

3. If your calculations fall in the "Great Danger" area, stay home. If you're caught in this situation at camp or while hiking, remain in your tents. Leave them only to do essential camp work and for the shortest time necessary.

Trail-Breaking

Whether hikers are skiing, snowshoeing or just walking, at times they may have to break a cross-country trail through heavy snow. Travel in single file, taking turns in the "lead." At a given interval or distance, the lead person should step off the track and let the group pass until the person can take up the rear position where the going is easier on a well-packed trail. Keep rotating each member through the lead, trail-breaking position so no one gets over-tired.

Unless the trail is well marked or you know the route well, it may be easy to lose your way. In some cases, you might prefer travelling across country using a map and compass. Many obstacles that block your path in summer will be buried under snow and ice. You should be able to see a greater distance in a hardwood forest without leaves on the trees.

Following frozen streams, rivers, and lakes may seem easy and an ideal route, but do this very carefully. Stay away from frozen water, if possible, unless you're absolutely sure the ice is safe.

Transporting Gear

For transporting bigger, bulkier and heavier winter gear, a toboggan or sled will make travel much easier. In fact, for many youths, it may be the only way to travel; the added weight and bulk of their gear in a backpack would make travel extremely difficult.

Loading a Toboggan or Sled

It's important to know how to load and lash equipment onto a sled or toboggan properly. New plastic sleds that wrap up around the sides work well for the gear one or two people would carry. You may need to drill a number of holes along the sides to provide lash points for securing equipment.

Here's a proven method for loading a toboggan. Spend time making a neat, secure job before you set out. It will save time repacking on the trail.

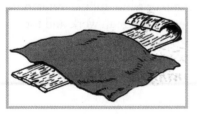

1. Lay a large piece of tarp or plastic groundsheet on the toboggan. It should be large enough to wrap completely up and over all your gear. You can also use this tarp or groundsheet as a shelter or a windbreak at the campsite.

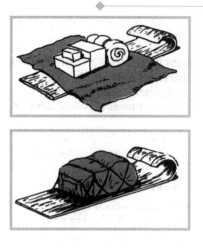

2. Distribute the load equally so the toboggan will track properly. Make sure the load is packed squarely, nothing sticks out over the edges, and it is not top heavy.

3. When the load is in place, wrap it snugly with the tarp or groundsheet, then lash it to the toboggan. Start lashing rope at the front of the toboggan, crossing over the top, down through the side ropes or holes, back up and over and so on, toward the rear. Bring the lashing rope back up to the front of the toboggan in the same manner and secure it with a clove hitch.

4. After you have completed the lashing, secure shovels, axes, spare skis and snowshoes on top of the load. Keep this extra equipment to a minimum!

Another loading option involves using hockey duffel bags secured with bungee cords to the toboggan. A duffel bag allows quick access to gear without unwrapping.

Towing a Toboggan

Towing a toboggan with a rope works well when you're going up a hill or along a flat trail; it doesn't work when you're going downhill. Your toboggan may run you over, or at least keep bumping into your heels.

It's easy to adapt your toboggan or sled for towing. By replacing the ropes with aluminum poles and fastening them to your hips with a hip belt, you'll be able to ski, snowshoe or walk quite easily and still have free movement of your arms and hands. To do this, you will need: a padded hip belt from an old pack; two clevis pins and rings; two wall brackets (conduit or pipe — the kind used to fasten pipe to a wall); and three lengths of lightweight aluminum conduit or old aluminum tent poles (two long and one short). Two lengths must be long enough to provide sufficient distance between you and your toboggan; this will allow room for an extended stride when skiing. (This length will vary from person to person.) The wall brackets must be at least one size larger than the diameter of the poles to allow them to move freely.

You will need one short piece of aluminum to go across the front of the toboggan, as well as two copper, aluminum or plastic elbows the proper diameter for the poles. Use screws to fasten the wall brackets to the front of the toboggan.

If necessary, drill holes in the hardwood toboggan and the ends of the poles for the clevis pins. (You may need a small piece of wood to screw into, and reinforce, the front of a plastic sled.) Cut poles to the proper length, drill clevis pin holes in one end, then fasten an elbow to the other. Join the elbows to the shorter piece of aluminum, making a large "U" with right angle corners. Use the wall brackets to fasten the shorter piece (the bottom of the "U" to the front of the sled/toboggan) and fasten the hip belt to the opposite ends of the poles. Now step in between the poles, fasten the hip belt and you're ready to roll!

Snowshoes

Snowshoes are an important part of winter hiking equipment. Many makes and models are available. New, lightweight, compact models are replacing traditional, wooden models made famous by trappers and Native peoples. New models use a light-weight metal alloy for the frame, and neoprene or polyethylene solid decking to maintain floatation (i.e. keeping the snowshoe from sinking into snow). They are smaller, making them much easier to manoeuvre — especially in tight areas.

lightweight model

Choose snowshoes carefully; you may have an unhappy time on the trail if you buy poor quality, an improper size or a model unsuited for you. Fragile, poorly maintained or poorly manufactured snowshoes can result in broken or bent frames, or sagging webbing. The snowshoe frame must be fairly light and flexible, but tough and capable of holding its shape.

Lightweight, felt pack boots with soft, flexible soles (large enough to let you wear two pairs of wool socks without binding your feet in any way) are favourite snowshoeing footwear. Make sure your boots have no heel; these would grind into the snowshoe and quickly ruin its webbing.

The Bearpaw and the Algonquin are the two most common snowshoes available today, aside from modern lightweight models.

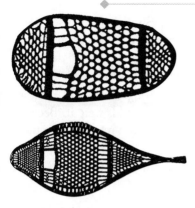

1. *Bearpaw*. This is a short, wide, oval shoe that may or may not have some turn-up at the front.

2. *Algonquin* (sometimes called Maine, Michigan or Huron). These have a tear-drop shape with a broad and slight upturn to the front, and a long, narrow tail.

The following table shows what weight different snowshoe types and sizes can carry.

Type	Weight with Pack	Size
Bearpaw (standard)	57 - 68 kg	33 cm x 71 cm
	68 - 79 kg	33 cm x 84 cm
	79 - 91 kg	38 cm x 76 cm
Algonquin	57 - 68 kg	31 cm x 122 cm
	68 - 79 kg	33 cm x 122 cm
	79 - 91 kg	35 cm x 122 cm

Flotation is the degree to which a snowshoe will keep you from sinking into the snow. As a rule, a large snowshoe of nearly any shape works well in deep snow on level ground. When the snow is deep and loose, and the ground is flat with little or no rough terrain, flotation is crucial.

If you are going to snowshoe on hilly ground, you'll need traction. Traction is improved by the position of the toe cord which governs how deep the front of your snowshoe will sink. Attaching metal devices to the bottom of your snowshoe will also improve traction; some newer models include this feature. Attach these devices directly under the ball of your foot so the full weight of your body will ensure a good grip or bite.

Tracking means how well the snowshoe follows your foot. Each time a snowshoer raises a foot, the snowshoe's toe should rise up while the tail drags directly behind. The key to good tracking is the ability of your boot toe to move through the snowshoe toe hole. Snowshoes with a high turned-up toe usually track best, since the snowshoe's toe doesn't catch in the snow. The tail should be heavier than the toe. When you lift a snowshoe by its binding, the tail should drop immediately.

Dimensions always involve a compromise. Longer and wider snowshoes obviously have a greater flotation, but the size adds weight. Because dimensions also affect the snowshoes' performance, you must be careful to choose the best size and weight.

Length. Long snowshoes track better but are difficult to handle when making turns.

Width. A snowshoe more than 25 cm wide will tire you because you will be walking with your feet far apart.

Weight. Because size adds weight, use as small and light a snowshoe as possible. Remember: you have to lift and move it with every step.

Front or toe turn-up on the snowshoe reduces the possibility of the snowshoe catching in snow. If there is too big a turn-up, the snowshoe may bang your shins.

Snowshoe bindings are as important to snowshoes as ski bindings are to skis. Bindings must allow the toe of the boot to move up and down easily through the snowshoe toe hole. At the same time, the binding should hold the foot firmly and allow no side play.

One way to bind your foot to a snowshoe is to loop a length of 2 cm wide lamp wicking over your toes, under the toe cord on either side of the toe hole, then diagonally across the toe, tying the two ends above the heel.

Manufactured harnesses work best for most snowshoers. A harness is a simple leather pocket or toe cap, open at both ends and lashed to the stringing of the shoe. The toe fits into the cap, and the straps from either side run back around the ankle.

Caring for Snowshoes

If you use your snowshoes only occasionally, maintenance is easy and can be done once a year.

At the end of the winter season, paint a coat of marine spar varnish on the wood and webbing. Allow this to dry, then rub lightly with fine steel wool or sandpaper. Now apply a second coat of varnish. (The sanding is important. It helps the coats to hold together well.) When finished, the wood and webbing should appear shiny.

Don't varnish your binding harness. If these are leather, treat with mink oil or a good silicone leather treatment. New, lightweight models require little maintenance other than simple cleaning.

Snowshoe Materials

Traditional snowshoes usually have a wood frame made from white ash; lacing is raw untanned cowhide. Although rawhide is tough and will withstand considerable wear, it loses much of its strength when wet.

Some manufacturers use neoprene or nylon cord for lacing. Both of these are waterproof, though nylon tends to wear out quickly on crusty snow.

Metal or metal alloy frames are becoming more popular today. These frames are often anodized or coated to prevent snow from sticking to them.

Plastic snowshoes may give problems because of limitations of the material. The snowshoe may be too flexible, may break in cold temperatures, or may develop a bowed appearance with the toe and heel pointing up. However, plastic snowshoes are inexpensive and lightweight.

Mal de Raquette

"Mal de Raquette" (snowshoe illness) is the name French Canadian coureurs de bois gave to a special type of cramp that slows or disables snowshoers. Its effects can last for days. Novice snowshoers may experience cramped muscles from overexertion. Thigh and calf muscles seldom used in ordinary walking may soon react to the unusual gait of snowshoeing. Rest and massages with liniment will usually help to lessen the cramps.

To avoid mal de raquette, or recover from it, begin your snowshoeing with short trips, and gradually build up to long trips.

Skis or Snowshoes

Many people today own cross-country skis or snowshoes. If you don't have either, many outfitters offer rental equipment at reasonable prices — a great option for those just starting out. Renting also allows you to try different models.

Your group may choose to use both skis and snowshoes for a winter adventure. If you're travelling on snow in a group, allow extra time. Don't expect to travel great distances, especially if skiers are new to the sport.

It is quite easy to learn to snowshoe; it can be mastered in a day. But learning to cross-country ski requires more teaching, time, patience and practice. Learning can be frustrating when others expect too much. Both skiing and snowshoeing require quite a bit of skill and fitness before you set out on a major outing. Training and experience on a number of short, day trips will prepare everyone for a more challenging trek.

Making Camp

Although the guidelines are quite similar, selecting a campsite for winter camping takes longer than finding a summer site. It's important to be well organized, with everyone doing something. Youths who stand around idly with nothing to do are more susceptible to frostbite or hypothermia. When they're busy, they'll stay warm and accomplish tasks much quicker. There's no shortage of tasks when you're winter camping!

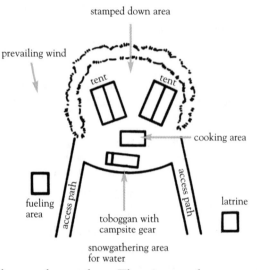

Setting Up Camp

Here is what a sample duty roster may look like:

1. Two people unpack the toboggan, light the stove, and put water on for a hot drink. Three people stamp out an area for pitching the tent or building shelters (first wearing snowshoes, and then without snowshoes) until snow is firmly packed down. Prevent overheating by adjusting or removing clothing as mentioned earlier in this chapter.

2. As soon as the snow is packed down, three people pitch tents or begin building shelters.

3. By this time, everyone should be ready for a break, and the water should be ready for a hot drink.

4. Once tents are set up or shelters are built, stow sleeping gear inside to keep it dry and free from snow. Unroll sleeping bags and allow them to recover their loft.

5. Avoid using tents/shelters as a gathering place. (When people gather there, they track in snow, which melts on sleeping bags and equipment. This makes an uncomfortable and potentially dangerous situation.)

To finish developing your campsite and to increase wind protection, build a snow wall around the stamped down edges of the campsite. Equipment (except sleeping bags, clothes, etc. which are placed in the shelter) should be placed on toboggans or ground sheets. This will keep it together, and prevent it from getting lost in the snow. Place all group equipment on the toboggan near a tent, and cover at night.

If you are camping in wooded country, check the trees above and around your tent. Dead branches, or large amounts of snow or ice may fall on you or your shelter, causing damage or injury. The danger is especially critical when the wind picks up, or if temperatures turn mild.

Trail Tip:

Liquid fuels freeze at a much lower temperature than water, therefore they become super cold but stay in a liquid state. Do not spill on exposed flesh.

Tents

Select tents for winter camping that are specifically designed to meet winter conditions. Four-season (or "mountaineering") tents are built much stronger than most summer tents. Generally they have four or more intersecting poles that form a sturdy, snow-shedding structure. Most have a fly that covers the entire tent and one or two vestibules, depending on the number of doors. Vestibules are great for storing extra gear and changing out of wet clothes.

Some more expensive models use a windproof, waterproof and breathable material which offers a single wall construction. This eliminates the fly and reduces the weight. Four-season tents, like their summer counterparts, must offer good ventilation. When winter camping, you need ventilation, not to keep you cool but to allow condensation to move outside. Otherwise it will freeze inside the tent. You still have to consider the tent's weight, the number of people it will accommodate, space, and warmth — just as in summer.

When you pitch your tent, look closely at your surroundings. This is important. Which way is the wind blowing? Which way do most storms come from? Pitch your tent with its back to the wind and bad weather.

Summer tents are not designed for winter's harsher conditions; they may be damaged by heavy snow and wind. This doesn't mean you have to purchase an expensive four-season tent or stay home during the winter; there are other ways to enjoy winter camping, such as making a quinzhee or other snow shelter.

Pitching Your Tent on Hard Ground

When you can't drive in tent pegs because of frozen ground, try using long nails or spikes. If these are too heavy to carry, you'll need some other method of holding your tent down. One way is to tie the guy lines to heavy rocks or logs; another is to cut poles from dead branches, lay the poles alongside each tent, and tie the guy lines to them, anchoring the poles with heavy rocks or logs.

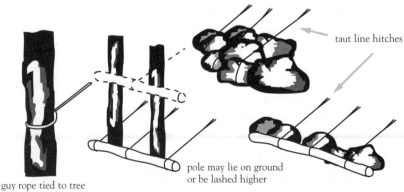

taut line hitches

pole may lie on ground or be lashed higher

guy rope tied to tree

Pitching a Tent on Snow

When the ground is covered with snow it may not be firm enough to hold tent pegs, or support your tent. If you encounter this, use "dead men" to hold your tent firmly in place.

Make "dead men" from stubby sticks, rocks or short pieces of logs. Bury these objects in the snow after tying the tent guy lines to them.

Crossed sticks also work well. Dig a hole (about 30 cm deep and 30 cm in diameter) in the snow. In the bottom, place two crossed sticks

Heavy log   Rock buried in snow   "Dead men" crossed
                                                  sticks buries

about 30 cm long and 2.5 cm in diameter. Now loop a short piece of line around the sticks and tie a bowline in each end of the line. The two ends of the line should extend to just above ground level. Fill in the hole and stamp down the snow. Loop the guy line through the two bowline loops, using a taut line hitch just as if you were tying the guy line to a tent peg.

Lean-Tos

Gone are the days when campers would simply cut down trees and gather green boughs to make shelters whenever and wherever they wished. However, with proper guidance and permission from a landowner, why not

gather green boughs for an "emergency shelter" after conducting selective thinning? Actually, selective thinning is a good environmental practice.

Your group can make other lean-tos by using tarps and ropes, with snow banked up around the sides for extra protection and insulation. These shelters can vary in size and shape to meet the needs of your group, but keep them low and small enough to contain the heat generated by three or four people.

If you choose to build a lean-to using either of these methods, be sure to return the site to its original state before leaving.

Treebase Shelter

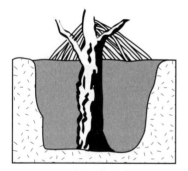

A tree that has been partly buried by a drift can make an excellent emergency shelter. Dig the snow out from around the tree and down to the base. Make the space large enough so you can sit or lie comfortably. In an emergency, cover the top with branches and evergreen boughs.

Snow Shelters

Snow is an excellent insulator. You can shape it into a shelter to provide a solid, quiet, and even comfortable place to spend a night. However, snow shelters take both time and energy to build.

Youths and adults will find building and sleeping in snow shelters both challenging and exciting. Snow is such a good windbreak and insulator that with the body heat from a couple of people and perhaps a burning candle, the temperature inside the shelter may stay above freezing.

Snow Trench

One of the quickest and easiest snow shelters to make (when the snow is at least 45 cm deep) is a snow trench. Simply dig a trench down to ground level, approximately 2.5 meters long and 1 meter wide. Dig a second trench, about 2 meters long across one end to form a "T."

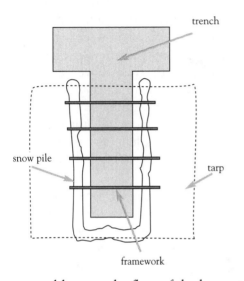

trench

snow pile

tarp

framework

Pile the snow you remove from the trenches along the sides of the *longer* trench to make them higher. Use your skis, poles and/or snow-shoes as a frame, placing them across the longer trench. Cover them with a tarp or a groundsheet for a roof. Pile a little bit of snow along the edges of the tarp/groundsheet to hold it in place and keep it from flapping in the wind. Place a second tarp or groundsheet on the floor of the longer trench, then add your mattress and sleeping bag. Now you're set for the night! The shorter trench provides access to the sleeping trench and serves as a place to cook and eat. Getting down below the snow level protects you from the wind, and the snow walls provide excellent insulation.

Quinzhee or Snow Dome

Quinzhees take lots of time and energy to build, but they're well worth the effort. The thick snow walls and roof provide excellent insulation and shelter — much better than a tent. All you need is a shovel, then dig in!

Building a quinzhee involves high energy output; usually resulting in perspiration. Adjust or remove layers of clothing to vent the moisture and regulate your body temperature.

You can make quinzhees with just about any type of snow as long as there is enough of it. Light, fluffy flakes will have to "settle" a little bit longer than sticky snow, but they contain more air and provide better insulation.

Before starting to build a quinzhee, determine how many people will sleep inside. This will tell you how big to make your snow pile. A quinzhee for three or four can be carved out of a snow pile roughly 2-2.5 meters high and 3-4 meters in diameter. When building the pile, clear an area the diameter you have chosen for your shelter right down to ground level, or stamp the snow down as much as possible, forming a solid base. Then throw the snow back into the cleared area or onto the compacted area, and build your pile. This may seem like extra work but when you

turn the snow over and over with your shovel or stamp it down, it actually speeds up the snow settling process. Complete your snow pile, then let it settle for as long as possible (at least two hours) before hollowing it out.

Plan your day allowing lots of extra time for building your quinzhee or snow dome. Get an early start. Try to arrive at your trailhead early enough to allow sufficient time to hike for one or two hours to your campsite, then an hour to build your snow pile before lunch. Let the pile settle for several hours while you cook and eat your lunch, explore the area and gather wood for your campfire.

When you've completed these camp tasks, it's time to resume work on your quinzhee. Gather a number of sticks (at least 12) that are approximately 45 cm long. Then walk around the shelter sticking them *straight* into the pile until the ends are flush with the outside wall. These will help you determine the thickness of the wall as you hollow the quinzhee out. When you hit the end of a stick when carving the quinzhee out, stop! You've reached the desired thickness for the wall. Next, decide which is the lee (or sheltered) side of the quinzhee, and begin hollowing it out there. This will be your door. Keep the door as small as possible — less than 60 cm high and wide. As you remove the snow from the centre of the pile, build two walls extending out from the quinzhee, one on each side of the door. These walls will help prevent wind and snow from blowing into the shelter. They can be filled later and hollowed out to form a tunnel entrance if you wish.

When hollowing out the quinzhee you have two options:

1. Remove all the snow right down to the bare ground. This will allow heat from the ground to warm the quinzhee a little and will provide lots of space for people to sit and sleep.

OR

2. Do not remove all of the snow from the inside. Leave enough snow to build a large sleeping platform just *a little bit higher* than the height of the door. This creates an air lock with the warmer air staying on top of the platform not being able to escape through the doorway where the cold air will lie. This method leaves you with less inside space, but it also means less space to heat and, therefore, a warmer shelter.

Because some people find the confined space inside a quinzhee uncomfortable, option #1 is their choice. For those willing to sacrifice space for warmth, option #2 works better.

When you've finished hollowing the quinzhee out, make a door. To contain the heat generated by your bodies and the candles, either cut a snow block or place your packs in the door. *Don't forget* to pull out several sticks in the roof. These will create air holes and will ensure you have an adequate fresh air supply.

Snow Cave

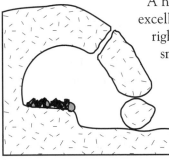

A hole dug into the side of a deep drift makes an excellent emergency shelter. Remember to dig at right angles to the prevailing wind so drifting snow won't block the entrance. Use a block of snow or roll a large snowball to block off the entrance hole, but make sure you've made several air holes in the roof before settling in for the night.

> **Caution!** *Never build snow shelters anywhere near snowmobile trails or close to a roadway where snowplows may venture.*

Other Shelters

Bivy sacks are one-person shelters that you slide your sleeping bag into for added protection from the elements. Tarps are also excellent for building shelters to house one or more campers.

Snow Shelter Tips

If you do decide to build a snow shelter during a winter camp, these tips will make the experience more pleasant.

1. Be sure you have plenty of ventilation. Poke two or three air holes in the roof using a stick or ski pole. For lighting, avoid gas lanterns. Use a candle lantern.

2. Building a snow shelter can be hot work. Take your time and adjust your clothing to let any extra heat or moisture escape. When you've finished building your shelter, remove any damp clothing and replace it with fresh dry clothes. Hang damp clothing in the sun or breeze to dry.

   While building your shelter, your body generates lots of heat and keeps you warm. When your work is complete and you're sitting back relaxing, your body doesn't generate the same volume of heat. It's time to put on lots of thick insulating layers and a hat. These will keep you warm.

3. Building snow shelters takes much longer than setting up a tent. Make sure you allow lots of extra time.

4. When hollowing out a quinzhee or snow shelter, put on waterproof clothes and a hood. These will keep your clothes as dry as possible.

5. Make sure you have a groundsheet to place under your mattress and sleeping bag to prevent them from getting wet.

6. First-time winter campers may choose to build their shelters close to home or a backup building. This works well as it helps reduce the element of risk and increases the camper's comfort level.

Bedding

A sleeping bag keeps you warm by capturing the heat generated by your body. The amount of heat the sleeping bag will trap is determined by the "loft" or thickness of the bag and the insulation material. The other factor making a comfortable sleep involves the amount of space inside that your body must heat. Closer fitting sleeping bags, such as the "mummy" style, are generally warmer than large rectangular types with lots of empty space inside. A good quality winter sleeping bag should have: a hood complete with a draw string; a boxed foot area; a draft tube along a good quality, two-way zipper; and a draw string at the shoulders.

For most winter camping, you will want a sleeping bag rated to -20°C or colder. (See sleeping bag section in Chapter 5 for more information.)

Increase your comfort level by following this advice:

▲ Because clothes get damp from work or play, it is important to change all of your clothes right down to the skin before gong to bed. The dampness will draw heat from your body.

▲ Place a waterproof reflector groundsheet under your mattress.

▲ Use a good mattress (Ensolite™, Airolite™ or Therm-a-rest™ types are best). Avoid air mattresses (they have too much empty space for you to heat) and open-celled foam pad (these absorb and retain too much moisture).

If you don't have a winter sleeping bag, you may be able to borrow or rent one from an outfitter. Another alternative is to improvise by placing two heavy summer sleeping bags, one inside the other. Place them so that the zippers are on opposite sides to minimize drafts through the zippers. To reduce the amount of open space inside these bags, campers can simply reach down beside their legs and pull the extra material up underneath. Wear a hooded sweater and/or a tuque.

Tests prove that up to 75 percent of a person's body heat is lost downwards, and only 25 percent is lost through the top of the sleeping bag. What does this mean? *To sleep warmly, you need three layers under you for every layer on top.* Place a lightweight waterproof groundsheet directly on the ground, then add your mattress, followed by your sleeping bag.

Whatever type of sleeping bag you use, remember to air it out every morning as early as possible. During the night, your body gives off a great deal of moisture which may be absorbed by your bedding. If you don't air out your bedding thoroughly, it will stay damp and lose some of its insulating abilities.

Avoid drinking tea and coffee (diuretics) before going to bed, and make sure you empty your bladder before turning in. Once you're in bed, you won't want to get out again until morning. But, if your bladder fills, get up and go. Otherwise, your body will use up energy heating the liquid; in the process, you might get cold. Some seasoned winter male campers take a leak-proof plastic bottle to bed with them. They use this to urinate into rather than having to get dressed and go outside. If you choose this method, make sure you clearly identify what the bottle is used for!

Place your boot liners inside your sleeping bag to keep them warm and dry when winter camping.

Before going to bed, prepare a hot water bottle by putting some hot water or juice in a *leakproof* plastic bottle. Then, put the bottle inside a wool sock. This will also give you something warm to drink during the night if you are cold.

Night Wear

Before leaving home, decide what you will wear to bed and place these clothes inside your sleeping bag. Here, they will be easy to find. Wool socks, polypropylene long johns, and/or fleece pants and a sweater work well. You may even wear these clothes next day.

Before climbing into bed at night, change all your clothes — right down to your skin! Hiking, skiing, snowshoeing and shelter building all generate heat and moisture, so the clothes you have been wearing will probably be damp or wet. If you wear these clothes to bed, you'll feel cold and clammy as the moisture draws the heat from your body. Your sleepwear should include a hat or hooded sweatshirt, especially if your sleeping bag does not have a hood.

Keep your mouth and nose outside your sleeping bag, or your breath will condense inside and form a layer of frost. If you're worried about frostbite on your nose, stick a piece of gauze across your nose with adhesive tape. This is a quick and easy safety precaution.

Get dressed and undressed inside your sleeping bag. This will keep you warm and prevent you from contacting the snow/tent walls with bare skin — not a pleasant experience!

Fires for Cooking and Warmth

Fires fulfil many functions. They provide warmth and light or heat for cooking and drying. Most people find a cheerful fire mentally uplifting.

As a source of warmth, a fire has limited value in winter. When you're standing or sitting near a fire, you can only warm one side at a time. A reflector fire, however, when built in front of a lean-to will reflect heat into the shelter, providing some warmth and comfort for the occupants.

When using a fire for winter cooking, location is very important. As with summer camping, position your fire well away from tents and equipment. Build your cooking fire in a sheltered place out of the wind. This will keep the wind from blowing away its heat; it will also prevent sparks from blowing onto your tent, tarp or gear.

Before lighting the fire, dig an area in the snow down to the ground level, or build a log platform for your fire. If you don't do this first, your fire will soon melt the surrounding snow, sink into a hole and probably go out.

Lighting a fire in winter may prove difficult; so take homemade firestarters with you. Carry a small supply of dry kindling, wood shavings and dry tinder in a small plastic bag as an emergency supply. When collecting firewood, look for wood that hasn't been buried in the snow. Find dead, dry, twigs and branches on the bottom of evergreen trees, or standing dead wood. Wood that is lying down will contain ice crystals. These must be melted, then dried out by the fire's heat before the logs will burn easily. These logs make a great log platform, but not fuel.

The firewood you need for cooking a meal can be gathered and broken by hand. You can break larger branches by stepping on them. Simply place one end on a rock (or a raised object), or place the branch between two trees and lever the branch until it breaks.

Stoves

A camp stove is often better than an open fire for cooking.

A pressurized, one- or two-burner stove operates well in cold temperatures. (*Note:* Pressurized stoves may require a priming paste to pre-heat and vaporize the fuel in the generator in extremely cold conditions. Squeeze the paste into the bowl underneath the generator and ignite.) Unpressurized stoves may not work as well in winter temperatures. Before moving a stove or adding fuel, be sure to turn it off and let it cool down. Liquid fuels freeze at a much lower temperature than water so they remain in liquid form even at very low temperatures. If spilled on your skin, cold fuel will make a painful, freezing burn. It's easiest and safest to do repairs and initial refueling at home before setting out. Most stove fuel tanks carry enough fuel to last a weekend under normal cooking conditions.

Caution! Do *not* use gas stoves, heaters or lanterns in a tent or snow shelter! The risks of damage and/or injury due to carbon monoxide poisoning and burns from spills or fire in the confined area are much higher than if you use them outside. Many manufacturers print a warning on their product stating: "Use only in a well ventilated area."

Light

Quite often, moonlight reflected off snow provides all the light you need, especially on a clear night. If you need additional light, a candle lantern may be helpful. Gas lanterns also work well but are for outside use only. Flashlights are great for finding items in a pack, but keep them in an inside coat or pants pocket so the batteries stay warm and functional. Cold batteries have a very short life span.

Food and Menus

Winter camping menus are a little different than summer outing menus. You'll need lots of calories to keep your body warm and provide extra energy for skiing, snowshoeing, shelter building and setting up camp.

During cold weather, campers want quick, easy to prepare and clean up, nutritious meals that provide enough calories to replace those burned during the day — 5,000 or more, depending on activities.

Refrigeration isn't a concern during winter, but freezing some foods can cause a problem. For example, it's pretty difficult to get frozen eggs out of the shell! Avoid fresh vegetables or eat them early before they have a chance to freeze. As in summer hiking, keep the weight and bulk of food supplies to a minimum unless you're pulling it on a toboggan or sled.

It's easier to do food preparation and packaging in the warmth of your kitchen rather than outside during a bitter snowstorm. Before leaving home, remove excess packaging, cut meat, and peel vegetables. You may even pre-cook some of the vegetables to reduce your cooking and waiting

Trail Tip:
To speed up cooking time in winter, pre-cook meals at home.

time in camp. Many people do all their cooking at home and freeze their meal in a freezer bag. At camp, all they have to do is reheat or boil the meal right in its bag.

Most grocery stores offer boil-in-a-bag meals, and camping stores sell dehydrated meals; these are usually very tasty. For dehydrated meals, simply add the required amount of boiling water, let it sit, then eat. If you really want to keep your clean-up to a minimum eat your meal right out of the bag. Use the boiled water for a drink and to clean your mug and spoon when you finish.

Some people still enjoy preparing and cooking their entire meal in camp, regardless of the weather. They may decide to cook a nice hot breakfast of bacon and eggs complete with toast and hash browns, or prepare a delicious one-pot stew with thinly sliced meat and vegetables. However you decide to prepare meals, make sure you allow enough time to get everything ready, eat and clean up.

Gas stoves are much faster and easier to regulate than campfires for cooking. You'll appreciate this early in the morning when you want a cup of hot coffee, or along a hiking trail when a cup of soup would really "hit the spot."

Build a cooking/eating platform with snow, and place your toboggan or logs on top to prevent your hot stove or plate from melting into the snow. If you choose to cook over a campfire, allow extra time to gather wood, build the fire, and get good coals glowing.

Here are a few menu suggestions:

▲ Instant oatmeal/porridge

▲ Bacon, cheese and an egg on an English muffin

▲ Prepared biscuit and pancake mix with molasses, pancake syrup or honey

▲ Dehydrated milk, juice crystals, tea, coffee, hot chocolate

▲ Instant cup of soup

▲ Dried or frozen meats

▲ Fish in a cornmeal batter

▲ Peanut butter with pita bread or crackers

▲ Macaroni and cheese

▲ Tuna or chicken

▲ Dried fruit, raisins, nuts, small pieces of chocolate, pretzel sticks in a trail mix

▲ Granola bars

▲ Egg powder for scrambled eggs

▲ Sardines

▲ Instant potatoes or packaged potato mixes

▲ Biscuits

▲ Small canned goods and hard candy.

Try other methods of cooking as well: shish kebabs, foil dinners, reflector or Dutch ovens. These provide new challenges and variety to traditional menus.

Hot beverages, such as tea, coffee, soups, or hot chocolate, and quick snacks, such as granola bars and GORP (good old raisins and peanuts), not only give energy and heat but also boost sagging morale. Try drinking hot Kool-Aid™ or juice too.

Storage

Store food in winter as you do in summer. Don't bring food into your sleeping area, including GORP which you may have stored in your pack. Hang food and garbage in "bear bags" at night. Although some animals may be hibernating, many other scavengers aren't. (Chapter 4 provides additional information on meals and storage.)

Water for Cooking

Take the same precautions for purifying water in winter as you would in summer. (See the water purification section in Chapter 5 for more.) Melting clean snow or ice for water or hot drinks works well; just make sure you boil it for five minutes or treat it first. As soft snow makes very little water for its bulk, dig deeper and use granular snow. Ice is even better if it is available, but chip it first for melting. If possible, start with a little bit of water in the pot. This will speed up the process.

If you are near a river or lake, chop a hole through the ice to get your water. Cover the water hole with loose snow to keep it from re-freezing and mark it so no one will get a wet foot or leg. Make your water hole do double duty by using it for ice fishing.

Avoid dehydration. Drink four-six litres or more of water per day to replace moisture "breathed out" or perspired.

Sanitation and Hygiene

Consider how you are going to dispose of garbage and waste water before setting out. Careful planning can eliminate most garbage before you even leave home. How? Buy your food in bulk when possible. Remove all outer packaging and repack in leak-proof, reusable containers.

When camping, burn all garbage (where possible) if you have a fire, and pack out non-burnable items. If you have canned goods, burn empty cans, crush them with a rock or your foot, then pack them out.

Mark out an area for collecting snow to melt for water. Don't go into the area for any other reason.

Carefully pour waste water from wash-up or cooking into a hole dug for that specific meal. Dig the hole 15 cm to 20 cm deep (about 6-8 inches) into the ground if digging is possible. If it isn't, dig a deep hole in the snow to ground level before pouring. Strain dish water through a terry cloth to collect food scraps. Burn these in the campfire or pack them out in the garbage. Drain waste water well away from your campsite, areas where you will be collecting snow for water, or any other water sources (even if frozen).

Wash dishes as soon as possible after you eat a meal. As soon as you serve your food, scrape out the cook pot, fill it with soapy water and put it back on the stove along with a second pot of clear water. Boil the water in both of these pots while you're eating.

The first pot is for washing; the second is for rinsing. Add a teaspoon of Javex™ (bleach) to the rinse water. Unless you rinse your dishes a second time in clear hot water, a slight taste of bleach may remain on the dishes. You can avoid this by having two rinse water pots: one with bleach and the second without. (See dishwashing section in Chapter 4 for more details.)

Personal cleanliness is a must, especially in a winter camp where it is tempting to forego the morning and nightly washes because of the cold. Wash when you get up, before meals, after doing camp chores and after using the latrine. This routine is important to health, sanitation and safety.

Keep a pot of water on the edge of the fire at all times; use this for washing or for when you need warm water (e.g. first aid). Also keep a plastic wash basin, soap and towels handy.

Latrines

When you camp in areas where outhouses are not available, mark off a latrine area. This area should be well off any trail, away from the rest of the campsite and any water source. In winter you won't be able to dig into the ground to make a cat-hole (a hole for body wastes), so follow these steps:

▲ Dig a hole in the snow.

▲ Line it with a plastic bag.

▲ Collect the solid waste and paper.

▲ Seal the bag, and double bag it (allowing it to freeze if temperatures permit).

▲ Pack it out.

Urinate into cat-holes and cover them over before leaving. Small, plastic garden trowels are great for digging cat-holes in the snow.

Trail or Camp Hints

Cold Metal

Be careful not to touch cold metal with your bare hands, or put a cold metal cup to your lips. You may lose some skin or part of your lip. If you do touch cold metal and feel yourself sticking to it, stay calm. Don't move. Get someone to pour lukewarm water over the "stuck" area until you can gently pull yourself free.

Sleeping Quarters

Place campers with the lightest weight sleeping bags away from the door and between two other campers with heavier sleeping bags.

Small Items

Small camp equipment can disappear quite easily in the snow. When you finish with an item, put it away in your pack or on your toboggan. Tie a piece of coloured flag tape to these articles to make them easier to find.

Fire-Making

If the snow isn't too deep, scrape it away to bare ground where you plan to build your fire. Place stones or logs on the ground for a base on which to build the fire. If you don't make a base, the fire's heat will thaw the ground and make a muddy mess.

Let your parka or jacket hang loose on hikes. If you become too warm, "pump" in fresh air by grasping the parka at the bottom, pulling it outwards and bringing it back several times. When you're resting, tighten the parka cord or sash slightly to keep in the heat.

To avoid chills during regular rest stops, find a sheltered spot, pair off and sit back-to-back on packs with a ground sheet around each pair. This back-to-back method provides lots of warmth.

If your feet are wet from perspiration or melting snow, change your socks and insoles immediately. Find a sheltered area out of the wind, and change quickly.

Winter Tools

Take extra care when handling an axe in cold weather. Even the sharpest blade may bounce off a piece of frozen wood or glance off a knot. The blade edge may also chip and nick.

A Swedish bow saw (also known as the Swede saw) or a light-weight collapsible, folding saw is useful for winter camping. A good saw will cut easily even if there is frost in the wood.

Axes, saws, knives and shovels can easily be lost in the snow. Designate a specific location for storing tools. If you're working away from your campsite, place your axe or saw where it won't get covered in snow (e.g. on a toboggan or sled).

Stay Safe on the Ice

Your knowledge of the winter environment, including ice, will help ensure your activities stay enjoyable and safe.

Understand the Environment

Ice forms on fresh water when the surface water temperature falls to 0°C. Salt water and water containing dissolved impurities freeze at a lower temperature. Freezing also depends on various factors, including the following:

▲ Air temperature

▲ Solar radiation

▲ Wind speed

▲ Snow cover

▲ Waves, currents, and tides

▲ The size and depth of the body of water

▲ Underwater vegetation.

For example, a small lake freezes earlier in the winter than larger lakes. Fast-moving rivers freeze later in the season than placid ones, or perhaps not at all.

Characteristics of Ice

The better you understand ice, the safer you will be on it. Your understanding should be based on the colour of ice and on other aspects that determine its strength.

Colour

The colour of ice is an indication of its quality and strength.

▲ *Clear blue:* strongest.

▲ *White opaque or snow ice:* formed when water-saturated snow freezes on top of ice, making an opaque white ice that is usually only half as strong as clear ice.

▲ *Grey ice:* the greyness indicates that water is present, usually from thawing.

Strength and thickness

Clear blue ice is the strongest type of ice. Its strength increases as the temperature drops further below 0°C. However, if the temperature drops very quickly (such as overnight), internal stress within the ice itself can weaken it. Likewise, removing snow from an ice surface may result in a temperature drop that weakens the ice. Thus, if you clear snow from lake or pond ice for hockey or skating, consider this ice to be only half as strong as it appears.

Large vehicles (pickup trucks or cars) compress the ice when they drive over it. The ice returns to its original qualities after the load is removed. The movement of the vehicle across the ice also creates a wave in the water under the ice that weakens it. After vehicles have been on the ice, recheck its thickness.

Some recreation departments and community groups measure ice thickness in areas for public use during winter months. Find out if this service is available in your community or in areas to which you are travelling.

Small group activities: 20 cm thick.

Operation of snow machines: 25 cm thick.

Operation of heavy vehicles: 40 cm thick.

If you must determine ice thickness yourself, drill test holes 15 metres apart in a river or 30 metres apart in a lake. When going onto the ice to drill these holes, proceed with caution in case the ice starts to break under you.

Before conducting an activity on ice, measure the thickness to determine whether it is strong enough to support the people and equipment. Check to make sure the ice is uniformly thick. Use the following guidelines for blue ice thickness.

Ice Rescues

If someone has fallen through the ice, it is crucial to act quickly and correctly. The longer the person is in the water, the slimmer the chances of survival.

Rescuing a person on or in ice may be very dangerous. Follow these guidelines to stay safe yourself while effectively helping the person:

1. If at all possible, do not go onto the ice yourself. The ice may give way; then there will be two people in the water instead of one. It's always safest to perform the rescue from a secure place on shore.

2. If the person has fallen through in the middle of a large body of water, consider whether you can quickly get help for the rescue.

Trained professionals (such as police, fire, or ambulance workers) are better prepared to deal with rescues from an ice surface.

3. If you must go out onto the ice, carry a long pole or branch to test the ice in front of you. Do this by hitting the ice or putting pressure on it with the extended end of the pole. Wear a PFD, if available. Take along something to reach or throw to the person, such as a pole, weighted rope, or line with an aid on the end. Even a tree branch can work.

4. When approaching a break in the ice through which the person fell, lie down and slowly crawl toward the hole. This distributes your weight over a greater surface area and should prevent you from falling through. Stay as far away from the breakthrough site as possible while attempting the rescue.

5. From a secure position on land or lying on the ice, extend or throw the emergency rescue device to the person. While extending the aid, stay low to avoid slipping on the ice or slipping toward the hole.

6. Tell the person to keep kicking while you pull them out. This will help propel the person out of the hole while you're pulling.

7. When you get the person out of the water, move him to a secure position on shore or where you are sure the ice is thick. Re-warm the person in dry, warm clothes in a warm place, and give him warm fluids. If necessary, call emergency medical assistance.

If a rescued person is conscious, get the victim ashore quickly and find a warm place to remove the victim's clothes. Put the victim into a bed with warm water bottles, or into a bed warmed by an electric blanket. This will help restore circulation. Give the person hot drinks.

If the victim is unconscious when drawn out of the water, give artificial respiration. When the person is breathing, put them into dry clothes and warm the victim as soon as possible.

If you break through ice, stay calm. If the ice is thin, don't try to climb back on it. Instead, spread your arms out over the surface and wait for help. If you're alone, carefully break the ice until you have a solid surface in front of you. Then, with arms fully extended and taking as much weight as possible, try to roll out full length sideways. If you have a pocketknife and you can reach it, open it with one hand and your teeth. Use it as an ice pick to pull on as you roll.

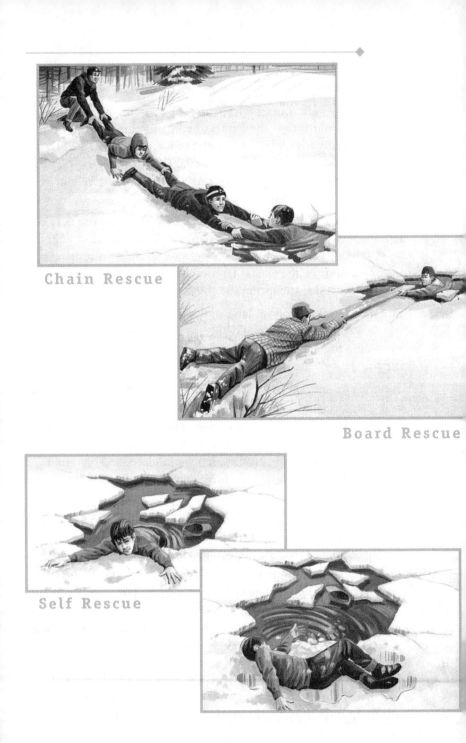

Chain Rescue

Board Rescue

Self Rescue

Rope Rescue

Ladder Rescue

(See Chapter 13 for more information.)

Snowblindness

The term "snowblindness" is misleading because you don't actually become blind. Here are the symptoms, from mild snowblindness to more severe cases:

▲ Gritty feeling in the eyes

▲ Eyes become hot and sticky

▲ Eyes begin to water, and vision blurs

▲ Sharp pain develops and you want to shrink away from light.

The sun doesn't even have to be shining for someone to get snowblindness. Most cases occur on slightly overcast days when there is little shadow.

Polarized or amber-coloured glasses help prevent snowblindness.

If you don't have any sunglasses but feel symptoms of snowblindness, keep your eyes fixed on a dark object ahead, such as a dark canvas covering, a loaded toboggan, or the back of a companion walking ahead of you. A trail-breaker developing eye trouble should fall back to the end of the line.

If you can't avoid looking at bright snow, you can give your eyes some help by almost closing the lids and looking through your eyelashes.

To cut down on glare, blacken your cheekbones and nose with a mixture of charcoal and grease. Some people find this helpful.

Camp treatment for snowblindness consists of applying cold compresses (or ice wrapped in gauze) to eyes. Shield the eyes as effectively as possible. In serious cases, the patient should be kept in a darkened place for as long as necessary.

Carbon Monoxide

Carbon monoxide poses a danger in snow shelters as well as tents.

Carbon monoxide is odourless and highly poisonous. It offers no advance warning of its killing potential. Unconsciousness may follow quickly after a sudden severe headache, dizziness and sickness. You can recognize carbon monoxide poisoning readily by one symptom — the cherry red colour of the victim's face.

To help someone in need, move the person quickly into fresh air and give artificial respiration. Keep the patient warm with blankets and hot drinks.

Cold Injuries

Low temperatures can lead to cold injuries, particularly when there are high winds or when the body becomes wet. Try to prevent cold injuries by dressing appropriately and not staying in the cold too long. Hypothermia and frostbite can occur together or separately.

Frostbite

Frostbite is a cold injury occurring in specific body parts exposed to the cold. In frostbite, body tissues freeze. In superficial frostbite the skin is frozen, but not the tissues below. In deep frostbite both the skin and underlying tissues are frozen. Both types of frostbite are serious.

Frostbite can usually be prevented with common sense. Follow these guidelines:

▲ Avoid exposing any part of the body to the cold.

▲ Wear a hat and layers of clothing.

▲ Drink plenty of warm fluids or water.

▲ Avoid alcohol.

▲ Take frequent breaks from the cold.

Depending on the circumstances and how long the person is exposed to the cold, frostbite may occur by itself or along with hypothermia. Signs and symptoms of frostbite include:

▲ Lack of feeling in the affected area.

▲ Skin that appears waxy.

▲ Skin that is cold to the touch.

▲ Skin that is discoloured (flushed, white, yellow, blue).

The specific care for frostbite involves the following:

1. Cover the affected area to keep it warm until you can immerse it in water.

2. Handle the area gently. Never rub it, because rubbing causes further damage.

3. Warm the area gently by immersing the affected part in water warmed to 40.5°C. If possible, use a thermometer to check the water.

4. Keep the frostbitten part in the water until it looks red and feels warm.

5. Bandage the area with a dry, sterile dressing. If fingers or toes are frostbitten, place cotton or gauze between them. Avoid breaking any blisters.

6. Get the victim to medical care.

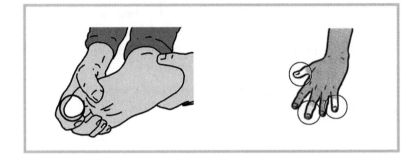

Hypothermia

When hiking, be aware of the danger of hypothermia. Hypothermia is a cooling of the body to the point at which the body's natural rewarming mechanisms cannot be maintained. This condition may occur if a person is dressed inappropriately for the cold, stays in the cold too long, or becomes wet from perspiration or falling into water.

Hypothermia is a significant threat when winter camping. A person could be in danger of hypothermia if exhausted, wet, exposed to wind, or undernourished. Under these conditions, the air doesn't have to be cold or below freezing — a moderate temperature of 5°C to 10°C can cause hypothermia.

To avoid hypothermia, stay dry. Put rain gear on before it starts to rain. Make sure it is waterproof, not just water repellent. Rain gear must provide adequate ventilation, otherwise a camper will become wet from perspiration, defeating the purpose of rain gear.

Protect yourself from the wind. Make sure you have warm, windproof clothing, including a good hat. Put on a dry sweater *after* working or playing, not before.

Avoid exhaustion. Set a reasonable hiking pace that won't leave people overly tired by mealtime. Play games, but avoid ones that require a lot of exertion. You need lots of energy reserves to stay warm and to fight off chills (early signs of approaching hypothermia).

Make sure you have some high energy food to nibble on while hiking, and drink lots of water to avoid dehydration.

Hypothermia can start either slowly (building over the entire day) or quickly (falling into freezing water). Early symptoms include: feeling chilly, feeling tired, or irritability. Uncontrollable shivering may follow. If you take no action to warm the victim and he remains exposed but the shivering stops, the hypothermia has reached a very dangerous stage!

How to Prevent Hypothermia

Protect yourself from hypothermia in the following ways:

▲ Don't start an activity in, on, or around cold water unless you know you can get help quickly in an emergency.

▲ Have PFDs at hand whenever you are near cold water. A PFD will help you float in a rescue position if you fall; some styles even provide insulation against cold water.

▲ Wear layers of clothing, and a hat. As much as 60 percent of body heat loss occurs through the head.

▲ Carry matches in a waterproof container. You may need to build a fire to warm up after a fall into cold water.

▲ Carry a chocolate bar or high-energy food containing sugar. Glucose stimulates shivering — the body's internal mechanism for rewarming itself.

▲ If you must snowmobile over ice-covered lakes and rivers, wear a buoyant snowmobile survival suit.

Caring for Someone with Hypothermia

Anyone in cold water, or someone who wears wet clothes for a long time, may develop hypothermia. Children under 12 and the elderly are particularly vulnerable. You need to recognize hypothermia's symptoms in order to act quickly and get emergency help. Bluish lips and shivering may be the first warning signs you see. Other signals include a feeling of weakness, confusion, a slow or irregular pulse, numbness, slurred speech, and semi-consciousness or unconsciousness. Exposure to cold water is a severe physical shock.

Follow these guidelines to help someone suffering from hypothermia.

1. Treat the person very gently and monitor breathing carefully.

2. Remove wet clothes, dry the person, and move him or her to a warm environment.

3. Wrap the person in blankets or put on dry clothes. Do not warm the person too quickly by immersing him or her in warm water. Rapid warming may affect heart rhythms. Remember that hypothermia can be life-threatening.

4. If available, put hot water bottles, heating pads (if the person is dry), or other heat sources on the body, keeping a blanket or towel between the heat source and skin to avoid burns.

5. If the victim is alert, give warm liquids to drink.

Take Positive Action

It takes time (up to eight hours) to warm a seriously affected hypothermia victim. Even after a victim's body begins to feel warm, cold blood circulating from the extremities (head, feet and hands) back to the body's core can produce an "afterdrop" — a continued lowering of body temperature.

In many cases, a victim won't even realize what is happening. Some people may deny that anything is wrong.

After any serious brush with hypothermia, end the outing *immediately*. If one person has fallen victim to hypothermia, probably others are in danger too.

Winter Survival

Probably you have never had to survive in the cold without a shelter, fuel, and sleeping bags. But this emergency may arise one day.

Whenever you're in an emergency situation without the usual protection, don't panic. Get organized. As a reasonably fit, knowledgeable, thinking person, you should be able to survive if you follow several steps prepared by David Dehaas (*Outdoor Canada*, May, 1982).

Trail Tip:

Liquid fuels freeze at a much lower temperature than water therefore they become super cold but stay in a liquid state. Do not spill on exposed flesh.

1. *Deal with your immediate problems first.* Find water, firewood and shelter. Attend to whatever first aid emergencies that come up, and prepare your signal fires.

2. *Assess your situation.* Every emergency involves different problems, and every situation provides a set of opportunities. Decide what has to be done and when. Be systematic.

3. *Establish discipline.* This is important whether alone or in a group. Don't let anyone, including yourself, waste precious energy by panicking. It's important that everyone works together for survival.

4. *Marshall your resources.* Find out what you have in your pack. How can you use it to improve your situation? Save, conserve, and ration whatever you have.

5. *Ration your physical and mental resources.* Manage your reserves carefully. Think about what you are doing, what can you expect to gain, and what can you expect to lose by choosing a certain action. Solve each problem thoroughly and capably.

6. *Keep your spirits up.* This is particularly important within a group. Sing, laugh, play counting games or anything else that maintains good spirits. Highlight your accomplishments and stress the positive.

7. *Don't surrender to your problems.* Keep up appearances by washing when you can, preparing food properly, and using civilized behaviour.

8. *Handle one problem at a time.* Once you have decided you need a shelter, build it. Don't stop halfway through and do something else.

9. *Consider your long-term course of action.* Assess your situation carefully and plan alternatives if necessary.

10. *Take action.* When you have decided something, carry through with it. Do what you think is best in light of the conditions.

Signals

Smoke makes a good signal; rescuers can see it for long distances. Three signal fires is an internationally recognized method of alerting others of an emergency.

Signal mirrors or polished metal have probably attracted more rescuers than any other method. A mirror's reflection is visible from many kilometres away on a sunny day. Carry a signal mirror in your survival kit.

You can make a signaling mirror from a piece of polished metal by drilling a hole in the exact centre of it for aiming purposes. Even at night, a flashlight or candle directed at the mirror can be very effective.

Here's how to use a signal mirror in bright sunlight. Hold the mirror in one hand close to your face. Hold up a finger from your other hand, sighting on your target (rescuer). When the sun reflects on your finger, the distant target should see the flash.

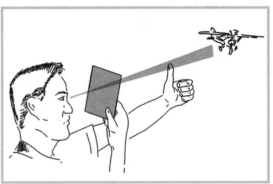

Survival Kits

Carry a survival kit with you on all winter hikes or camps. The items in the kit are only helpful if you have the necessary knowledge and skills to use them. (See survival kit section in Chapter 3 for more details.)

CHAPTER 9

▶ Ropes and Spars

Rope Work

Rope is essential to many outdoor activities like camping, canoeing, sailing, skiing, rock climbing, and pioneering. Rope is one of the most basic materials in our society; learning how to use it properly is a valuable skill.

In pioneering projects, rope work is essential when fastening odd sized or awkward shaped logs and branches together to build temporary or semi-permanent structures. "Pioneering" is the word used to describe the work done by old-time military engineers who went ahead of the army on foot to build bridges and towers with rope and timber.

Types of Rope

There are three basic types of rope.

- ▲ Laid rope
- ▲ Woven rope
- ▲ Sash cord

Laid Rope

Natural and synthetic fibres are often twisted into yarns, the yarns into strands, and the strands into ropes so the twists are stable and flexible. This process is called "laying." The method permits using shorter lengths of natural fibres to make uniformly strong rope. Ropes made like this come in all sizes.

Woven Rope

Synthetic fibres are often braided or woven into rope in smaller diameters.

Sash Cord

This cord is made from cotton, and woven and glazed with starch or a similar product. Avoid this cord, as well as binder twine, for pioneering projects. Both are unreliable and clumsy.

Proper knot-tying is important in pioneering and other rope work; the strength and security of a job may depend on it. Successful knot-tying involves using the right knot at the right time, and tying it correctly. The right knot holds when you want it to hold (it has lots of contact points for friction), ties and unties quickly, and has a specific use. The wrong knot may loosen when you put a strain on it, or it may jam so hard you cannot untie it.

The more knots you tie, the faster and better you'll become. Practise with a piece of rope about two meters long and 6-12 millimeters in diameter. First-hand experience is always the best when learning knot-tying, but we provide instructions and diagrams for several important and useful knots.

Types of Rope

Ropes are made from natural or synthetic fibres to achieve maximum strength, flexibility, and uniformity for specific purposes. It's important to know the proper kinds of rope to use for different jobs — what you don't know *may* hurt you. A nice thick rope may be rotten; a thin, strong nylon rope may burn your hands as it slips through.

Manila and hemp are the two most popular natural fibre ropes. The most common synthetic (man-made) ropes are nylon, polyester, and polypropylene. Some characteristics of these ropes are found in the chart to the right.

You must look after all rope carefully to ensure its durability and safety. Keep it clean and free of mud or grease. Replace worn spots by splicing (see p.211). Uncoil and coil rope properly, and watch for kinks. Prevent its untwisting or frazzling by whipping, taping or melting the ends. But most important, identify any rope that is unsafe for normal use. Destroy it.

Parts of a Rope

A piece of rope doesn't have parts such as a head, body or tail. To understand knot-tying, think of rope as having three sections: two ends and a standing part. Some knots are formed by two ends (reef knot), some by the end and the standing part (bowline), and some by the standing part alone (sheepshank).

Some knots seem to be made up of many parts. But even the most difficult knots can be broken down to three basic terms: bight, standing part and free end.

Characteristics of popular types of rope

TYPE	NYLON	POLYESTER	POLYPROPYLENE	NATURAL FIBRE
Cost	high	high	medium	medium low
Ease of Knotting	fair/good	fair/good	very poor	good
Tensile Strength	high	high	medium	low
Effect of Water on Strength	loss	slow gain	gain	varies
Stretch	high	low	low	low
Shock Absorption	good	fair	poor	very poor
Flexing Endurance	good	good	poor	poor
Behavior on Water	sinks	sinks	floats	sinks
Resistance to Sunlight	fair	good	poor	varies
Resistance to Heat	fair	fair+	poor	varies
Approximate Melting Point	2200°C	2500°C	1600°C	burns
Resistance to Wet Freezing	fair+	good	poor	very poor
Resistance to Damp Storage	good	good	good	very poor
Resistance to Chemicals	fair (avoid acids)	fair (avoid alkalis)	fair (avoid solvents)	very poor
Electrical Insulation (Dry)	poor	good	good	poor

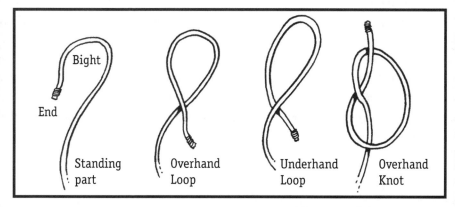

Bight

End

Standing part

Overhand Loop

Underhand Loop

Overhand Knot

Whipping

Before using a rope, "whip" the two ends to keep them from unravelling. To whip the ends of a rope, use a piece of twine or cotton fishing line about 15 cm long. Make it into a loop and place it at the end of the rope. About 6 cm from the end, begin wrapping the twine tightly around the rope. When the whipping is as wide as the rope is 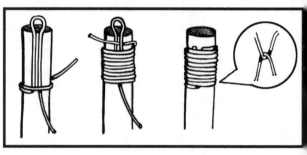 thick, slip the end through the loop, pull the end of the loop hard, and trim off the twine. Then whip the other end of the rope.

For a permanent type of whipping, use sailmaker's whipping. Unlay the rope 5 cm. Make a bight in a 1 metre length of twine, and place it around one of the strands. Re-lay the rope. Wind the twine tightly around the rope end for a sufficient number of turns. Carry the bight originally formed back over the end of the same strand around which it was laid. Pull twine ends tight and tie them with a square knot between the rope ends. Trim ends of twine.

Kinds of Knots

There are many kinds of knots; some are used for specific purposes as indicated by their names, while some are useful for almost any kind of work. No matter what they're called, they are all knots, bends or hitches.

A **knot** is a knob made in a rope to serve as a stopper, such as a figure eight or an overhand knot. But the term is used very loosely.

A **bend** unites two rope ends.

A **hitch** is a temporary noose made by tying a rope to itself or around a timber, usually to anchor the rope or to tether an animal or boat.

Sometimes different names describe the same knot; people in different trades call knots by various names. For example, the sheetbend, the weaver knot, and the weaver's hitch are all the same knot.

Note: You can make the knots in this section with either natural or artificial fibre ropes.

Knots for Joining

The *woven figure-eight bend* or the "S" knot are good for joining two ends of ropes or lines in either natural or artificial fibres.

The "S" Knot

1. Start by placing the ends of the two ropes parallel to each other.

2. Using one free end, make four round turns over both ropes before passing the end down the centre of the knot.

3. Take the second end, make four similar turns over both ropes, and pass the end down the centre of the second knot.

4. Pull both standing parts, and the two knots will slide together to form a secure "S" knot.

Woven Figure-Eight Bend

This knot can substitute for the "S" knot when you don't require the highest security and strength.

1. Make a figure-eight in the top rope as shown in drawing 1 (see p.202).

2. Thread the end of the other rope exactly as shown in drawing 2 (see p.202).

3. Partially tighten, making sure that the lines remain parallel without twists. This makes the knot both pleasing to look at and compact.

4. Thoroughly tighten by repeatedly pulling each end and standing part. Note that the standing parts emerge on diagonally opposite sides of the knot.

DRAWING 1

DRAWING 2

Warning! DO NOT tie a figure-eight the "easy" way by simply twisting a figure-eight in the doubled ends of a pair of ropes. If you do, the standing parts will emerge together and you will have one of the weakest knots known.

Knots for Attaching

The *half-S* and *modified timber hitch* are two knots or hitches you can use on either artificial or natural fibre rope. They are good for attaching a rope to a pole or some other kind of timber.

Half-S

The half-S is a secure slip knot or hitch which you can use to fasten a rope to a ring or a pole. The half-S is identical to the first part of the "S" knot shown earlier (*Knots for Joining*).

1. Start with a bight around or through the securing object (ring or pole).

2. Bring the end of the rope around to the standing part, and make four overhand loops over both ropes before passing the end down through the centre of the knot.

3. Pull the standing part to tighten the knot. (See diagram)

Modified Timber Hitch

This knot can be used with both artificial and natural fibre rope. It's good for raising logs or dragging them along the ground, or tying to a post or spar. Unlike the regular timber hitch, it will hold under slack conditions.

1. Bend the end of the rope around the pole twice, then around the standing part and through the loops just formed.

2. Take at least four turns around both ropes on the post.

3. Make the last turn at the front near the standing part.

4. Tighten the knot before using.

Knots for Loops

Sometimes you may want to throw a loop — a running loop, a noose, or a permanent loop — around something. Use the *half-S* (as shown previously), the *8-1/2 loop*, and the *locking bowline* with both artificial and natural fibre ropes.

The 8-¹/₂ Loop

This knot is used for tying a loop that will not slip at the end or middle of a rope.

1. Form a bight by doubling the end of the rope back toward the standing part.

2. Take the bight and bend it around the end and standing part over itself and up through the loop formed by the bight. (See diagram)

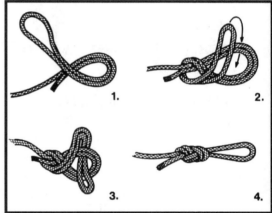

Locking Bowline

The locking bowline is used for tying a loop at the end or in the middle of a rope. It is much more secure than the regular bowline, especially if you're using stiff or slippery rope. Use it also when you need to tie a non-slipping rope around either an object or yourself.

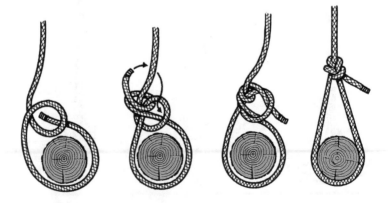

1. Pass the rope around the object or your waist.

2. Form an overhand loop. (See diagram) Push the end of the rope up through the overhand loop and around behind the standing part.

3. Follow up through the loop a second time, passing the end behind the standing part and then down through the overhand loop. (See diagram)

4. Make the knot as tight as you can.

Knots for First Aid

The *reef knot* is useful for first aid.

Reef or Square Knot

The reef knot is used in first aid for tying bandages. It lies flat, holds well, and is easily untied. Never use the reef knot when someone's life is at stake. Keep this knot for tying pack-ages and first aid.

1. Begin with an over and under crossing. (See diagram A)

2. Bring the ends back above in a second similar crossing. (See diagram B)

3. The completed knot is snugged up by pulling on the ends. (See diagram C)

Knots for Joining

Two knots which may be used for joining natural fibre rope are the *sheetbend*, and the *fisherman's bend*. Use these knots with natural fibre rope only.

Sheetbend

The sheetbend is valuable when joining ropes of different thickness. It got its name from sailors who used it to attach the ropes used to rig a ship.

1. Form a bight or loop on the end of the heavier rope, and hold it in your hand.

2. Pass the end of the thinner rope up through the bight from below.

3. Bring the end of the thinner rope over, around, and under the bight; then slip it under its own standing part where this enters the bight. (Note that both rope ends are on the same side.)

4. Hold the bight with one hand, and tighten the sheetbend by pulling on the other rope's standing part.

Fisherman's Knot

Fishermen use this knot to join strands of gut. It's one of the best knots for tying fine lines together.

1. Tie an overhand knot in one of the ropes, but do not pull it tight.

2. Pass the other rope end through this overhand knot and alongside the first rope's free end.

3. Tie an overhand knot in the second rope around the standing part of the first rope.

4. Pull each of the two overhand knots tight separately.

5. Pull the whole knot tight by pulling on each pair of ropes below the overhand knots. This will interlock the two overhand knots.

Knots for Attaching

Three knots which can be used for attaching in natural fibre ropes are the *clove hitch*, the *two half-hitches*, and the *timber hitch*.

Clove Hitch

The clove hitch is a widely used and important pioneering knot. Scouts use it for starting and finishing most lashings.

1. Bend the rope end around the pole, then bring the end forward over its own standing part.

2. Bend the rope end once more around the pole beside the first turn, then pass it under the second bend.

3. Push the loops close together, tighten the clove hitch by pulling hard on the end and the standing part of the rope.

Two Half-Hitches

This knot is good for fastening a natural fibre rope to a post or ring.

1. Bend the end of the rope around a pole, then over and under its standing part.

2. Now pass the end down through the loop you have formed.

3. Make the second half-hitch in front of the first by bringing the rope end over, under, and through the loop formed.

4. Push the two half-hitches close together and up against the pole.

5. By pulling in on the standing part, you will tighten everything.

Timber Hitch

The timber hitch is another excellent pioneering knot. It's used when two timbers need to be hitched together. It's also fine for raising logs, for dragging them over the ground, or for pulling them through water. It will only hold under pressure.

1. Bend the end of the rope around the pole, then under and over its own standing part through the loop just formed.

2. Make a bend near the rope end, and twist the end a number of times around the part of the rope next to it.

3. Push the timber hitch firmly up against the pole, then tighten it by pulling hard on the standing part.

Knots for Loops

Use the *slip knot*, the *taut-line hitch*, and the *regular bowline* when making loops with natural fibre rope.

Slip Knot

Some common uses for the slip knot include tying string around a package, and tying up a rolled tent.

1. Bend the rope in a large loop around the item you wish to tie up.

2. Tie the end of the rope around the standing part with an overhand knot.

3. Pull the overhand knot tight, then push it up against the item to be tied.

4. Tighten the whole knot by pulling the standing part.

Taut-Line Hitch

The taut-line hitch can be tied on a line that is taut or tight. Since it will only slide one way, campers often use it on tent guy ropes. For

this reason, it's sometimes called the guy line hitch. This knot is simply a clove hitch with an extra turn in the direction of the strain on the standing part.

Bowline

The bowline is a rescue knot that you tie around yourself or throw to someone who needs a lifeline. Originally it was used to tie a line to the bow of a ship.

1. Pass the rope around your waist and hold the short end in your right hand.

2. Make a simple overhand loop in the length and hold it with your left hand.

3. Pass the short end through the hole from the bottom.

4. Bend the end around the length, and pass it through the small loop just formed and alongside its own continuation. (See diagram)

5. Tighten the bowline by holding onto the bight formed by the rope end and pulling hard on the standing part.

Extra Knots

The *butterfly* and the *sheepshank* knots can only be made with natural fibre rope.

Butterfly Knot

This knot gives you a loop that won't slip and which may be tied without using the end of the rope. It's used as a harness for hauling heavy loads and for climbing.

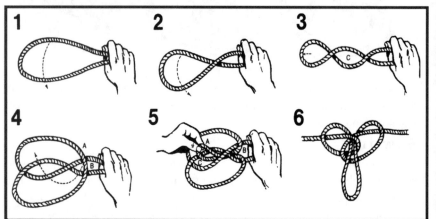

1. Make a bight in the rope in one hand and hold it, as shown.

2. Make one twist in the bight to form holes A and B.

3. Make another twist in the same direction and produce hole C.

4. Fold part A up to B.

5. Pass A down through hole B and produce hole C.

6. Pull the bight through and tighten it.

Sheepshank

Use this knot for shortening a rope without cutting it, or for strengthening a weak part in a rope.

1. Take up the slack, as shown in Diagram 1.

2. Form an underhand loop as shown in B (Diagram 2), slide it over the bight "Bl" and pull it tight. Repeat at the other end.

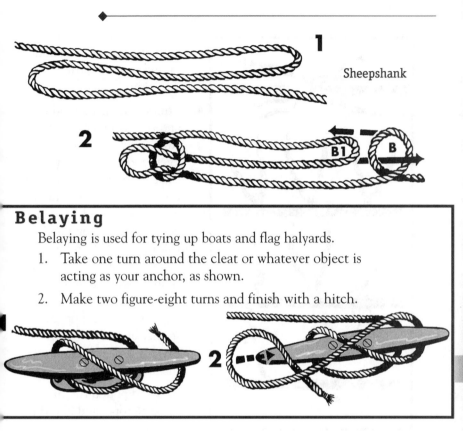

1

Sheepshank

2

B1   B

Belaying

Belaying is used for tying up boats and flag halyards.

1. Take one turn around the cleat or whatever object is acting as your anchor, as shown.

2. Make two figure-eight turns and finish with a hitch.

2

Splicing

A splice is used to mend a damaged rope or to fasten one rope to another. A good splice maintains up to 95 percent of the rope's strength and is even stronger than a knot. The basic idea is to unlay or untwist the strands which make up the ends of two pieces of rope, then to join all the strands together to make up one strong piece of rope.

Long Splice

The long splice allows the rope to run through a block, and should be made only with two ropes of the same size. It takes a long time to make and uses a lot of rope. (See diagram on next page.)

1. Unlay both rope ends about 15 turns and place them together, alternating the strands of each end.

2. Using opposite pairs, unlay one strand (4) and fill its place with "its" partner strand (2).

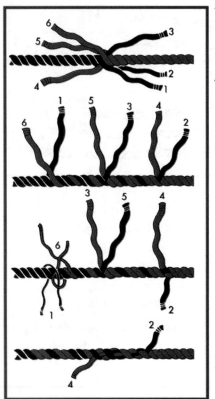

3. Repeat this operation with another pair of strands (1 and 6), in opposite directions.

4. Trim the longer strand (4) and tie each pair of opposing strands 2 and 4 with an overhand knot, tucking each strand twice. The tuck then goes over one strand, under the second and out between the second and third. Strands 1 and 6 are halved. Strands 3 and 5 are simply tied with an overhand knot. Strands 1 and 6 are halved, and opposite strands are tied with an overhand knot before tucking.

5. Roll and pound the tucks into the rope, and clip the strand ends.

Short Splice

The strongest method for joining two ropes is the short splice. You can make it quickly, and it wastes very little rope. It has a disadvantage; it cannot pass through a block.

1. Unlay the rope a few turns and alternate the strands.

2. Tie the strands down to prevent further unlaying.

3. Tuck strand 1 over an opposing strand and under the next strand.

4. The tuck of strand 2 goes over the first strand 5, under the second, and out between the second and third.

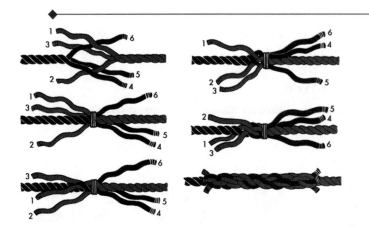

5. Repeat the operation with the other two strands (1 and 3) from the same rope end. Remove the tie and repeat the operation on the other rope end.

6. Make two more tucks for each strand, roll the tucks and clip the ends.

Back Splice

Use the back splice to make a woven end on the rope so it won't unravel.

1. First lay the ends over each other in a crown knot (Figures 1-3), so they point from the crown knot back along the length of rope.

2. Tuck them over-and-under fashion, as you did with the short splice.

3. Trim the ends and smooth the splice by rolling it on the floor with your foot.

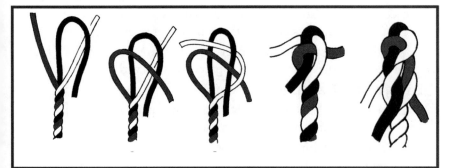

Prepare the "unfinished" ends of any rope before using. Back splicing is a good method of preventing a rope from unravelling, but it may make it more difficult to thread the rope through a block or a pulley.

Eye Splice

Use the eye splice in the end of a rope used for mooring or when you need a permanent loop.

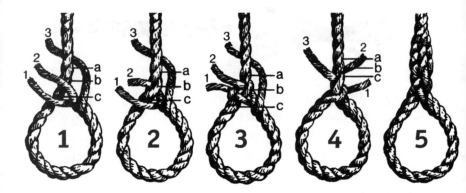

1. Unlay the end of the rope.

2. Tuck strand 2 over strand C, under B and out between A and B.

3. Tuck strand 1 once over B and under A.

4. Tuck strand 3.

5. Tuck each strand, in turn, twice more. Clip the ends.

Lashings

For extended camping trips, you may choose to make a few pieces of camp equipment. Camp furniture and gadgets are fun to make — they show your inventiveness and add the comforts of home.

Whether you're making a pioneering project, a raft, a dock, or a bridge, you'll need to know how to lash the parts together with rope.

Diagonal Lashing

Use a diagonal lashing to bind together two spars which tend to spring apart and which don't touch where they cross.

1. Start the lashing with a timber hitch around both spars.

2. Tighten the timber hitch, bringing the two spars together.

3. Take three or four turns of the lashing around one fork and three or four turns around the other fork.

4. Take two frapping (tightening) turns around the lashing at the point where the spars cross.

5. Finish off the lashing with a clove hitch around the most convenient spar.

Square Lashing

The square lashing is used to lash spars which cross at a right angle, touching where they cross.

1. Start with a clove hitch around the upright spar immediately under the cross-piece.

2. Twist the rope end into the length, then "wrap" the rope around the crosspiece and the upright, binding them together.

3. In wrapping, the rope goes on the outside of the previous turn around the cross-piece, and on the inside of the previous turn around the upright.

4. After three or four tight wrapping turns, make two or three frapping (tightening) turns between the timbers. Pull them tight.

5. Finish with a clove hitch around the end of the cross-piece.

Remember: Start with a clove hitch, 3 or 4 wrappings, frap twice, and end with a clove hitch.

Tripod Lashing

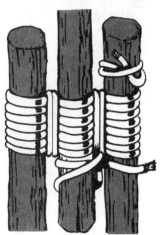

1. Place three timbers next to each other and attach the rope to the outside leg with a clove hitch at the proper place.

2. Bind the poles with seven or eight wrapping turns around each and two frapping turns between the poles to form the hinge pivots.

3. Finish off the tripod lashing with a clove hitch on the other outside leg.

4. Spread the legs to the proper position for use.

Shear Lashing

This lashing is used to bind parallel spars and to form "shear legs" which support things like bridges.

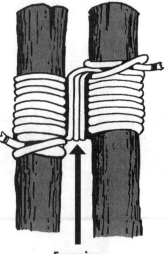

Frapping

1. Place the two timbers next to each other.

2. Tie a clove hitch around one of them at a convenient place from the top.

3. Bind the two timbers together by making seven or eight loose turns of the rope around them — one turn beside the other.

4. Make two frapping (tightening) turns around the lashing turns between the two timbers. Fasten the rope with a clove hitch around the second timber.

5. Open out the timbers.

CHAPTER 10

▶ Map and Compass

Early explorers to Canada knew how important it was to carefully take note of their surroundings in this new and uncharted land. They used their notes to prepare maps and guides for settlers who would follow.

Aboriginals used many techniques to give directions, and the explorers and pioneers quickly learned and applied these to their maps to mark portage points, locate good trapping areas, find easy transportation routes, and to indicate sources of food and water. Soon, early Canadians marked the locations of unusual landmarks, rock formations, animal paths, water routes (including waterfalls, rapids and forks), and the kind of terrain they traveled.

Today many jobs demand mapping and charting skills, including urban planning, northern development and transportation. These path-finding and map-making skills make practical and enjoyable Scouting activities. Knowing how to use a map to plan a hike, or how to find a location using a compass can acquire life or death importance, especially if you're exploring, hiking, or camping in remote territory. Orienteering challenges young people seeking adventure and fun with friends. It also provides a perfect opportunity to see our great country.

Maps

A topographic map shows details of a portion of the earth's surface drawn to scale on paper. The features shown fall into four main divisions:

▲ *Water:* including the sea, lakes, rivers, streams, ponds, marshes, swamps, glaciers and snowfields.

▲ *Relief:* including mountains, hills, valleys, cliffs, slopes and depths.

▲ *Culture:* including cities, towns, villages, buildings, railways, highways and land boundaries.

▲ *Vegetation:* including wooded areas, orchards, vineyards and cleared areas.

Map makers use colour to tell the difference between land and water, and forest and cleared land. Contour lines tell the height of various areas above sea level. Blue horizontal grid lines are called "northings"; vertical ones are called "eastings." Both help pinpoint locations.

A map must be drawn to a uniform scale if it's going to truly represent the surface of the ground. Distances must all appear on the map in the same proportion, and the map user must know what that proportion is. Beginners need to understand scale well. If they don't, they could form wrong ideas about what the terrain actually looks like. They could judge size and distances on the map incorrectly and get into serious trouble.

Canadian maps, like those of other countries, show scale as the proportion of map distance to true distance. On maps with a scale of 1:250,000, one centimetre on the map represents 250,000 centimetres on the ground.

If all maps were drawn to the same scale, it would be easy to compare actual areas and distances on the ground. But maps have many different uses and so there are many different scales. Canadian topographic maps come in four scales:

   1:25,000   (or 40 mm to the kilometre)
   1:50,000   (or 20 mm to the kilometre)
   1:125,000   (or 8 mm to the kilometre)
   1:250,000   (or 4 mm to the kilometre).

All Canadian topographic maps include a graduated scale on each sheet. This scale usually shows the distance in both kilometres and miles.

Many modern maps also give distance in metres and yards. The scale at the bottom of a topographic map demonstrates several ways to measure distances.

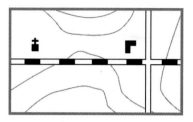

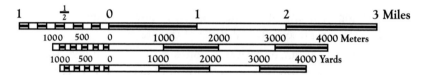

SCALE 1:50,000
1.25 Inches to 1 Mile approximately

Direction

You'll usually find north at the top of the map, south at the bottom, east to the right, and west to the left. These are the "true" or "astronomic" north, south, east and west. They are different from magnetic directions. A set of arrows on the map's border will show the difference in degrees between true directions and magnetic directions. This difference is called "magnetic declination." (See page 224 for more on magnetic declination.)

Contours

A topographic map does not show landscape in the same way a photograph or a painting does. With practice, a map reader will be able to pick out small features, like streams or bridges, and learn to recognize symbols for many others which identify specific terrain (see page 221 for more on map symbols.)

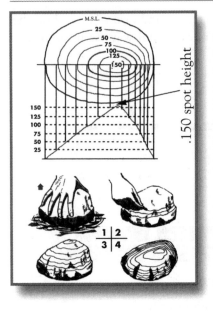

Hills and valleys are shown on the flat surface of a map by *brown* contour lines these connect points of equal height throughout the area presented on the map. Lines are numbered to show the height of the ground in metres (or feet) above sea level. For example, a map reader following the course of a contour line would go neither uphill nor downhill but would stay on the same level.

The drawing illustrates an imaginary hill which rises from sea level to 150 m this is how it would appear on a map and how it would appear in cross section. Where lines are far apart, the ground slopes gently. Where they lie close together, the hill is steep. When lines are crowded, they show a cliff.

At the top of a large hill, the map may show a number, called a "spot location," which represents the altitude of the crest.

The vertical distance between contour lines is called the "vertical interval" or "contour interval." The horizontal distance between contours is called the "horizontal equivalent."

Map Symbols

All maps have a reference that displays symbols and abbreviations. They may all appear in a margin of the map, or some may appear in the margin with the remainder on the back. These symbols tell details of the terrain and various features of the area.

The colours used are symbolic too. Everything in *black* indicates manufactured structures (roads, towns, bridges, boundaries and dams). Water, such as rivers, lakes and swamps, appears as *blue*. Valleys, hills and mountains are in *brown*. On some maps, woodland areas are shown in *green*, and main highways in *red*.

Map Symbols

⚒	Open pit, mine
~	Index contour
⌒	Fill
═══	Cut
┼──┼──┼	Power line
•······•······•	Telephone line
┼═┼═┼	Railroad
▄▄▄	Hard surface road
═══	Improved road
∷∷∷∷	Unimproved road
------	Trail
═╪═╪═	Bridge
---┤├---	Footbridge
⌒⌒	Perennial streams
o o⌐	Water well-Spring
⬭	Lake
≋	Marsh (swamp)
▪▪▐	Buildings (dwellings)
▪▪⊞	School-church-cemetery
▫☐▮	Buildings (barns, etc.)
Brown	Sand area
Green	Woods
⸴. ˜‿	Orchard
≋≋≋	Scrub

Ordering Maps

The best topographic maps for hiking have a scale of 1:50,000. These are available for your area. Of course you'll have to know the specific section of the country for which you want the map. These maps are available at many camping and "outdoor" stores.

Orienting or Setting a Map

A map is "oriented" when it is placed to correspond in direction with the ground it represents. Map readers can tell in which direction they're facing by any of the following methods.

1. *By the compass.* (See page 227 to find out how to orient a map using a compass.)

2. *By objects.* If you know your position on the map and can identify the position of some distant object, turn your map so the lines on the map between your position and the object point to the distant object.

3. *By a watch and the sun.* In the northern hemisphere, if Daylight Saving Time is in effect, first set your watch back to Standard Time. Place the watch on something flat with the hour hand pointing toward the

sun. True south is midway between the hour hand and the figure 12. True north is directly opposite. (This is a very rough way to check directions.)

4. *By the North Star.* In latitudes below 60 degrees N, the bearing of the North Star (also called Polaris) is never more than 2° degrees from true north.

Map Date

All maps show the date when they were prepared and printed. No map is ever truly up-to-date, for cities grow larger, new buildings are built, roads are widened, and new dams are created. Check your maps to make sure that they are the most current ones available.

Charts

Just as there are topographical maps for use on land, there are navigational charts for use on water. "Charting" is an interesting and complicated field, beyond the scope of this publication.

To read a chart, begin by finding the line which points north, as in topographical maps. This line is part of a circular pattern, called a "compass rose." The compass rose not only shows true north but also magnetic north.

The Compass

The first compass was probably a rock or stone containing magnetized ore which, when suspended on a thong or vine, would always point in the same direction. Although no one knows who first discovered the compass, the Chinese seem to have understood its secrets years before Europeans learned to steer without using the sun and the North Star. According to some historians, Marco Polo brought back the knowledge of the compass to Europe from Cathay in 1260.

Compass Bearings

The direction measured by a compass from one point to another is called a "bearing." Bearings can be expressed either in "compass points" or in degrees.

The principal compass points are easy to find. Compass needles point north. When you're facing north, south is directly behind you, west is on your left, and east on your right. Intermediate points have logical names. For example, northeast is half-way between north and east, north-northeast is half-way between north and northeast, and east-northeast is halfway between northeast and east. It's convenient to use compass points when you're referring to approximate directions. For example, you might say, "Vancouver is southwest of Edmonton."

For really accurate compass work, measure bearings in degrees. Compasses are divided into 360 units called "degrees," which are measured clockwise around the circle from north (which is 0 degrees), through east (90 degrees), and so on until you get back to north, which can also be called 360 degrees. (It's correct to say north is both 0 degrees and 360 degrees; it's the same bearing.)

How a Compass Works

Many types of compasses exist. The orienteering-type compass used for illustrating many of the sections in this book is good for both hiking and orienteering. In orienteering compasses, the needle housing rotates on a base plate. A base plate helps you read the compass and serves as a direction pointer in the field. The edge of the base plate has measuring scales. These prove useful both when you read the compass and when you make maps.

The magnetized needle — balanced on a pinpoint and free to swing around — is the most important part of any compass. When the needle is undisturbed, Earth's magnetism makes it point towards magnetic north. The end is either painted (black or red), stamped with the initial N, or shaped like an arrowhead.

Parts of a Compass

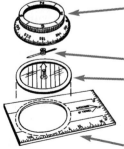

Top of compass housing with cardinal points on upper rim, degrees on outer rim in two degree portions.

Magnetic needle with red north end.

Bottom of compass housing (transparent in some models) with orienting arrow and meridian lines.

Base plate with direction of travel arrow and metric and inch scales.

True Bearings and Magnetic Bearings

A compass needle doesn't point to true north. Instead, being magnetic, it orients itself to the Earth's magnetic field; this converges on the north magnetic pole, located off the northern tip of Bathurst Island in the Canadian Arctic (1300 km south of the north geographic pole).

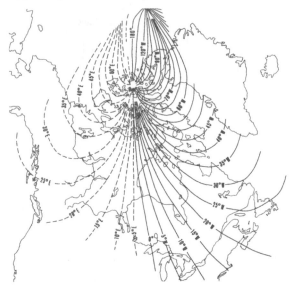

If you're close to a line which runs near Thunder Bay and Churchill, you're in luck! Why? Your compass will show true north and magnetic north in almost the identical direction. If you're east of that line, your compass will point west of true north, while, if you're west of the line, it will point east of true north. The number of degrees west or east of true north that the compass points to is called "declination."

The chart shows how declination varies across Canada. Figure out the approximate declination where you live by estimating which of the lines (called "isogonics") passes closest to your home. The number and direction on that line represents your declination. Thus, the declination for Newfoundland is about 25 degrees west. This means that in Newfoundland, the compass needle points approximately 25 degrees west of true north. For a more accurate measure of declination, look at a recent topographic map of your area. The declination will be shown by a set of arrows on the border of the map. (When you look at the arrows, you'll see that there is also an arrow pointing to "grid north." The difference between grid north and true north is too small for you to be concerned about.)

When you're working with a map and compass, you must convert the true bearing between two points (as measured on the map) to the magnetic bearing (as shown on the compass), and vice versa. To understand how to convert between true and magnetic bearings, remember that bearings are measured in degrees *clockwise from north.*

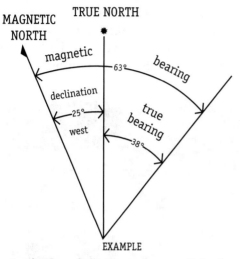

EXAMPLE

true bearing + declination west = magnetic bearing

38°   -   25°   =   63°

When the declination is west, the compass needle points to the west of true north. (So there are more degrees between magnetic north and the bearing line than there are between true north and the bearing line.) Therefore, when the declination is west, the magnetic bearing is always greater, by the amount of the declination, than the true bearing (i.e. magnetic bearing equals true bearing plus declination).

When the declination is east, the opposite is true, and the magnetic bearing is always less, by the amount of the declination, than the true bearing (i.e. magnetic bearing equals true bearing minus declination).

Here's a simple rhyme which will help you remember the difference between true and magnetic bearings:

> *Declination west, magnetic best (greater)*
>
> *Declination east, magnetic least.*

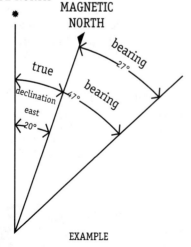

EXAMPLE

true bearing - declination east = magnetic bearing

47°   -   20°   =   27°

Finding a Bearing

Face the direction for which you want to know the bearing. Hold the compass level in front of you with the direction arrow of the base plate pointing in the direction of your bearing. Twist the compass housing until the north part of the needle lies over the north marker on the bottom of the housing. Then read the degree number on the edge of the housing where it touches the direction arrow line. This is your bearing, but it's a magnetic bearing.

To find your bearing from true north, adjust your reading as described in "true bearings and magnetic bearings." For example, imagine a compass bearing in Ottawa is 45 degrees. Since magnetic north is 14 degrees *west* of true north in Ottawa, the true bearing is 31 degrees (45 degrees *minus* 14 degrees).

If you already know the magnetic bearing (direction) you want to follow, set the compass to that direction (in degrees) by turning the compass housing until that degree number is opposite the direction of travel line. Hold the compass level in front of you and slowly turn your body until the north part of the needle lies over the arrow on the bottom of the compass housing. Now raise your eyes in the direction where the arrow is pointing, find a landmark and walk straight to it. When you reach this landmark, check your direction with the compass. Now, pick another landmark and go to it.

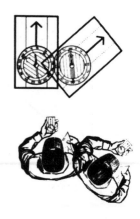

Using a Map and Compass

Follow these three simple steps when using an orienteering compass and map together.

Step One

Place the edge of the base plate of your compass on a route from starting point A to destination X. The direction of travel arrow must point in the direction you want to go.

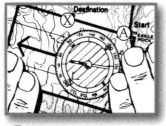
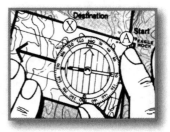

Step Two

Holding the base plate firmly on the map and ignoring the needle, turn the compass housing until the north arrow on the bottom of it is parallel with the map's north-south lines, with north to the top. Find the degree number at the base of the direction arrow; this is your true bearing.

To convert to a magnetic bearing, either add westerly declination to this number or subtract easterly declination depending on your locality. Then, reset your compass housing to the new number. Your compass is now set on your magnetic bearing.

Step Three

Hold the compass level in front of you with the direction arrow straight ahead. Turn your whole body until the north part of the compass needle covers the north arrow on the bottom of the housing. The direction arrow now points to your destination. Follow it. (Remember, every standard topographic map of Canada has an inset in the margin which states the magnetic declination for that map area.)

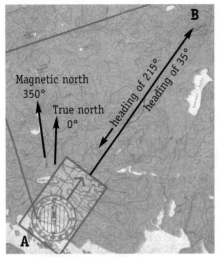

Magnetic north
350°

True north
0°

heading of 215°

heading of 35°

A

B

Plotting a Course

If you're given a true bearing to follow (e.g. 35 degrees), here's how to plot a course on a map. Place your compass on the starting point (A) and orient it to the map's grid lines. A bearing of 35 degrees, including a detour around a steep hill, takes you to your destination (B). A bearing of 215 degrees (35 degrees plus 180 degrees) brings you back to base.

Locating your Position on a Map

If you want to plot your location onto a map, use the following steps:

Step One

Look at the outdoor scene spread out in front of you. Pick out a tower, house, small lake, or other object that you can find on your map. Hold the compass horizontally so the direction arrow on the transparent plate points directly towards the object in the field.

Step Two

While holding the compass base plate, turn the housing until the north (red) end of the needle points to the letter "N" and is parallel to the engraved arrow inside the compass housing.

Step Three

Adjust for magnetic declination (usually found on the map margin). You are working from magnetic to true bearing, therefore, subtract for westerly declination and add for easterly.

Step Four

Place your compass on the map so that either long edge of the transparent plate intersects the object mentioned in Step One. Using this object on the map as a pivot, rotate the entire compass until the engraved arrow inside the compass housing points to north on the map. Do you want real accuracy? Then, compare the vertical grid lines on the compass housing to be sure they're perfectly parallel to the meridian lines on the map (also called eastings). Any true north-south line may be used as a meridian line.

Step Five

Draw a line on the map along the edge of the transparent plate which intersects the sighted object. Your position on the map is somewhere along this line.

Step Six

To determine your exact position on this line, pick out a second object in a different direction from that picked in Step One. Proceed through steps one, two, three, four and five. You will now have two intersecting lines. You are at the point of intersection.

Orienteering

What is orienteering?

It's the sport of finding your way through rugged country using a map and compass. Orienteering is a fundamental Scouting skill because it stresses outdoor activities like hikes, rambles and camps away from built-up areas.

Begin orienteering on a small scale with a couple of short cross-country hikes through easy territory. Your group might also want to try orienteering within city limits, providing a detailed map is available. As your orienteering skills increase, you will be more comfortable planning longer and more ambitious trips through tougher terrain.

Orienteering Techniques

You can't always walk in a straight line when you're orienteering. Bodies of water, cliffs, and heavy deadfalls sometimes get in the way. "Aiming off" is one way for getting around these obstacles. Instead of taking a bearing exactly on the point you wish to reach, you aim off; that is, you take a bearing on a point to the right or to the left of where you actually want to go.

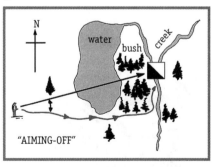

"AIMING-OFF"

In the diagram, the orienteer has aimed off to the right of the point wanted. He has decided to head for the creek where he will make a left turn to head straight for the original object.

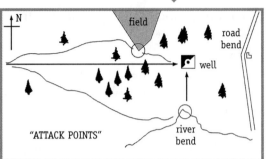

Sometimes the point you want to reach is clearly marked on your map, but it is difficult to see on the ground. This is when to use "attack points." These attack points are usually large, easily seen landmarks, either off to one side or slightly behind the point you want. In the diagram, either the corner of the field or the bend in the river could serve as an attack point to reach the well.

Finding your Direction

If something happens to your compass, you can still find your direction. The sun rises in the east and sets in the west. The actual compass point at which it rises varies a bit in the summer and winter. However, at six o'clock in the morning, the sun is due east; at twelve noon it is due south, and at six in the evening, it is due west. At nine in the morning, it is southeast and at three in the afternoon, southwest.

The moon rises in the east and sets in the west. Except for these points, using the moon to find direction is a bit tricky.

Here are two methods to find direction.

Watch Method

1. Lay a watch on the ground.

2. Place a match or a short piece of straw upright against the edge of the watch (stick the match into the ground if you can).

3. Turn the watch until the shadow of the match or straw falls exactly along the hour hand (i.e. until the hour hand points directly to the sun).

4. Divide the angle between the hour hand and the figure 12 in half.

5. Between 6 a.m. and 6 p.m. Standard

Time, a line from the centre of the watch through the half way mark between the hour hand and the figure 12 will point true south.

6. Scratch a line on the ground or stretch a string southward from the centre of the watch. This is your north-south line.

Here's how the watch method works. At twelve noon the sun is located in the south. It takes 24 hours for it to come back to this position, but in the meantime, the hour hand of your watch has gone around twice. If you have a 24-hour watch, all you would need to do is point the hour hand at the sun, and the figure 12 would point south. But since, there are only 12 parts on your watch, you use the halfway point between the hour hand and the 12.

Step five requires the use of Standard Time, but, if your watch is on Daylight Saving Time, you can still use the same method. Divide the angle between the hour hand and the figure one to find south.

Finding North Another Way

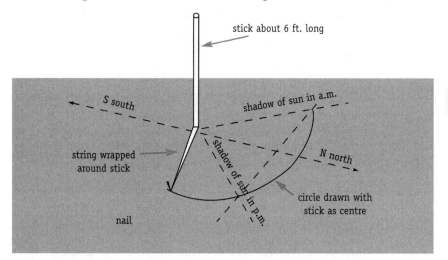

stick about 6 ft. long

S south

shadow of sun in a.m.

string wrapped around stick

shadow of sun in p.m.

N north

circle drawn with stick as centre

nail

If you do not have a compass or watch but the sun is bright, you can find true north in this way.

1. Push a short pole or a straight stick into the ground, making sure that it is vertical by holding a weighted string beside it.

2. Loop the string (lace, thong, vine etc) around the base of the pole.

3. Holding the string tightly, measure the length of the pole's present shadow.

4. Tie or hold a sharp stick or nail to the string at this precise point.

5. Draw a half circle, either starting at the tip of the present shadow or marking this point with a stake.

6. The shadow of the pole will shorten until it is noon by local standard time. Then it will start to lengthen again. Watch for the moment it once more meets the half-circle. Mark this point with the second stake.

7. A line connecting the pole with a point halfway between the first and second marks will run north and south. South will lie toward the sun.

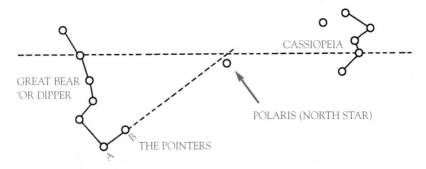

Where Is West?

There is an even quicker method of telling directions from shadows. All you need is sunlight or moonlight strong enough to cast its shadow.

1. Stick your pole into the ground as before.

2. Mark the top of the shadow, perhaps with a pebble or a twig.

3. Five or ten minutes later, mark the tip of the new shadow.

4. A line joining the second mark with the first will, in the Northern Hemisphere, generally point west.

This method is surprisingly accurate in the middle of the day when it is sunny. The line runs a bit south of west in the morning, and in the afternoon it runs somewhat north of west. If you use this method during a full day of travel, the inaccuracies will average themselves out.

Using the North Star

Before you can use the North Star to find directions, you have to be able to locate it in the night sky. The easiest way is to find the Big Dipper and its pointer stars and then find the North Star as shown on page 232.

If you can see the Big Dipper, but not the North Star itself, you can locate where it is approximately by following the line of the two pointers for a distance of five times the distance between the two pointers.

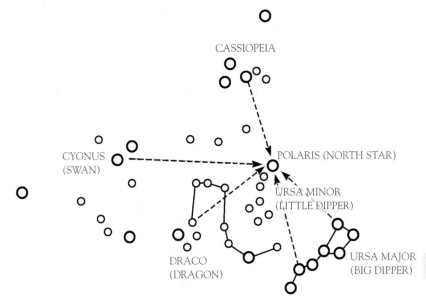

The North Star gives true north. If you're facing it, you are looking directly north. It is the one star in the sky which stays in one place. The others circle around it (once in 24 hours) in a counterclockwise direction if you're facing north. If you think of the sky as an umbrella turning around very slowly, then the North Star is the point where the umbrella's centre handle goes through.

Even if parts of the Big Dipper are hidden by clouds, trees or a mountain, you can still find the North Star in each of these three ways:

1. Through the stars furthest apart in the head of the dragon (Draco).

2. From the double star in the middle of the Big Dipper handle to the centre of Cassiopeia.

3. Through the pointer stars in the middle of the Northern Cross (part of Cygnus).

Bringing the North Star to the Ground

You might be able to see the North Star high up in the sky, but here's how to bring it down to the ground to navigate accurately using it.

1. Place a long stick in the ground.

2. With a shorter stick, sight across the top of the two sticks at the North Star exactly as if you were aiming a gun.

3. When the tops of the two sticks and the North Star are in a direct line, push the short stick into the ground.

4. A scratched line, a piece of string or another stick connecting the bottom of the short sighting stick and the long sighting stick, will point north.

5. Another line at right angles will point east and west.

Your Compass as a Watch

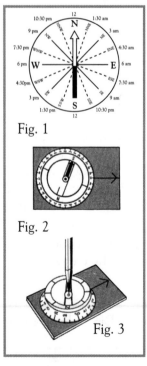

Fig. 1

Fig. 2

Fig. 3

You can tell what time it is (roughly) with your orienteering compass. The sun moves 15 degrees in one hour (360 degrees in 24 hours). Figure 1 shows you the bearing of the sun at any hour of the day. Here's how to use your orienteering compass as a watch.

Step One

Place your compass on a level surface in the sun.

Step Two

Turn the compass housing until its "S" is exactly above the north end of the magnetic needle. (See Figure 2)

Step Three

Place a pen, pencil, match stick or other thin, straight object upright over the middle of the compass (Figure 3). The shadow of the pen will indicate the bearing of the sun, and by using Figure 1, you will know what time it is.

Estimating Distance

Knowing how to estimate distances and sizes is a useful skill. You can make hikes or rambles more interesting with guessing games, and hand-made maps of your surroundings can become more accurate.

Here's a valuable tip. Objects often seem closer or farther away than they really are, depending on how clearly you see their outline. If snow or water is between you and the object (such as a tree or a house), or if you're looking up or down at it, your estimating may also be made less accurate. Following are some hints to remember when judging distances.

An object seems *farther away* when:

▲ It's in the shade.

▲ It's across a valley.

▲ It's the same colour as its background.

▲ There is a heat haze.

▲ You're lying down or kneeling.

An object seems *nearer* when:

▲ The sun is behind you.

▲ The air is very clear.

▲ It's a different colour from its background.

▲ The ground is flat or covered with snow.

▲ It's larger than the other objects close to it.

▲ You are looking across the water.

Visible points seem nearer by night than they do by day.

Learning to Judge Distance

There is a way to ensure your estimates are fairly accurate. First, learn the exact length of your pace (one walking step, measured from heel to heel or toe to toe). Try to learn to pace an exact three metres with five of your paces. If you always pace off distances this way, 1665 of your paces will equal one kilometre.

Start by estimating short distances and then pace them off to check your guess. For safety, use a quiet road, a field or a meadow for your practice. Remember that your eye measures distance "as the crow flies" or from eye to object. This method does not allow for irregularities of the ground, and so ground distance may be greater than visual distance.

Here's an extra hint to remember when estimating: at 700 metres, a person looks like a post. At 650 metres, the head is not yet visible, but, at 550 metres, the head appears as a dot. At 450 metres, the person looks bottle-shaped, while, at 350 metres, you can see leg movements. At 250 metres, you can see a face, and, at 200 metres, you can recognize details of clothing. At 100 metres, you can see the eyes and mouth clearly.

Personal Measurements

Not many people carry a tape measure with them in a camping kit, but your own personal measurements can act as a ruler. Take note of these measurements, and check them regularly. Why? Your human body is always changing. With a friend and a tape measure, mark the measurements suggested here.

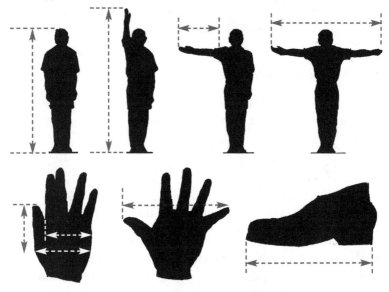

▲ Height

▲ The distance from your eyes to the ground.

▲ Your reach from the tops of your outstretched fingers.

▲ Your reach from armpit to outstretched fingers.

▲ Your reach across from outstretched fingertips.

- ▲ The span of your hand from thumb to little finger.
- ▲ The length of your foot.
- ▲ The length of your step.
- ▲ The width of your thumb.
- ▲ The width of the nail of your forefinger.
- ▲ The span of your thumb and forefinger.
- ▲ The span of your elbow to the wrist.
- ▲ The span of your elbow to your fingertips.

Once you have these measurements, find a measurement on your body that is exactly one centimetre. (It may be the width of one fingernail.) Then find exactly ten centimetres. Finally, find one metre. (It may be the distance from outstretched fingertip to your chin or opposite shoulder.)

Some Judging Methods

Here are some more ways for judging distances and heights fairly accurately. These make practical use of some basic geometry taught in school.

Pencil Method

Ask a friend (whose height you know) to stand against an object for which you want to find the height. Follow these steps:

1. Hold a pencil or short stick at arm's length, and sight across the top of it to the top of your friend's head. (See diagram)

2. Move your thumb down on the pencil until you sight across it to your friend's feet.

3. Raise your arm until your line of sight over your thumb touches the top of your friend's head.

4. Note where your line of vision across the top of the pencil cuts the object you're measuring.

5. Move your arm again, and repeat step four.

6. Keep repeating steps four and five, counting as you go up, until you reach the top of the object.

The number of sightings you took of your friend represents the number of times higher the object is than your friend. Multiply that number by your friend's height to find the height of the object.

Height by Shadow

Here's how to guess the height of a tree by its shadow.

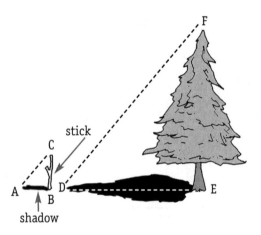

1. Get a stick of known length and notch it in metres and centimetres.

2. Stand the stick upright in the sun and measure the length of the shadow.

3. Measure the length of the shadow cast by the tree.

4. Multiply the stick length by the length of the tree's own shadow.

5. Divide by the length of the shadow cast by the stick. The result is the height of the tree.

Here's the formula:

> Tree (T) height =
> Stick length (SL) x tree shadow (TS) divided by
> Stick shadow (SS)

Or

$$T = \frac{SL \times TS}{SS}$$

For example, if the stick's length is two metres, the tree's shadow is 20 metres long, and the stick's shadow is five metres long, then:

$$\frac{2 \times 20}{5} = \frac{40}{5} = 8 \quad \text{The tree is 8 metres high.}$$

Line of Sight and a Measured Stick

Here's another method you can use to measure a building or tree.

1. Measure along the ground from the base of the building out far enough so you can sight the top of the building from ground level at a comfortable angle.

2. Mark this distance off in nine units of equal length (e.g. nine measured stick lengths).

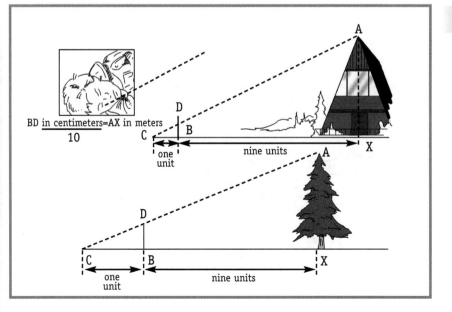

$$\frac{\text{BD in centimeters}=\text{AX in meters}}{10}$$

3. Nine stick lengths out from the building, stand your stick upright and ask a friend hold it.

4. Measure off one more unit past the stick.

5. Put your head to the ground. Getting your eye as close to the ground as possible, sight the top of the building.

6. Where your sighting line cuts the stick, have your friend make a mark.

7. Measure the number of centimetres from that mark to the ground. Divide by ten which will equal the height of the building in metres.

Estimating the Width of a River

Here's a useful method for groups wanting to erect a pioneering structure. (Golfers can also use it.)

1. Pick out a point across the river, such as a tree (A).

2. Drive a stake (B) into the ground on your side of the river in line with the tree.

3. Walking parallel to the river bank, make a base line of any convenient length, say 40 metres.

4. Drive a stake (C) into the ground.

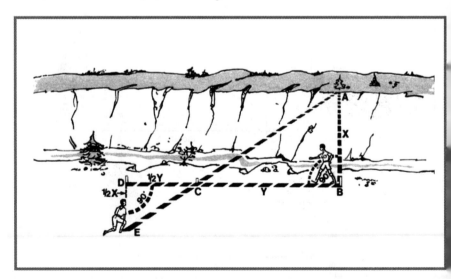

5. Continue along the bank in the same direction for half the first distance you measured (20 metres).

6. Mark the spot D.

7. Make a 90 degree turn (your back to the river) and walk inland until you can sight your first stake C in line with the tree across the river.

8. Mark the spot E.

9. Measure the distance between the stakes D and E.

10. Double this distance and you will have a fairly accurate estimate, as long as your sighting measurements and angles are correct.

Global Positioning System

Charting your progress on a map as you travel through woods or along a river can be difficult. It may leave you looking at your map in frustration, and wondering, "Just exactly where am I?"

Modern technology can take away the frustration. A small, reasonably lightweight, hand-held device, when programmed properly, will tell you your location. Called Global Positioning System (GPS) receivers, these devices collect radio signals transmitted by satellite. When the receiver makes contact with *at least three* of the 24 satellites circling the earth, it can triangulate your position to within several meters! If it makes contact with four satellites, it can even tell you your altitude! This information appears on a small screen on the face of the GPS unit for easy and accurate reading.

To find your position on a map, you must apply the information on the screen to your map by using longitude/latitude coordinates or Universal Transverse Mercator (UTM) information — included on many topographical maps. This means that the information provided on the maps must be compatible with the receiver.

You can program a GPS to provide direction to one specific destination (referred to as a waypoint) or a series of waypoints that you must pass through to reach your final destination. To find the location of these waypoints and any obstacles in your way, you'll still need a map. Plot your course on the map and enter the waypoints into the GPS using coordinates or grid points taken from the map.

You can even use a GPS unit without a map. Just head off into the woods and the device will track and record your route. When you're ready to return, it will give directions to retrace your steps back to your starting point.

A GPS unit will show you the direction to travel, the speed you are travelling, and your estimated time of arrival; it will tell you if you go off track, and which way to go to correct your error. (**Note:** These units require batteries to operate and are, therefore, not designed or suitable for continuous operation. Use them as a reference tool to check and confirm your location periodically or when you're unsure of your location.) A compass is still the best tool to use for walking a given bearing, although the bearing may be taken from your GPS unit.

The GPS unit comes into its element when on a large lake or when crossing a large open area where accurate reference points are not present. For example, a GPS unit can be very helpful if you have just paddled out onto a large lake and are trying to find a small outlet stream three kilometres away. With map and compass, you can take a bearing and do your best to stay on course. This is difficult even for experienced paddlers under calm conditions, but it becomes even more difficult as the distance increases or if a breeze is blowing. Once your GPS unit has the necessary information, it will continue to provide accurate direction and let you know if you stray off course. It will even tell you how to get back on course.

A compass provides you with direction to a position in relation to north (the direction a compass needle points). A GPS unit provides you with your current location and directions to another waypoint from your current location.

Each of these three tools (map, compass and GPS) are of limited use when you use them independently. However, when you use all three tools together, each one complements the other and provides excellent and accurate information for navigating.

▶ Water Safety

How can you be safe when you're in and around water? Many people will shrug and tell you "just use your head." And yet in Canada, hundreds of people drown every year. Is this common sense? Water safety may be simple, but besides using common sense, people must learn a few rules and understand the importance of practising them whenever they're in and around water.

Leader Note

Wear Your PFD! It's Scouting Policy

Youth and adults who take part in Scouting boating activities must wear Transport Canada approved, properly fitting PFDs or lifejackets at all times. This rule applies to all boating activities in small craft six metres or less (powered and non-powered). It also applies to canoes longer than six metres.

Scouts Canada's *By-law, Policies and Procedures* and Scouts Canada's *Camping/Outdoor Activity Guide* has very specific requirements that apply to all members who participate in water activities. Please read them.

It's easy to understand how non-swimmers can get into trouble, but records show that many supposedly good swimmers drown as well. Being able to swim is important, since a swimmer will have a better chance of saving himself in an emergency. But it takes more than being able to swim. Ignorance and stupidity in the water cause most deaths.

Everyone should know basic water safety and rescue procedures. Because accidents do happen, someday a life may depend upon you. You may be the only person there who knows what to do in a water emergency.

Know and practise these rules of water safety.

1. Learn to swim. Don't rely on floating aids (toys, life-belts, etc.) to keep you up.

2. Swim with a buddy — never alone.

3. Don't get into rough play in the water.

4. Don't fake trouble.

5. Read and obey warning notices.

6. Learn and respect the limits of your strength in the water.

Where to Swim

Whether your favourite swimming spot is a lake, river, pool, pond, or the seaside, make sure that it's safe. The ideal swimming area is one that's supervised by qualified lifeguards. But since you can't always have this, go to an area that you know is safe, but don't go alone.

A Safe Swimming Area

Depth

The bottom should be solid and gradually sloping to a depth of 3 m or less. Deeper water is dangerous because if you do get into trouble, few rescuers will be able to dive deep enough to reach you on the bottom. Swim parallel to the shore. If you're going to try a distance swim, have two people travel beside you in a boat.

Weeds

It's safer and more pleasant to swim in an area that is free of weeds. But if you ever get tangled up in weeds, don't panic and don't struggle. Use easy movements to get your body on top of the water and move yourself slowly out of the weeds.

Currents

Currents are usually found in rivers, and you should stay away from them. Throw a small stick into the water; it will show you the direction and approximate strength of any current. If you do find yourself swimming where there is a current, don't swim against it. You'll only exhaust yourself. Swim with the current and, at the same time, diagonally towards shore.

Undertows

Undertows are found in large lakes, rivers and oceans, and may be dangerous. An undertow is a deep current traveling outwards underneath the surface of the water. It can drag a swimmer downwards and away from shore. Again, don't struggle against an undertow. Let it carry you out a little as you swim diagonally towards the surface.

Tides

Don't swim in tide-bound or secluded coves or inlets. You can become trapped, and there may be no one to help you.

Surf

In the sea, the swelling surf will move you away from the shore. Swim towards the shore in the troughs (or valleys) of the waves until they begin breaking, then ride in on top of a wave. On a beach, dig your hands into the sand to brace yourself against the undertow.

Hidden Dangers

Before swimming anywhere, check the bottom for dangers such as holes, rusty cans, tree stumps or sharp rocks. To do this, wear shoes and wade in slowly, exploring the bottom carefully. Never jump or dive. Many serious accidents have happened to swimmers who didn't bother to look before they leaped.

When to Swim

Time

The warmest and most pleasant hours for swimming are late morning and early afternoon.

Weather

Never swim during thunderstorms or in bad weather.

Sun

Cooling off in the water after being in the sun is very refreshing. But tak
it easy and don't start off too vigorously. Your body has to adjust to the ne
temperature of the water. Swim just a few strokes at first, then you ca
gradually increase.

After Dark

Swimming after dark is dangerous because people can't see you if you ge
into trouble. If you were to go under, no rescuer could possibly find you
Motor boats are another great danger to you at night, because their drive
can't see swimmers in the darkness.

After Meals

You can swim, within reason, after a light snack. After a heav
meal, any strenuous activity can be exhausting and cause nausea, fatigue an
muscle cramps. This can be dangerous if you're swimming, so wait at lea
one hour after eating a heavy meal.

After Vigorous Activity

Often a swim is most pleasant after some vigorous activity such a
a game of tennis or a long hike. Just a word of caution: It's better to wait an
cool off. Don't dive straight into the cold water. Either wade in or cool o
slowly by first splashing water over yourself.

Supervised Areas

Pools

Each public swimming pool will have its own set of rules. Here are th
ones that apply to everyone. They're designed to prevent accidents.

1. Non-swimmers and poor swimmers must stay in shallow water.

2. Don't dive into shallow water.

3. At the deep end, dive from the end of the pool, not from the sides.

4. Don't play on the float lines.

5. Don't take part in rough fooling around.

6. Don't run on the deck.

7. Use the diving board one at a time.

8. Respect and obey the lifeguard.

Waterfronts

Each beach area will have its own set of rules, but here are some general ones to follow.

1. Swim within area boundaries.
2. Swim only when the safe swimming flag is up.
3. Don't play on the float lines.
4. Dive only where marked.
5. Don't take part in rough fooling around.
6. Respect and obey the lifeguard.

The Lifeguard

The lifeguard is there to explain and enforce water safety rules. He or she is trained to help anyone who gets into trouble, but a lifeguard's main job is to prevent accidents. Don't talk to the lifeguard unless you have to; it may take his mind and his eyes off his work.

Swimming Strokes

The standard swimming strokes are:

1. The front crawl
2. The back crawl
3. The elementary backstroke
4. The breaststroke
5. The sidestroke and trudgen (scissor-kick).

Before trying to learn any of these you should be able to swim 6 m on your front and back, using a basic swimming style.

Learning to Swim

The best thing you can do to stay safe in and around the water is to learn to swim. Learning to swim is fun for everyone!

Swimming can open up a whole new world of enjoyment and recreational activity. The Canadian Red Cross Society offers water safety and learn-to-swim classes through municipalities, camps, fitness facilities, and private organizations.

Knowing how to swim is important even if you don't intend to swim regularly. It may even save your life at some time when you hadn't planned to swim. Many drownings in Canada occur each year when the person never intended to be in the water.

The Buddy System

A buddy system should be used to be sure participants in an aquatic activity, particularly children, can be accounted for at all times. You can use this system whenever you are supervising a group in the water. Every person is paired with another person of about equal ability, and they are asked to stay near each other and watch out for each other. Periodically you call for a "Buddy check," and each pair holds their hands up together. Count the number of pairs to be sure everyone is accounted for.

Camps, municipal pools, and other programs often use an organized buddy system for the same purpose. Participants check in at the "buddy

board" before entering the water and check out when they leave the water, allowing supervisors and lifeguards to know who is in the water and to have an accurate count to compare with the count during a buddy check.

Prepare Before You Head to the Water

Preparation includes being personally prepared, checking your equipment, and checking the environment.

Personal Preparedness

Being personally prepared involves having the correct knowledge, skills, and attitude. Follow these guidelines:

▲ Through the Red Cross or other agencies, learn about swimming, boating, and first aid; and be sure that others in your group are well informed.

- ▲ Know the rules of the recreational site.

- ▲ Teach your children about water safety. Even very young children can learn basic safety rules.

- ▲ Plan water activity with your children ahead of time to ensure that you will not be distracted or interrupted while you supervise them.

- ▲ Know your swimming limits, based on your own level of capability.

- ▲ Learn the safe and proper way to dive, and know when and where it is safe to do so.

- ▲ Have an emergency plan in case of a water emergency, regardless of how well you swim.

Check Your Equipment

- ▲ Keep boating equipment in repair and ready for use.

- ▲ Ensure that your pool has access to a telephone. The gate into the pool area should be self-latching and self-closing, and at least 1.2 metres high.

- ▲ Have a first aid kit at the site and know how to give first aid.

- ▲ Apply sun protection, and dress appropriately for the weather conditions.

- ▲ Have the appropriate safety equipment readily available and in working order, and know how to properly use it.

- ▲ Wear your flotation device.

Check the Environment

- ▲ Swim in supervised areas.

- ▲ Avoid swimming in open water with strong currents, heavy boat traffic, or excessive debris in the water.

- ▲ Always check the depth before entering the water.

- ▲ Check for inclement weather.

▲ Know the local water hazards. In some urban or industrial settings, for example, swimming is not recommended if the daily pollution count is high. Check with local authorities.

▲ In winter, telephone your local community authority for ice safety reports.

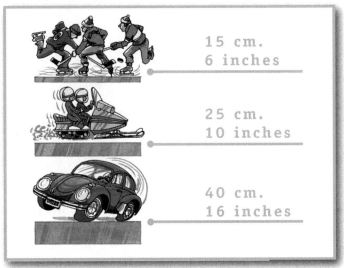

15 cm.
6 inches

25 cm.
10 inches

40 cm.
16 inches

Personal Safety

▲ If you feel cold and are shivering, stop and warm up. Have something hot to drink.

▲ Swim with a buddy.

▲ Refrain from the use of alcohol and other drugs when you are swimming.

▲ Always enter feet first if you do not know the water depth.

▲ Stay within your swimming capabilities.

▲ Watch out for the "dangerous too's": too tired, too cold, too far from safety, too much sun, too much rough play.

▲ Do not chew gum or eat while you swim; you could easily choke.

▲ Give children your undivided attention.

Be Sun Smart

Summer is a great time to be outdoors, but the sun's rays can be harmful to skin. When you or your child is swimming or playing outdoors, you should take precautions against the damaging effects of the sun's rays. Exposed skin during winter activities is equally as susceptible.

It doesn't matter how old you are or what colour your skin is. You are still susceptible to skin damage from the sun.

Why should you be concerned? When skin is exposed to the sun, it can be damaged by two different ultraviolet rays in sunlight:

▲ Ultraviolet B (UVB) rays affect the outer layer of skin, causing sunburn.

▲ Ultraviolet A (UVA) rays go deeper into the skin, possibly causing damage that may result in the development of cancer at a later time.

UVA and UVB rays are both known to damage the skin and cause cancer. The most dangerous part of the day is from 11 a.m. to 4 p.m.

What Can You Do?

Reduce your exposure to the sun. To be protected from the sun's rays, be sure that you and your family:

▲ Wear a hat with a wide brim or peak.

- ▲ Wear sunglasses. Sunglasses are sunscreen for your eyes and provide important protection from UV rays. Ophthalmologists recommend sunglasses that have a UV absorption of at least 90%.

- ▲ Wear light clothing to cover as much skin as possible.

- ▲ Use sunscreen with a minimum sun protection factor (SPF) of 15, and reapply it frequently (every 3 to 4 hours). Sunscreen should be applied 15 to 30 minutes before exposure to the sun.

- ▲ Use sunscreen also on cloudy and hazy days. Clouds do not block UV rays.

- ▲ Remain in shaded areas, especially if you don't have sunscreen.

- ▲ Take extra care around the water. Water reflects the sun's rays and can cause sunburn.

- ▲ Keep infants under one year old out of the sun altogether.

- ▲ Drink lots of water or juice to prevent dehydration.

How Do You Choose a Sunscreen?

When choosing a sunscreen, read the label carefully and look for:

- ▲ SPF of 15 or higher, as recommended by the Canadian Dermatology Association and the Canadian Cancer Society.

- ▲ The word "waterproof" or "water resistant."

- ▲ Protection against both UVA and UVB.

- ▲ The Canadian Dermatology Association seal of approval.

Note: If a rash appears after using the sunscreen, contact your physician.

PFDs and Lifejackets

Statistics on water-related fatalities in Canada show that most drowning casualties never intended to be in the water. Many were either enjoying boating activities or playing near the water. Because they did not intend to enter the water, they were not wearing the most important piece of safety equipment: a lifejacket or personal flotation device (PFD).

The Department of Transportation (DOT) requires that there must be one approved PFD or approved lifejacket for each person in a craft (under 5.5 metres). Flotation devices should be WORN by everyone in the boat.

What's the Difference Between a Personal Flotation Device (PFD) and a Lifejacket?

Lifejacket

A lifejacket will hold the wearer in an upright position and will keep the face of an unconscious victim above the water.

Personal Flotation Device

A PFD is less bulky and less buoyant than a lifejacket. A PFD will not necessarily roll a person into a position where the head is out of the water. PFDs are preferred for active sports such as canoeing or fishing because they allow for greater movement.

Self-Rescue

Because of the risk of falling into the water, non-swimmers should wear a lifejacket or PFD whenever they are near water. This flotation device makes self-rescue or rescue by another more likely and easier.

Self-rescue can mean reaching safety by yourself or staying afloat long enough for someone to help you. In both cases, be prepared by knowing how to survive a sudden, unexpected entry or problem in the water.

The method you use for self-rescue depends on factors such as the water temperature and the presence of currents. The following sections describe self-rescue techniques for deep water and cold water.

Self-Rescue in Deep Water

In deep water, try to move to safety if you can. If you cannot, call out or signal for help. Stay on the surface by swimming, using surface support skills, or floating. Follow these guidelines to decide what to do:

▲ Consider swimming for safety if no one responds to your call for help within a few minutes. You can swim for safety if you are in known water and the distance you need to swim is appropriate for your swimming skills, your energy level, and the conditions at the time. Remember, distances over the water often appear shorter than they actually are.

▲ Treading water to stay at the surface requires less energy than swimming, but more than floating. Treading water may result in less heat loss than motionless floating on the back.

▲ Motionless floating is useful for conserving energy while waiting for help or while resting. This is an effective survival skill in calm, warm water (20°C to 24°C).

Motionless floating is not recommended for self-rescue in cold water (10°C or lower) because much heat is lost through the head when it is fully or partially submerged. This results in a lowering of the body's core temperature.

Swimming Self-Rescue

Following are some tips for a swimming self-rescue:

▲ Check whether there is a current, wind, or tide you can use to your advantage in planning your swimming route. An onshore current or wind may aid your progress toward shore.

▲ Use any buoyant object to help you stay afloat while you swim.

▲ Although a PFD or lifejacket may make swimming a little more difficult, do not remove it.

▲ Unless you are in warm water, swim with your head up because of the heat loss that will occur when the head is submerged in cold water.

▲ Do not swim too fast. Pace yourself and keep your breathing relaxed and controlled.

Self-Rescue After a Boat Incident

If you are in a boat that swamps or capsizes, think carefully before you choose to swim to safety. In general, it is safer to stay with the boat and wait to be rescued.

Self-Rescue in Cold Water

Cold water is more dangerous than warm, but you can use different survival skills to reach safety or stay at the surface until rescued. First, you need to know the effects on the body of sudden immersion in cold water. Several reflex "shock" responses occur because of the immediate drop in skin temperature.

▲ The gasp reflex causes a sudden breathing in followed by involuntary hyperventilation. This may cause water to be breathed into the airway.

▲ The ability to hold the breath is greatly reduced.

▲ Heart rate and blood pressure both increase.

Continued exposure to the cold causes a rapid decline in strength and in the ability to use the fingers, hands, and limbs. This makes it more difficult to hold onto rescue aids.

Because of the immediate effects of cold water, the priority is to get out of the water as fast as possible. If you can, use a quick burst of energy to get out, remove wet clothing immediately, and dry off and keep warm.

If you cannot get out immediately, take action to extend your survival time while waiting to be rescued. Follow these guidelines.

▲ If you expect to be in the water a long time, move slowly and deliberately to conserve heat. Because your strength and ability to move will diminish, any manoeuvre that requires strength should be done right away.

▲ Keep on any clothing that will help you conserve heat.

▲ If you are not wearing a PFD or lifejacket, tread water.

If you are wearing a PFD or lifejacket, use the HELP or Huddle position to reduce heat loss while waiting for rescue.

Cramps

Cramps are a threat in cold water self-rescues. Cramps occur when your muscles become cold or tired from swimming. The muscle contracts suddenly, usually in the arm, foot, or calf. Try to relax it by not moving, by changing position of the limb, or by massaging the area. To massage a cramp of the calf muscles, take a deep breath, roll face-down, extend your leg and flex your ankle, and massage the cramp.

Rescue of Others: Decision-Making

When you recognize a distressed swimmer or drowning casualty, you must first check for hazards in the area.

Hazards

In any rescue situation, there may be hazards in the environment that could endanger you or cause further danger to the casualty. Remove such hazards from the area when you can, or remove the casualty from the hazards:

▲ Water

▲ Poisonous gas, such as engine exhaust or chlorine gas

▲ Other poisons

▲ Live electrical wires

▲ Debris, broken glass

▲ Extreme cold or heat

▲ Animals

The Ladder Approach to Rescue

After considering hazards and before starting the rescue, you need to decide which rescue method to use. No one technique works in all instances, as you will see in the following sections.

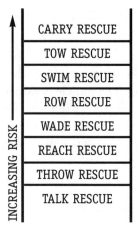

The general principle for decision-making is to use the least risky method that will work and for which you are equipped.

This principle can be easily understood in terms of the ladder approach . Start at the bottom rung of the ladder: use that method if it will work, or take a step up to the next rung and try that one. Consider every rung before moving to a higher, more risky rescue method, and always use the lowest rung possible.

These types of rescues are described in the following sections.

Talk Rescue

From a dry, safe location, give the person clear, simple instructions about what to do, along with verbal encouragement.

▲ From a crouched position, tell the casualty, "Watch me, keep your head up, kick your feet, and grab the side..."

- ▲ Eye contact and positive encouragement can have immediate results on a casualty at close range, without putting you in any danger.

Throw Rescue

If the casualty is a short distance away and a suitable buoyant object is available, throw the object so the casualty can grasp it for support.

- ▲ Be careful not to hit the casualty on the head when throwing the object.

- ▲ Encourage the casualty verbally, and direct him or her toward safety.

- ▲ Remember that wind and waves make it harder to throw accurately.

Reach Rescue

If you can find a suitable rescue aid, extend it and pull the casualty to safety. If the casualty is close enough, even a towel can work. A pole or branch can work with a casualty who is farther away.

- ▲ A buoyant object works best, because it can help support the casualty in the water so that you don't have to both lift and pull. A rope attached to the buoyant object can extend your reach even farther.

- ▲ Keep your centre of gravity as low as possible.

- ▲ Anchor yourself by holding onto a solid object such as a tree root, ladder, or dock with your free hand to prevent being pulled into the water.

Wade Rescue

When the casualty cannot be rescued from shore and if the water is shallow, wade into the water with a rescue aid and extend it to the casualty.

- ▲ Minimize the risk by keeping your feet on the solid bottom at all times or by grasping a solid object such as a dock or ladder with your free hand.

- ▲ With others to help you, form a human chain by taking hold of each other's wrists. The rescuer nearest the casualty extends the rescue aid and encourages the casualty. Another rescuer guides the chain back to shore.

Row Rescue

The row rescue is riskier because you do it in open water from a small boat.

▲ Try to manoeuvre the boat so that you approach the casualty from downwind to lower the chances of pushing the boat into the casualty and causing injury.

▲ Follow the ladder approach to first talk to the casualty, then throw him or her a lifejacket, PFD, or boat cushion. If necessary, reach a paddle or throwing line to the casualty.

▲ When the casualty has grasped the rescue aid firmly, decide whether to row to shore towing the casualty in the water or to help the casualty into the boat. The choice you make takes into account the casualty's condition and size, the boat's stability, your distance from shore, the water temperature, your skill, and the number of rescuers.

How a small boat is used in a rescue depends on the size and type of boat.

▲ Canoes can be very unstable and should be used only by experienced canoeists in a rescue. It is very difficult to get a casualty into the canoe.

▲ Inflatable boats have varying stability. Those with outboard motors are more easily manoeuvred and are easily used in a rescue.

▲ Kayaks, rowing sculls, and paddleboards have limited stability, but the casualty can hold on to them to be towed to safety. You can also use them as a buoyant rescue aid to support the casualty in the water.

▲ Powerboats that are not too large or difficult to manoeuvre work well for rescues. When near the casualty, cut the power to avoid injuring the person.

▲ Rowboats are easy to manoeuvre and are stable. The casualty can be helped into the boat over a square stern. Rescue breathing can be given over the stern to a casualty still in the water.

▲ Sailboards should be sailed to a casualty only by skilled board sailors. However, the sail can be taken off, and the board used as a paddleboard for a rescue.

▲ Sailboats require experience and skill to be used for a rescue. To approach the casualty, manoeuvre the boat from downwind and stop alongside the casualty. Depending on the size and shape of the sailboat, the casualty may be brought aboard or towed to shore in the water.

▲ Personal watercraft can be used in an emergency to transport a casualty to safety if the person can be brought aboard. Otherwise, the casualty can hold onto the watercraft until further help arrives.

Swim Rescue

You may have to enter the water during a rescue if the casualty's condition gets worse, if the casualty cannot be reached with a throwing assist, or if no craft is available for rescue.

▲ Enter the water with a buoyant rescue aid (such as a rescue tube or flutter board) and swim to the casualty.

▲ Minimize your personal risk by stopping before you reach the casualty and pushing the buoyant aid to the casualty from a safe distance away. Avoid even indirect contact with the casualty.

▲ Move back as the casualty grasps the aid, maintain eye contact, and encourage the casualty to kick or paddle to safety while holding onto the aid.

Tow Rescue

When you try the swim rescue, the casualty may not be able to propel himself or herself to safety while holding the buoyant rescue aid.

▲ Pull from the other end of the rescue aid to tow the casualty to safety.

▲ As this indirect contact brings you close to the casualty, ensure your own safety by being ready to move away quickly at any time.

Carry Rescue

If all else fails, you may have to use the carry rescue. This may occur if the casualty cannot support his or her head above the water while holding onto the rescue aid, if no rescue aid is available and the casualty is not responding to verbal encouragement, or if the casualty is unconscious.

▲ Calm the person before making contact. Throughout the rescue, keep reassuring the casualty.

▲ Never make contact with a violently struggling person. Try to calm the person or wait until he or she is subdued and just starting to submerge.

▲ Always maintain control of your own body and that of the casualty. If you think you're losing control, break away and start over.

▲ There are many types of water rescue carries. Some offer only minimal assistance, whereas others directly control the casualty. An assistive carry, such as an armpit carry, should be used when the casualty is conscious and can provide some help to the rescuer. A more controlling carry, such as a cross-chest carry, should be used with an unconscious casualty.

Rescue of Others: Rescue Skills

The ladder approach helps you to decide what kind of rescue to make. The rescue skills themselves — how to do the rescue — are described in this section. This process begins with using an assistive aid and entering the water, and includes removing the casualty and follow-up care and activities.

Assistive Rescue Aids

An assistive rescue aid is an object you use in the rescue, whether it is to extend or throw to the casualty. It allows the casualty to grasp onto something and be pulled to safety, and it may provide buoyant support as well.

Your choice of what assistive rescue aid to use depends on the situation and the available aids. Different techniques are used with the different assistive rescue aids.

Choosing an Assistive Rescue Aid

Consider the following factors when choosing an assistive rescue aid:

▲ Availability. The object must be readily available at the moment needed.

▲ Buoyancy. Floating objects support the casualty higher in the water and let you rest if needed during the rescue.

▲ Manageability. The assistive rescue aid must be easy to handle on land and in the water, and easy to transport to the casualty.

▲ Strength. The assistive rescue aid must be strong enough to accomplish the rescue.

▲ Your own fitness and strength. Be sure you can carry and use the assistive rescue aid effectively.

▲ The immediate surroundings. Make sure the aid can be manoeuvred in the available space.

Types of Assistive Rescue Aids

Assistive rescue aids include the following:

▲ Lifejackets and PFDs. Because of their buoyancy, these are effective aids that can be thrown or extended to the casualty.

▲ Throw bags. Throw bags are a white-water rescue aid. They consist of a bag with a length of rope that streams out of the bag while in flight. With practice, you can throw these bags a good distance accurately.

▲ Kickboards. Kickboards and flutter boards are available in many facilities and can be used as assistive aids.

▲ Improvised buoyant aids. Buoyant objects such as large plastic bottles, plastic coolers, gasoline cans, paddles, boards, and branches can all be used in rescues. Poles, oars, paddles, and sticks make good extensions because they are usually light and strong and can be extended easily to the casualty.

▲ Reaching poles. Reaching poles are used when the casualty is within reaching distance. Poles vary in length and material. Some are lightweight, and some are electrically insulated. Reaching poles with a hook on one end are called "shepherd's hooks."

▲ Ring buoys. Ring buoys are required at pools and beaches in many provinces and territories. They are also found at many docks and marinas. A length of rope (appropriate for the environment) allows them to be thrown to someone at a distance.

▲ Rescue cans and rescue tubes. Rescue cans (buoys) and tubes come with a length of rope and strap that slips over the shoulder. These can be used as reaching assists or as aids to tow or carry distressed swimmers or drowning casualties.

▲ Clothing as Towing Aids. Shirts and pants can be used as towing assistive rescue aids if you must enter the water to reach the casualty. Swim with the pants or shirt over your shoulders, with the legs or sleeves stretched forward over your shoulders and back under your arms. If the casualty is calm, pass the legs or sleeves under his or her arms and back over the shoulders, and hold both sleeves or pant legs in one hand as you swim back to safety.

Using Assistive Rescue Aids

Assistive rescue aids are extended or thrown to the casualty. Follow the guidelines described in the following paragraphs.

To extend an assistive rescue aid to the casualty:

▲ Keep your centre of gravity low to avoid being pulled into the water.

▲ If the casualty is just out of reach, lie down at a 45-degree angle on the side of the dock or pool with legs spread for stability. With one shoulder over the edge of the dock or pool deck, you have the longest reach.

- If a rigid reaching pole or other aid is not available, use any material at hand such as clothing, a towel, or a blanket to reach to the casualty. You may have to "flip" the flexible aid to the casualty.

- After extending the aid, crouch or drop to one knee, staying as far from the water's edge as you can.

- Be careful not to jab a struggling casualty with the aid.

- Pull the aid back in hand over hand, moving gradually to the edge to secure the casualty.

- Only if no assistive rescue aid at all is available, reach with an arm from the position lying down with legs spread. Keep a firm grip on the pool edge, dock, or boat.

To extend a reaching pole to the casualty:

- Make sure the casualty can grab the pole without being injured.

- Control the pole to avoid injuring anyone around you.

- Stay low when reaching to ensure your own stability.

- When the casualty has grasped the end of the pole, bring it back in hand over hand.

- Let the casualty contact the edge of the pool or dock before using your hand to secure him or her. Reach out to a casualty only if he or she has trouble grasping the edge of the pool or dock.

To use a throwing assist:

- Secure the trailing end of the rope by a method such as tying it to a dock or making a knot at one end and holding it under one foot.

- For greater accuracy in the throw, tie a lightly weighted buoyant object such as a semi-filled plastic container on the end of the line. This throwing assistive aid should be prepared and in place. Do not spend time locating equipment when there is an emergency.

- Consider currents and other factors that can affect your throw. Throw upstream so that the current will carry the assisted aid to the casualty.

▲ Throw past the casualty with a pendulum swing. For greatest distance, throw at an upward angle of 45 degrees.

▲ After throwing, drop to one knee or lie flat on your stomach for greater stability.

▲ When the casualty has grasped the aid, pull it back slowly hand over hand.

▲ Let the casualty contact the edge of the pool or dock before using your hand to secure him or her. Reach out to casualties only if they have trouble grabbing the edge of the pool or dock on their own.

Keep a throwing rope on your dock, boat, or other setting. Keep the rope permanently knotted at the end and uniformly coiled to save time in an emergency.

Waiting to Be Rescued

There are two floating rescue positions you can use in cold water in a PFD. Because both of these positions are hard to maintain, you may want to practise them in warm, shallow water. Practise only when supervised by someone with the water safety skills so that they can assist you.

Heat escape-lessening position

In the HELP position, draw your knees up to your chest, keep your face forward and out of the water, hold your upper arms at your sides, and fold your lower arms across your chest.

Huddle position

This position is for two or more persons. Put your arms over one another's shoulders so the sides of your chests are together. Sandwich a child between adults.

Special Situations

If your boat capsizes, do not assume the HELP position; instead, try to climb up onto the boat to get more of your body out of the water. If you cannot get onto the capsized boat, position yourself on the lee (downwind) side of the craft.

If you fall into cold water and a swift current is carrying you toward some danger, swim to safety. If you are not in immediate danger but are far from shore, float on your back and go downstream feet-first. Let your PFD support you as you flow with the current. Swim to shore when appropriate.

Falling into Cold Water Without a PFD

If you fall into cold water without a PFD, you must get out of the water as quickly as possible before hypothermia sets in.

Respiration

Vital to the life of every cell in the human body is the intake of fresh oxygen from the atmosphere and the removal of carbon dioxide. The exchange of air between the lungs and the atmosphere is referred to as respiration.

Respiration is a double phase operation: breathing in (inspiration) and breathing out (expiration). These automatic actions are controlled by the brain. *When a person stops breathing Every Second Counts.*

Artificial Respiration

When normal breathing has ceased, artificial respiration is used to replace it. Start immediately. Time is important. Do not waste time trying to discover the cause, or to summon help, or, unless a dangerous situation exists, to move the victim.

The rescuer must make sure:

▲ The victim's air passages are cleared and kept open.

▲ Artificial respiration is started immediately.

▲ Air is entering the lungs.

Rescue Breathing

Rescue breathing refers to the techniques of mouth-to-mouth and mouth-to-nose artificial respiration. Air is passed directly from the rescuer to the lungs of the victim.

Basic Life Support: The ABCs

Basic life support is the term for first aid to keep the casualty alive until ambulance attendants or paramedic professionals arrive and give more advanced care. Whenever you encounter an unconscious casualty, regardless of whether the person is found on dry land or was rescued from the water, you must first check the casualty's airway, breathing, and circulation and give basic life support care if needed. It is easy to remember these steps because they are called the ABCs:

A: Airway

B: Breathing

C: Circulation

These are described in detail in the following sections. Try to check the ABCs without moving the casualty. If you must move him or her, roll the casualty gently onto the back, keeping the head and spine in as straight a line as possible.

A: Check the Airway

Be sure the casualty has an open airway. The airway is the pathway from the mouth and nose to the lungs. Any person who can speak or cry is conscious and has an open airway.

If the person is unconscious, you must ensure that the airway is open. To do this, tilt the head back and lift the chin. This moves the tongue away from the back of the throat and lets air reach the lungs. However, do not use the head-tilt method for a casualty you suspect of having a spinal injury. Instead, to avoid injuring the spine further, use the technique called the modified jaw thrust. The steps for the modified jaw thrust are:

1. Grasp the casualty's lower jaw on both sides of the face where it forms an angle close to the ears.

2. Using both hands, move the lower jaw forward (upward) without tilting the head backward.

3. If rescue breathing is required, DO NOT move one hand to pinch the nostrils closed; instead, seal the nose with your cheek.

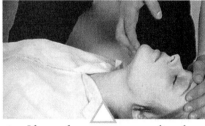

A. If you do not suspect a head or spine injury, tilt the head and lift the chin to open the airway.

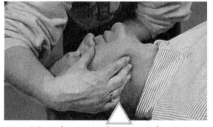

B. Use the jaw thrust technique for a casualty suspected of having a head or spine injury.

When the airway is open, check for breathing in the same manner as you do for a casualty not suspected of having a spinal injury. You can give rescue breathing while the casualty floats in the water with head and neck immobilized. However, if the casualty does not have a pulse, you must remove him or her promptly to the pool deck or beach and begin cardiopulmonary resuscitation (CPR).

When the person's airway is blocked by food or some object, you must remove the blockage first. **Note:** Personel performing CPR should have completed the recognized training certification course.

B: Check Breathing

Next, check for breathing. Someone who can speak or cry is breathing. Watch an unconscious person carefully for signs of breathing. The chest should rise and fall, but you must also listen and feel for breathing. Put your face close so you can hear and feel air coming out the nose and mouth while you watch the rise and fall of the chest. Take the time to look, listen, and feel for breathing for a full 3 to 5 seconds.

Rescue breathing is the technique of breathing for a non-breathing casualty.

If the casualty is not breathing, you must help the person to breathe by breathing air into the casualty's mouth. Follow these steps:

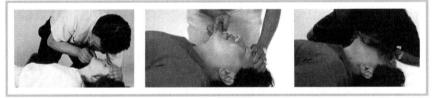

1. Gently tilt the casualty's head back with one hand and lift the chin with the other.

2. Gently pinch the casualty's nose shut with the thumb and index finger of your hand that is on the casualty's forehead.

3. Take a deep breath and make a tight seal around the casualty's mouth with your mouth.

4. Breathe slowly into the casualty until you see the casualty's chest rise. Each breath should last about 1 to 1 1/2 seconds. Pause between breaths to allow you to take a breath and to let the air

flow back out of the casualty's lungs. Watch the casualty's chest rise each time you breathe in to ensure that your breaths are actually going in.

5. If you do not see the casualty's chest rise and fall as you give breaths, you may not have the head tilted far enough back to open the airway. Retilt the casualty's head and try again to give breaths.

If your breaths still do not go in, the casualty's airway is obstructed, and you must clear it first.

Rescue breathing can be given to a casualty while still in shallow water, but is easier to do effectively if the casualty is out of the water.

Note: *Rescue breathing is used for a casualty who is not breathing but who has a pulse. You must check to see if the casualty has a pulse. If the casualty does not have a pulse, give CPR instead of rescue breathing alone.*

Rescue Breathing for Children and Infants

Rescue breathing for children and infants follows the same general procedure as that for adults. The differences are based on the child's or infant's different physique and faster heartbeat and breathing rate. The following is a summary of the differences:

▲ Use the head-tilt/chin-lift position to open the airway as for an adult, but move the head very gently. For an infant, use the neutral or "sniffing" position, and seal your mouth over both the infant's nose and mouth.

▲ For an adult, give full breaths in rescue breathing. For a child use smaller breaths, and for an infant use puffs of air. Breathe in only enough air to make the chest rise.

▲ Give rescue breathing to adults at the rate of 1 breath every 5 seconds (12 per minute); give rescue breathing to children at the rate of 1 breath every 3 seconds and to infants at the rate of 1 puff every 3 seconds (15 per minute).

▲ For both adults and children, check the pulse at the carotid artery in the neck. For infants, check the brachial pulse.

C: Circulation

The last step in a primary survey is to check the circulation. This step involves checking for a pulse and looking for severe bleeding and signs of shock.

If a person is breathing, the heart is beating and you do not need to check the pulse. If the person is not breathing, you must check the pulse. To check circulation, feel for the pulse in the carotid artery in the neck on the side closest to you. To find the pulse, find the Adam's apple and slide your fingers into the groove at the side of the neck. The pulse may be hard to find if it is slow or weak. If at first you do not find a pulse, start again at the Adam's apple and slide your fingers into place. When you think you are in the right spot, keep feeling for at least 5 to 10 seconds.

If the casualty does not have a pulse, you may need to perform cardio-pulmonary resuscitation if you are trained to do so.

This step in the ABCs also means looking for severe bleeding. Look for severe bleeding by looking at the casualty from head to toe. Severe bleeding must be controlled as soon as possible.

Sometimes an injured person may be bleeding inside the body. A casualty who is bleeding either externally or internally may go into shock. Shock is a serious condition when the body has lost a lot of blood. If the person is in shock, the skin may look pale and feel cool to your touch.

If you find that an unconscious casualty is breathing and has a pulse, do not leave the person lying on his or her back. Unless you suspect a neck or back injury, roll the casualty onto the side to keep the airway open. This is called the recovery position. In this position the casualty's tongue does not block the airway; vomitus, fluids and blood will also drain from the mouth and not block the airway.

National Safety Standard

Research shows that a person in distress in water uses up to 10 times the amount of energy he or she would normally use to swim a distance to safety. Most drownings also occur within 50 metres of the shore, dock, boat, or other safe area. Therefore you should learn to swim at least 500 metres in any stroke that is comfortable and effective for you. To be safe around the water, all Canadians should achieve this standard.

▶ Canoeing

Canoes continue to provide a safe, enjoyable way for modern day "voyageurs" to explore the wilderness. In fact, many canoe routes used today in Canada were discovered and travelled by First Nation peoples hundreds of years ago and later by the voyageurs.

The materials and designs have changed significantly since the early birch bark canoes, but the skills used to maneuver them, although somewhat refined, are very similar.

Canoes provide an excellent means to introduce youth to the outdoors. Whether the outing involves an afternoon paddle on a small pond or a week-long canoe trip in the wilderness, youth will gain a totally different perspective and appreciation of the outdoors.

Leader's Note

Be aware of, and follow, Canadian Coast Guard and Scouting regulations when participating in boating activities. Many courses are available that teach swimming and canoeing skills. Take one or more of them; they will increase the safety and comfort of youths and adults participating in swimming or canoeing activities.

Begin your canoeing in small, protected bodies of water and slow-moving rivers or streams. They are ideal for learning and developing basic canoeing skills. Remember these basic rules when getting started:

▲ Stay close to shore.

▲ Avoid crossing large lakes.

▲ Head for shore at the first sign of rough weather.

▲ Keep your weight low and centred.

Hull Types

Today, canoeists have many makes and models from which to choose. Designs and uses range from long, slim, lightweight racing models to short, stubby, rugged whitewater play boats. Canoes designed for recreational touring and tripping are most suited for Scouting activities. They're approximately 5.5 metres long, and capable of carrying two or three people and gear for an extended trip. The width or beam (widest point at the gunwales), the height of the ends, and the hull shape vary according to design and manufacturer.

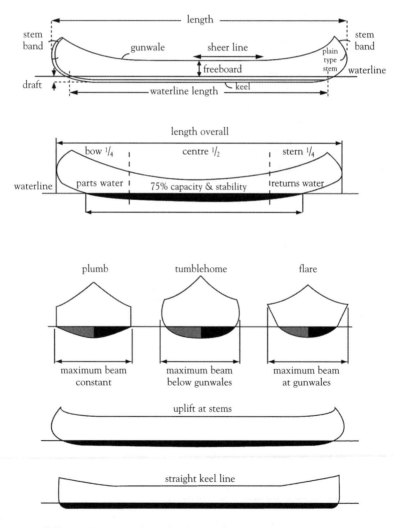

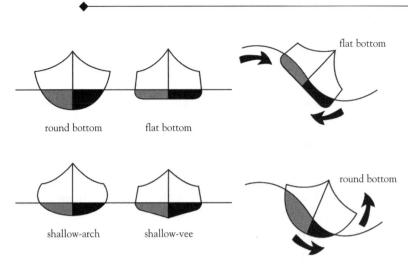

round bottom

flat bottom

flat bottom

shallow-arch

shallow-vee

round bottom

Length

Generally, longer and narrower canoes are the fastest. They track or travel in a straight line better and usually have a larger carrying capacity. Shorter canoes are usually lighter in weight and are more maneuverable, but slower.

Width

The width or beam of a canoe will help determine its performance. Wide canoes provide good stability and carrying capacity, but are fairly slow. Narrow canoes are much faster and efficient to paddle, but are less stable. The width of a canoe is usually measured in two places: at the beam (which is measured from gunwale to gunwale), and at the 10 cm waterline.

Depth

Canoes with a deep hull design will generally stay drier and will be able to carry large loads. However, canoes with this feature are often heavier than other models, and their extra height may make the boat harder to handle in strong winds.

Bottom

Canoes with a flat bottom offer great initial stability (i.e. they feel stable and secure on flat water). Canoes with a rounded bottom provide more secondary stability (i.e. they may not feel as stable when you first get in, but as you lean the canoe over it will balance on its side better and resist tipping).

Sides

Canoes have sides with one of three different shapes: flare, straight, tumblehome.

Flare

The canoe sides flare outward and are widest at the gunwales. This style will shed water, keep the paddlers dry and increase stability.

Tumblehome

A canoe with tumblehome has sides that slope inwards at the gunwales; the widest point of the canoe is often fairly low, near the waterline. This style is easier to paddle than many designs because the paddler doesn't have to reach as far, but its stability may be decreased.

Straight Side

This design is a compromise of the above two. Some canoes incorporate a combination of these styles to include a flared bow and stern with straight sides.

Entry Lines

The sharpness of the bow where the canoe cuts the water will also determine the performance of a canoe. A sharp entry line will cut through the water, while a more blunt bow will ride up on the water and add buoyancy to a canoe.

Rocker

The curve of the keel line from bow to stern is referred to as "rocker". A canoe with lots of rocker is quick and easy to maneuver, but it doesn't track as well. A canoe with little or no rocker will track well, but lacks maneuverability.

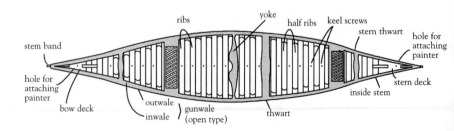

Materials

The canoe industry has evolved considerably from the days of the birch bark canoe. In the early 20th century, wood-canvas boats completely replaced birch bark models. As the aircraft industry developed, it had spin-off benefits for the canoe industry. Soon aluminum canoes started appearing. Although some boat manufacturers still produce aluminum canoes and wood-canvas canoes, most manufacturers use tougher, maintenance free and lightweight materials.

Common materials used today include: Royalex ABS™, polyethylene, fibreglass, kevlar, and carbon fibre.

Each material has its own advantages and disadvantages. Price, weight, durability, ease of repair and maintenance are all considerations when buying a canoe. It's also important to identify who will use the canoe and where you will paddle your craft. Visit a canoe store, talk to outfitters/guides, or attend a boat show to get answers to your questions. After speaking to local experts, you'll have a pretty good idea what type of canoe you need.

For occasional canoeing, why not consider rentals? Many outfitters offer a wide choice of excellent models. Some Scouting groups find that renting costs about the same, or even less than buying, storing and maintaining their own canoes for several years. Before making any purchase decision, weigh the advantages of owning and renting.

Canoe Accessories

Stay Afloat and Survive!

Flotation Devices

PFDs are generally much more comfortable than lifejackets for extended wear, but there's a big difference between the two flotation devices. A PFD will not keep the head of an unconscious person out of the water; that's what a lifejacket is designed to do. Remember, lifejackets/PFDs are not substitutes for adult supervision.

Scouts Canada's *B.P. & P.* makes a clear statement about flotation devices: "Youth and adults participating in small craft (6 metres or less) boating activities involving powered or non-powered boats must wear Transport Canada approved, properly fitted, personal flotation devices (PFDs)/life jackets at all times. Canoes exceeding the 6 metre standard will also be included in this policy." The Canadian Coast Guard also has specific policies relating to flotation devices.

Selecting a PFD/Lifejacket

Follow the checklist below when selecting a PFD/Lifejacket:

1. Is it Transport Canada approved?

2. Will it support the person it was made for?

3. Are all the snaps, belts, ties, tapes, and/or zippers on the PFD/life-jacket in good condition?

4. Is it easy to put on and take off?

5. Can you move your arms freely when wearing it?

6. Does it let you bend at the waist? (Can you touch your toes when wearing it?)

7. Can you see the ground at your feet and walk over obstacles easily?

8. Does it keep your head above water?

9. Relax in the water face down. Does it roll you to a face-up position?

10. Can you swim and manoeuvre easily in the water?

Wacky 'Expert' Camp Tip

While the Swiss Army Knife has been popular for years, the Swiss Navy Knife has remained largely unheralded. Its single blade functions as a tiny canoe paddle!

Paddles

Canoe paddles are made from many different materials, everything from wood to plastic and aluminum. Outfitters commonly use plastic and aluminum paddles because they're strong and maintenance-free. Wooden paddles, although they do require regular maintenance, are usually lighter in weight and much more pleasing to the eye.

Wooden paddles may be made from one single piece of wood or a number of different pieces laminated together. Paddles fashioned from a single piece of wood are usually made of hardwood such as straight-grained ash, maple or cherry. Laminated paddles usually combine both hardwoods and softwoods to reduce weight. Paddles are available in a wide variety of shapes and sizes. Round-tipped (beaver tail) and square-tipped blades are the most popular shapes.

Paddles come in various lengths to suit the canoeist's height. When choosing a paddle, stand it upright on the ground in front of you. The paddle should reach somewhere between your chin and your eyebrows. Another method for selecting the proper paddle size involves holding the paddle at the grip and shaft with the paddle raised above your head. Your arms should form right angles at the elbows when your hands are in the correct position.

Take care of your paddles. When not in use, hang them up, always out of the sun. Never use them as shovels or walking sticks. Don't lay them on the ground where someone might step on them; instead, lean them against a tree or building.

Caring for a Canoe

Preventive maintenance and careful handling will increase the life expectancy of a canoe and your canoeing equipment. Even low-maintenance, modern canoes should be protected from unnecessary abuse and excess exposure to the sun. Canoes spend more time out of the water than in, and during this time serious damage may occur through carelessness.

Keep canoes under shelter when not in use to protect them from sun, wind, snow and ice. Store them bottom up and level, on racks that are evenly spaced a half canoe length apart. If gunwales are not resting fully on the racks, a canoe may twist out of shape over time.

Towing

If you have to tow your canoe with a power boat, tie the towline to the forward thwart, run the line under the canoe, and tie it to the other end of the same thwart. Tie the towline to the line under the canoe. This will lift the canoe's bow and allow it to track directly behind the power boat.

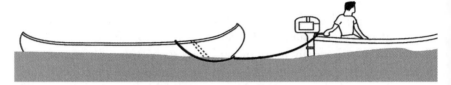

Keep Your Gear Dry

On a long trip, you may have to travel in heavy rain. Or you may have to cross a wide stretch of water in windy weather, taking some water into the canoe. (**Note:** If the weather becomes too severe, move off the water.)

If you're prepared, you can keep your packs and gear dry by using waterproof canoe bags or by packing your gear in plastic bags inside regular packs. Here's how to keep all your gear dry and secure. Place a groundsheet or small tarp on the floor between the gunwales, leaving enough material to wrap up and over the gear. Place the gear on the tarp, wrapping its sides up and over the gear. Finish by tying the tarp securely to keep it from flapping in the wind.

Are there puddles lying in the bottom of your canoe? Your gear doesn't have to get wet. Simply lay three or four, 5-cm diameter poles in the bottom of the canoe and place your gear on these.

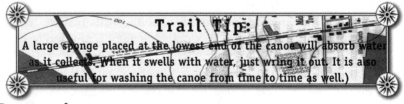

Trail Tip:

A large sponge placed at the lowest end of the canoe will absorb water as it collects. When it swells with water, just wring it out. It is also useful for washing the canoe from time to time as well.)

Portaging

"Canoes are meant to be paddled, not carried."

Most people would agree heartily, but to reach that perfect crystalline lake or to avoid a treacherous set of rapids, occasionally you must portage. It's nice to know what to expect before setting out, so you can prepare. Is it a steep portage? Is it through a bug-infested swamp? How good is the footing?

You'll find out this information by talking to other canoeists who have completed the same route recently. Topographical maps and their contour intervals can reveal many secrets. For more established routes, you may even find canoe maps or books. They'll give you a pretty good idea what to expect on the river. Here's some information to seek out:

▲ What's the river's rate of descent?

▲ Is the terrain along the edges steep or flat?

▲ Where are the rapids and falls? Other potential hazards?

▲ What information is available about portage trails? How long are they? What condition are they in? How steep are they?

▲ Where are the "put in" and "take out" spots?

Some rivers are more prone to spring flooding and flash floods after heavy rain. (Maps might warn of this problem.) These conditions may increase the level of difficulty, making portages necessary when they normally wouldn't be required.

If you find out that you'll probably have to portage during your canoe trip, prepare yourself. Learn and practise the necessary skills to make it as easy as possible.

For Starters

Make sure youth members are ready to tackle any challenge they face. Set aside an evening or an afternoon and create an interesting obstacle course. Get the youth to practise different carries (one- to four-person) within their capabilities. This "game" will give everyone an opportunity to learn; it'll also let you see what each youth is capable of managing.

The portaging method you choose will depend on:

▲ The strength and number of youths available to carry the canoe.

▲ The distance and terrain you must carry the canoe.

▲ The amount to be portaged.

▲ The canoe's weight.

One-Person Carry

For a short carry over flat ground, try moving a canoe by holding the gunwale, while the hull of the canoe rests on your hip. (In this case, the canoe doesn't go over your head.)

How do you do it?

Place the canoe flat on the ground, stand beside the centre thwart, and, using both hands, grip the gunwale, keeping one hand on either side of the thwart for balance. Lift the canoe until it rests on your hip and the side of your leg.

This lift is fairly awkward and requires some strength, but it's effective for short carries. Strong, tall Scouts and Venturers will manage it well.

The Traditional Portage Carry

If you've got a longer distance to cover, it's more efficient to carry your canoe on your shoulders. Getting it into position is the toughest part. Once the canoe is up there, it's fairly easy to walk, even over rough territory. Here's how to get the canoe into position.

1. With the canoe right side up, stand at the middle and pull the nearest gunwale up so the canoe is resting on one side with the bottom against your knees.

2. Bend your knees against the bottom and grab the middle thwart with one hand. Place your other hand on the gunwale just ahead of the centre thwart. Pull the opposite gunwale off the ground so the upper gunwale pivots against your upper legs. Keep pulling on the thwart until the gunwale that was along the ground is pulled up, and the canoe balances on your bent legs.

3. You are now ready to stand up using the large muscles in your legs to take the weight. As you straighten, swing the canoe onto your shoulders slipping your head and shoulders into the yoke. Then, extend your arms forward down the gunwales. Voilà!

If you have someone to help you, your partner can lift the upside down bow of the canoe as high as possible with the stern still on the ground as you duck under and into place. Once you're in position and comfortable, the person can let go; then you can raise the stern and set off down the trail.

Once you're up and walking, you may find you want a break if the portage is a long one. Some of the more established portage routes may have a canoe rest. This consists of two vertical poles, a couple of metres apart, with a horizontal pole joining them at the top. If you're lucky enough to find one, simply place the bow on the horizontal beam and step out from underneath. You might simply find a sturdy branch or a "V" in a tree and be able to place the bow there while you take your break. To lower the canoe, simply reverse the process described above.

Carrying can be very strenuous; make sure you don't overdo it. Take breaks whenever you feel the need.

Watch the trail carefully for obstacles like rocks, slippery mud, and low-hanging branches. You don't want to trip.

Two-Person Carry

If your lake is only a short distance away, each paddler may simply pick up the boat by the grab handles at each end (one person on each side of canoe) and walk. This means each paddler must carry half of the canoe's weight.

Longer Carries

If two canoeists want to carry the canoe in the upright position, here's how to do it.

The bow person turns his hand so his knuckles are against his leg with thumb pointing *back*; then he grabs the front of the canoe at the bottom. The stern person simply holds the bottom of the canoe at the back, but on the opposite side.

Tandem Shoulder Carry

For this portage method, both canoeists stand beside the canoe *on the same side*, facing the bow of the canoe: one at the bow, the other at the stern. The paddlers grab the gunwale nearest them and lift the canoe onto their thighs.

Using the same hand (either a left or right) each person reaches across the canoe and grabs the other gunwale. Now they can lift the canoe and swing it (upside down) onto their shoulders. The stern carrier should rest the stern thwart on her shoulders, while the bow person rests the bow deck on his shoulder. This will permit both to see where they're going. The stern person will carry most of the weight. This method works well when you have a strong person carrying with a weaker person.

Three- or Four-Person Carry

Are you canoeing with a group of youths, and the portage trails are wide?

When you have three people available to portage the canoe, position two people at the bow thwart or seat (one on each side where they can easily hold on), and the third person at the stern, holding the hull and top of the gunwale.

If you have four people, place two on each side opposite each other, holding onto the gunwale or thwarts — whichever they find most comfortable.

Portaging Secrets

▲ When lifting or setting the canoe down, do it on flat ground. Check for sharp rocks or other obstacles that may damage the hull of your canoe.

▲ Never load a canoe on shore; you'll only have to drag it into the water. This may damage it. Load your canoe in the water.

▲ Seasoned canoeists with the proper lightweight gear are often able to complete a portage in one trip: one person carries the canoe, while the other carries the gear. But there's no shame if you must make an extra trip. In fact, when travelling with young children, it's probably better to make several trips because it gives them an opportunity to stretch and explore. Make the portage part of the adventure.

▲ Load gear in as few packs as possible.

▲ Most canoe bags don't have pads for back protection. When packing canoe bags, put soft items closest to your back or cut a small piece of ensolite pad for use as a back pad inside the canoe bag.

▲ Waterproof canoe bags (complete with shoulder straps and hip belts) are excellent. Internal frame backpacks also work well. Place contents in waterproof bags first.

▲ Before unloading your canoe at a portage, look closely at how you've packed objects in the canoe for "trim." This will save lots of time when you're reloading at the end of the portage.

▲ Make each person responsible for carrying the same items at each portage. This will reduce the chances of leaving something behind.

▲ External frame packs cause problems in canoes. Besides not fitting well, they may damage the floor of the canoe.

▲ Use a dunk bag for odds and ends, like sneakers, water bottles, and extra rope.

▲ Pack lightly, just as when backpacking.

▲ Use short bungee cords to hold paddles in the canoe when portaging. It also keeps them from shifting around.

▲ Carry the lightest gear through first. This gives you a chance to see the trail.

▲ Don't try to carry too much. Portaging, just like canoeing, should be an enjoyable experience.

▲ One adult and two youths per canoe works well. The adult can carry the canoe while the Cubs or Scouts can carry the gear. Encourage everyone to help carry the canoe part of the distance.

▲ Don't carry gear in the canoe. It's neither good for the canoe, nor your back.

▲ Before making the first trip down the portage trail, secure all equipment you're leaving behind so it won't blow away.

▲ Fasten small items inside the canoe with bungee cords to prevent them from swaying. Loose ropes are potentially dangerous as they could drag on the ground and trip you.

▲ Wear sturdy footwear, especially on rough trails.

▲ Wearing your PFD while you portage may provide some cushioning when resting the thwart or yoke on your neck/shoulders.

▲ Keep a first aid kit at each end of your portage for convenient access.

The Yoke's on You

What's the key to making portaging as easy as possible?

Keep the amount of gear and weight to a minimum. Of course, this applies to the canoe as well. A lightweight model can reduce the weight you have to carry by as much as 15 kg or more.

Wacky 'Expert Camp Tip

You'll never be awakened by the call of a loon if you have an unlisted phone number

Launching

If you're standing on shore and want to launch a canoe without getting wet feet, each person can grab the gunwales at the middle of the canoe on either side and carry it (walking sideways) to the water. At the edge, just "feed" the canoe into the water, moving hands up the gunwales as the stern slides into the lake.

Boarding

Getting in and out of a canoe can be tricky. If you want to stay dry, don't hurry.

Make boarding easier by fastening your PFD or lifejacket while still on shore. Use a paddle to help distribute your weight when entering and exiting the canoe. At a dock, enter a canoe near its centre section. Place your paddle across the gunwales, anchoring yourself by holding your paddle and both gunwales. With most of your weight resting on the dock, place a foot in the centre of the canoe over the keel. Now, shift your weight from the dock to the foot inside the canoe. Next, bring your other foot aboard, and slide your paddle along the gunwales as you move into position while still keeping your weight low and centered.

Locations for Single Paddling

If you're paddling alone, position yourself in the center of the canoe just *behind* the centre thwart. If the water is calm the paddler should move close to one gunwale and kneel in the tumblehome or side of the canoe. This will reduce the waterline length of the canoe and make it more manoeuvreable. If the water is rough, a paddler should kneel in

the centre of the canoe just behind the centre thwart, straddling the keel line and keeping body weight low. If it is windy, a paddler may find it helpful to kneel just *ahead* of the centre thwart. This will keep the bow low and make the canoe more manageable.

Paddling strokes
The "J" Stroke

A stern paddler uses the "J" stroke to make the canoe go in a straight line. This stroke combines a power and a pry stroke into one smooth manoeuvre.

Begin it with a power stroke. As the paddle nears the end of the stroke, the power face of the blade is turned out and pried away from the canoe. This final prying stroke steers the canoe and puts it on the course the paddler chooses.

Here's how canoeists can check to see if they are doing the stroke correctly: the paddle should make a "J" figure in the water. A second check method involves watching the thumb on the grip hand at the top of the paddle. At the end of the stroke the thumb should be pointing *down* (away from the paddler) toward the floor of the canoe if the stroke is correct.

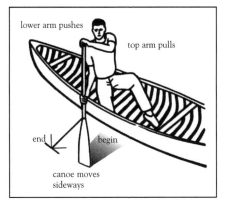

lower arm pushes

top arm pulls

end | begin

canoe moves
sideways

Pry Stroke

The pry stroke will move your canoe sideways away from your paddle.

Draw Stroke

The draw stroke is used to move the canoe sideways toward the paddling side.

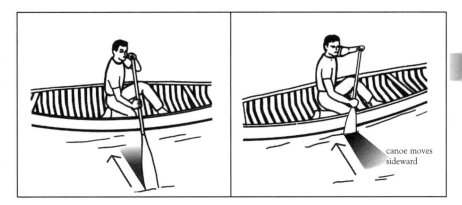

canoe moves
sideward

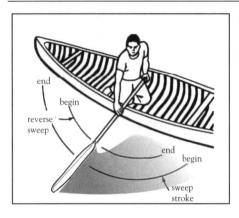

Sweep Stroke

The sweep stroke is used for partial and pivot turns.

Clothing

Avoid wearing heavy clothing and rubber boots when boating. If an accident happens, you don't want to have to struggle trying to remove a bulky jacket or boots.

Weather

Before setting out on any canoe or boating trip, check the weather forecast and plan your activities accordingly. A weather bureau in your area will be able to provide long-range forecasts.

Wise boaters watch out for any changes in temperature, wind direction and clouds. These usually indicate a change in weather. If you see foul weather approaching (like a thunder or lightning storm), get to shore as quickly as possible, and seek appropriate shelter.

If caught in a sudden storm, paddlers should move toward each other into the center of the canoe. Keep your weight low. Angle the bow of the canoe towards the waves at about a 45 degree angle to go up and over them. Don't head straight into waves as they may pour directly into the canoe.

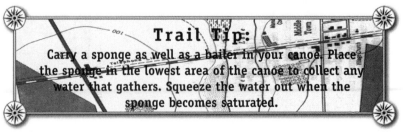

Trail Tip:
Carry a sponge as well as a bailer in your canoe. Place the sponge in the lowest area of the canoe to collect any water that gathers. Squeeze the water out when the sponge becomes saturated.

Overturned Canoes

If a canoe overturns, stay with it and hang on. If there are two or three people present, they should lock wrists over the top of the overturned canoe.

Self Rescue

The ability to re-enter a canoe from deep water is an important safety skill. There are several ways to re-enter, but the easiest for most people involves reaching over the gunwale near the centre of the canoe. Place

your hands on the bottom of the canoe, press down with your hands, and kick your feet to the surface. The hands should continue to press down, and the feet should kick until the canoe is under your trunk. Keep your head low, and when it's against the far side of the canoe, roll your body over into a sitting position on the canoe's bottom.

Swamped Canoe

Enter the swamped canoe in the same way as re-entering an empty canoe, but, before bringing your legs aboard, pause for a few seconds with arms and legs hanging over the gunwales until the canoe has stabilized. Then, bring them into the canoe. Sit on the bottom of the canoe directly in the center and paddle or hand-paddle the canoe to safety.

Basic Rescues: Reach, Throw, Row, Go, Tow

Anyone can give some sort of aid to a water accident victim. Even a weak or non-swimmer can learn to save a life by using reaching and throwing assists. (See Chapter 11, Water Safety, page 256 for more rescue tips.)

The manner in which the water rescue is performed should be considered in the following order:

Reach   with an object (oar, plank, pole, branch).

Throw   a buoyant object (preferably with an attached line).

Row   using a boat to rescue an offshore victim.

Go   swimming with a buoyant aid.

Tow   victim using a buoyant object.

For information on Respiration and Rescue Breathing, see Chapter 13, page 309.

Rescuing Others
Canoe-Over-Canoe Rescue

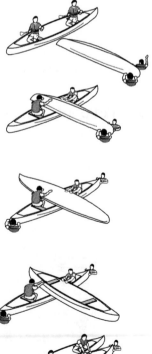

If you encounter an overturned or swamped canoe (or other small craft), make sure the occupants are safe. Once you know they are well, ask them to hold onto the overturned canoe as you gather any floating gear and place it in the rescue canoe.

Next, paddle your canoe into position at right angles to the overturned canoe, forming a "T" with the two canoes. Have the people in the water move to the end of the overturned canoe farthest away from your rescue canoe. They should hang on to the end, one on each side. You and any helper in the rescue canoe must position yourselves facing each other in the center of the canoe about one and a half metres apart.

Lift the overturned craft onto the gunwales of your rescue canoe. You'll need help from the people in the water. Ask them to push down and turn the canoe slightly to lift one gunwale out of the water. This will break the air seal. As they push down, you and your helper must lift the other end until you can slide the canoe completely out of the water across your gunwales. As you do this the people in the water must move to the ends of your rescue canoe and hold on until their canoe is back in the water. Turn the canoe over and gently slide it back into the water alongside your own canoe. Hold the gunwales of both canoes tightly together as the people in the water get back into their own canoe again.

This is an excellent exercise to practise in a pool or other safe setting.

Tired Swimmer Assist

When using a canoe as a rescue craft for a tired swimmer, extend a paddle, a pole, or a ring buoy to the victim. Don't reach for the person because of the possibility of being pulled off balance by the swimmer's struggles. You might need to block the victim or to apply pressure with your hand on the person's head or shoulder when the person comes alongside. This will keep the individual from trying to climb in over the gunwale.

To help a tired swimmer into your canoe, sit on the bottom near the middle. Shift your weight to the opposite side while using a high brace to help balance the craft as the swimmer climbs aboard.

An unconscious person, if not too heavy, can be lifted into your canoe. Grasp the victim's arms near the shoulder. "Jackknife" the victim's trunk into the canoe when it clears the gunwale, and then pull in the legs by lifting at the hips.

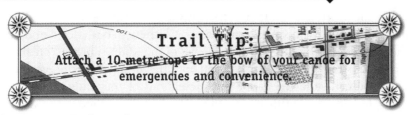

Canoe Tripping

Opportunities for canoe tripping abound! Many national and provincial parks now have back country canoe routes and campsites. Federal, provincial and territorial governments have joined forces to conserve and protect designated Heritage Rivers across Canada. These designated rivers often have campsites and picnic sites for public enjoyment.

Travelling by canoes, provided there are few or no portages, allows more flexibility when selecting gear. Weight and size are still a concern, but not as much as when backpacking. Of course the other concern is waterproofing your gear.

Here are some helpful tips for your canoe trip:

▲ It's easy to waterproof items. Just place everything inside plastic bags and then inside your regular pack. You might even buy special waterproof canoe packs or barrels for your gear.

▲ Place all maps and cameras in waterproof bags or specially designed cases.

▲ Equip each canoe with painters, bailers, paddles, and sound signaling devices as per Canadian Coast Guard regulations.

▲ Internal frame packs are easier to fit into a canoe than external frame packs.

▲ Fasten a pealess whistle to the zipper of each PFD for emergency signaling.

▲ Each canoe should have a rescue throw bag. Make or buy them, and practise throwing them over the water.

▲ Coil all loose ropes in your canoe and fasten them to the deck with shock cord. This will prevent the rope from wrapping around someone's leg if you capsize.

▲ Each person must wear a PFD or lifejacket. (*See B.P.& P.*)

Taking off with a group for a canoe trip isn't quite as easy as heading out on a camping trip. Be sure to assess the swimming and canoeing skills of each member. Everyone participating in a canoe trip should have swimming, first aid and canoeing knowledge, and skills appropriate to the outing. As well, make sure you have properly-equipped canoes.

International River Classification

Whitewater rivers are rated according to a uniform international river classification. The difficulty of a rapid is described by one of six categories:

Class I

> Moving water with a few riffles and small waves. Few or no obstructions.

Class II

> Easy rapids with waves up to one meter high, and wide; clear channels that are obvious without scouting. Some maneuvering is necessary.

Class III

> Rapids with high, irregular waves often capable of swamping an open canoe. Narrow passages that often require complex maneuvering. May require scouting from shore.

Class IV

> Long, difficult rapids with constricted passages that often require precise maneuvering in very turbulent water. Scouting from shore is often necessary, and conditions make rescue difficult. Generally impossible for open canoes. Boaters in covered canoes and kayaks should be able to perform the Eskimo roll.

Class V

> Extremely difficult, with long and very violent rapids. Complicated routes which nearly always must be scouted from shore. Rescue conditions are difficult and there is significant hazard to life in event of a mishap. Ability to perform the Eskimo roll is essential.

Class VI

> Difficulties of Class V carried to the extreme of navigability. Nearly impossible and very dangerous. Possible only for teams of experts, only after close study with all the precautions taken. Serious risk to life.

CHAPTER 13

▶ What is First Aid?

First aid is emergency help given to an injured or suddenly ill person using readily available materials. It can be simple, like removing a sliver from a child's finger and putting on a bandage. Or, it can be complicated, like giving care to many casualties in a motor vehicle collision and handing them over to medical help. But no matter what the situation, the objectives of first aid are always the same. First aid tries to:

▲ Preserve life

▲ Prevent the illness or injury from becoming worse

▲ Promote recovery.

First aid is made up of both knowledge and skills. Most of the knowledge you will find in this chapter can be learned by studying it. The skills are different. The best way to acquire first aid skills is to take a recognized first aid course from a qualified instructor. In an emergency where there are injuries, your ability to act calmly, assess the situation and give appropriate first aid will depend on your first aid skills. St. John Ambulance strongly recommends you take a first aid course to learn the skills of first aid.

Who Is a First Aider?

Anyone can be a first aider. Often the first aider at an emergency scene is someone who was just passing by and wanted to help. A parent can be a first aider to her child, a firefighter can be a first aider to an injured pedestrian, or an employee can be trained as a first aider for her place of work. A first aider is simply someone who takes charge of an emergency scene and gives first aid.

First aiders don't diagnose or treat injuries and illnesses (except, perhaps, when they are very minor). This is what medical doctors do. A first aider suspects injuries and illnesses and gives first aid.

What Can a First Aider Do?

A first aider gives first aid, but she can also do much more. In an emergency, where there is confusion and fear, the actions of a calm and effective first aider reassure everyone, and make the whole experience less traumatic.

Besides giving first aid, she can:

▲ Protect the casualty's belongings

▲ Keep unnecessary people away

▲ Reassure family or friends of the casualty

▲ Clean up the emergency and work to correct any unsafe conditions that may have caused the injuries in the first place.

Emergency Scene Management (ESM)

A first aider needs to follow a sequence of actions that ensure safe and appropriate first aid is given, and everyone's safety is protected. St. John Ambulance first aiders use emergency scene management (ESM) to do this.

ESM has four steps:

▲ *Scene survey.* Here you take control of the scene, get an idea of what has happened and what is going on, and get things organized so you can start helping any casualties.

▲ *Primary survey.* Here you assess each casualty for life-threatening injuries or illnesses, and give the needed life-saving first aid.

▲ *Secondary survey.* Here you assess the casualty for injuries or illnesses that are not life-threatening, and give appropriate first aid. Sometimes you don't have to do this step.

▲ *Ongoing casualty care.* Here you stay with the casualty until medical help arrives and takes over.

First Aid and the Law

Can a first aider be sued for giving first aid? Fear of being sued is one of the main reasons why people don't help when help is needed most. As a first aider, there are two "legal" situations in which you might give first aid. First, you may give first aid as part of your job — for instance, as a life-guard or first aid attendant. Second, you might simply be a passer-by who sees an emergency situation and wishes to help an injured or ill person.

Giving First Aid as a Passer-By

In Canada (except Quebec) and most of the United States, you do not have a legal duty to help a person in need — if you do not help an injured person, you are not at fault. But our governments want to encourage people to help others, so they recognize the Good Samaritan Principles. These principles protect you if you choose to help someone in need. Once you begin to give assistance, you are obligated to use reasonable skill and care based on your level of training.

Giving First Aid in Quebec

The Quebec Charter of Human Rights and Freedoms declares that any person whose life is in danger has the right to be helped. This means that you are required to help a person whose life is at risk, provided you do not put your own life, or anyone else's, in danger.

Principles of the Good Samaritan

You are a Good Samaritan if you help a person when you have no legal duty to do so. As a Good Samaritan, you give your help without being paid, and you give it in good faith (meaning you're helping because you care about the person and not for some other reason). Whenever you help a person in an emergency situation, you should abide by the following principles, each of which is discussed further below:

- ▲ You identify yourself as a first aider and get permission to help the injured or ill person before you touch her — this is called **consent**.

- ▲ You use **reasonable skill and care** in accordance with the level of knowledge and skill that you have.

- ▲ You are not **negligent** in what you do.

- ▲ You do not **abandon** the person.

Consent

The law says everyone has the right not to be touched by others. As a first aider, you must respect this right. Always identify yourself to a casualty and ask for permission to help before touching her. When you arrive at an emergency scene, identify yourself as a first aider to the casualty. If you are a police officer, nurse, first aider, etc., say so. Ask if you can help. If the casualty says "yes," you have consent to go ahead and help. If the casualty doesn't answer you, or doesn't object to your help, you have what is called **implied consent,** and you can go ahead and help. There are some special situations.

- ▲ If the casualty is unresponsive and relatives are present, ask for consent from the casualty's spouse or another member of the casualty's immediate family.

Although it might not seem to make sense that you would identity yourself to an unresponsive person and ask for consent to help her, this is what you must do. Always ask for consent before touching a casualty. If there is no response, you have implied consent to carry on and give first aid.

▲ If the casualty is an infant or a young child, you must get consent from the child's parent or guardian. If there is no parent or guardian at the scene, the law assumes the casualty would give consent if she could, so you have implied consent to help.

A person has the right to refuse your offer of help and not give you con sent. In this case, do not force first aid on a conscious casualty. Even if you d not have consent to touch the person and give first aid, there may be othe actions you can take, like controlling the scene, calling for medical help, etc

Reasonable Skill and Care

As a Good Samaritan, when you give first aid you are expected to use rea sonable skill and care according to your level of knowledge and skills. Whe in question, care that is given will be measured against what the reasonabl person with the same level of knowledge and skill would do. Give first aid wit caution so that you don't aggravate or increase an injury. Make sure you onl try to do what you know you can do, and that all your actions help the casu alty in some way.

Negligence

The Good Samaritan Principles say that, if you help someone who nee emergency medical care, you will not generally be considered negligent fo what you do or don't do as long as you use reasonable skill and care accordin to your level of knowledge. When you give first aid, use common sense an make sure your actions are in the casualty's best interest. Simply put, give th care that you would like to receive if you were in the casualty's position.

Abandonment

Never abandon a casualty in your care. Once the casualty accepts you offer of help, do not leave her. Stay with her until:

▲ You hand her over to medical help.

▲ You hand her over to another first aider.

▲ She no longer wants your help — this is usually because
the problem is no longer an emergency and further care is
not needed.

In summary, there is no reason not to help a person in need. By following the guidelines above, you will minimize the risk of being held negligent for your actions.

Safety and First Aid

The number one rule in giving first aid is, "Give first aid safely." Emergency scenes can be dangerous and you have to make sure your actions don't put you or anyone else in danger. Take the time to look for hazards and assess the risks of any actions you take. You don't want to become a casualty too!

There are three basic types of risks to be aware of:

▲ *The energy source that caused the original injury.* Is the energy
still active and could anyone be injured by it? For example,
where an injury has been caused by machinery, is the machinery
still running?

▲ *The hazards from secondary or external factors.* Are other
conditions present that could be a hazard? For example, at the
scene of a car crash, could there be an explosion or perhaps
injuries caused by passing vehicles?

▲ *The hazards of the rescue or first aid procedures.* Is there risk of
someone being injured by the rescue and first aid actions? For
example, if the casualty is much larger than you are, and you
have to move that person, can you do so without injuring
yourself?

Preventing Infection

A first aider and casualty are in very close contact with each other when first aid is given. This close contact means that an infection could pass from one person to the other. This risk of infection is a safety hazard a first aider always has to be aware of.

There is more risk of serious infection when blood and other bodily fluids are involved, as the viruses that cause AIDS (acquired immuno-deficiency syndrome), hepatitis B and other illnesses may be present. If you don't know if someone is infected with an illness, you should use safety measures called **the universal precautions** to minimize the risk of transmission.

The universal precautions are used in the health care professions to reduce the risk of infection for both the caregiver and the casualty. The universal precautions that apply to first aiders are: hand washing, wearing gloves, minimizing mouth-to-mouth contact during artificial respiration, and the careful handling of sharp objects.

How Big Is the Risk of Getting AIDS?

If a casualty has AIDS, it is highly unlikely you would get AIDS by giving artificial respiration or CPR without a mask. The risk is very low. It has never actually happened.

You Can Always Do Something

If you do not want to touch a casualty because of the risk of infection, is there anything you can do? Yes, there is plenty of first aid you can give.

For instance, you can:

▲ Take charge.

▲ Call bystanders and ask for help.

▲ Make the area safe.

▲ Send/get medical help.

▲ Give reassurance.

▲ Give information to ambulance officers.

The risk of infection to a first aider is extremely small. In a situation where you think the risk is high, there are still many potential life-saving actions you can take.

Sending a Bystander for Medical Help

If there is a bystander at the scene, it's best to send her to call for medical help. This lets you stay at the scene and give first aid.

Tell the bystander:

▲ To call an ambulance — give her the phone number.

▲ What's wrong with the casualty — give the worst possible situation to make sure the casualty gets the urgent care she may need.

- ▲ Where you are.

- ▲ To report back to you — this way you know the call for medical help has been made.

If possible, always send someone out to meet the ambulance. Leading the ambulance officers to the emergency scene saves a lot of time. Call an ambulance. Dial 911 and tell them an infant is unresponsive. The address is 321 Oak Street. Hang up when they tell you to, and then come back here.

History, Signs and Symptoms

Before you can give first aid, you need to assess the casualty to find out what is wrong. All your first aid actions are the result of what you find out in your assessments. History, symptoms and signs are the three ways you get information about a casualty.

History

History is all the information about the emergency situation and the condition of the casualty. You get this information by looking at the scene, talking to witnesses and to the casualty. The history answers the question, "What happened?"

Signs

Signs are conditions of the casualty you can see, hear, feel and smell. You may see the signs of injury or illness immediately, or you may discover them while examining the casualty.

Symptoms

Symptoms are things the casualty feels and may be able to describe. You cannot discover symptoms on your own — the casualty must somehow communicate them to you.

Shock

Any injury or illness can be accompanied by shock. Shock is a circulation problem where the body's tissues don't get enough blood.

Signs and Symptoms of Shock

Signs

- ▲ Pale skin at first, turns bluish-grey

- ▲ Bluish-purple lips, tongue, ear lobes, fingernails

- ▲ Cold and clammy skin

- ▲ Breathing shallow and irregular, fast or gasping for air
- ▲ Changes in level of consciousness
- ▲ Weak, rapid pulse — radial pulse may be absent.

Symptoms

- ▲ Restless
- ▲ Anxious
- ▲ Disoriented
- ▲ Confused
- ▲ Afraid
- ▲ Dizzy
- ▲ Thirsty, maybe
- ▲ Very thirsty.

> **It is not shock if...**the casualty is warm, the skin is dry with full colour, and the person is fully conscious.

Minimizing Shock

The following actions will minimize shock:

1. Give first aid for the injury or illness that caused the shock.
2. Reassure the casualty often.
3. Minimize pain by handling the casualty gently.
4. Loosen tight clothing at the neck, chest and waist.
5. Keep the casualty warm, but do not overheat; use jackets, coats, or blankets if you have them.
6. Moisten the lips if the casualty complains of thirst; don't give anything to eat or drink. If medical help is delayed many hours, give water or clear fluids to drink. Make a note of what was given and when.

7. Place the casualty in the best position for her condition. (See diagrams)

8. Continue ongoing casualty care until hand-over.

The above first aid for shock also prevents shock from getting worse. Whenever possible, add these steps to any first aid you give; this will minimize shock.

Positioning a Casualty in Shock

Putting the casualty in the right position can slow the progress of shock and make the casualty more comfortable. The position you use depends on the casualty's condition. The casualty should be as comfortable as possible in the position you use.

No Suspected Head/Spinal Injury; Fully Conscious

Place the casualty on his back with feet and legs raised — this position is often called the shock position. Once the casualty is positioned, cover him to preserve body heat, but do not overheat.

No Suspected Head/Spinal Injury; Less than Fully Conscious

Place the casualty in the recovery position. When there is a decreased level of consciousness, airway and breathing are the priority; the recovery position ensures an open airway.

Suspected Head/Spinal Injury

If there might be a head or spinal injury, steady and support the casualty in the position found and monitor the ABCs (airways, breathing, circulation) closely. This protects the head and spine from further injury.

As Injuries Permit

A casualty's injuries may not permit you to put her into the best position. For instance, raising the legs of a person with a fractured pelvis can cause more pain and aggravate the injury. Keep this person lying flat on her back. If possible, put her on a stretcher, or a backboard, and raise the foot of the stretcher. Always think of the casualty's comfort when choosing a position.

What Happens When a Person Chokes

Choking is a life-threatening emergency. When the air supply to the lungs is cut off, the person's face immediately becomes reddish. Shortly after, as oxygen in the body is used up, the face becomes grey and lips and ear lobes become bluish. This change in colour is called cyanosis. Soon, the person becomes unconscious and eventually the heart stops beating.

Signs of Choking

The most obvious sign of choking is grabbing the throat. The other signs are given in the illustration on page 305. Notice how they are different with good air exchange or poor/no air exchange.

You need to know how to recognize whether a choking person has good air exchange or poor/no air exchange because the first aid is different for each.

Choking with Good Air Exchange

▲ Able to speak

▲ Signs of distress — eyes show fear

▲ Forceful coughing

▲ Wheezing and gagging between coughs

▲ Reddish face

▲ Grabbing the throat.

Choking with Poor or No Air Exchange

▲ Not able to speak

▲ Signs of distress — eyes show fear

▲ Weak or no coughing

▲ High-pitched noise or no noise when trying to breathe

▲ Greyish face, bluish lips and ears

▲ Grabbing the throat.

Listen to how well the casualty speaks and for other sounds of a partly blocked airway.
Look for signs of good air exchange versus poor or no air exchange.

First Aid for Choking

Choking Adult – Conscious Who May Become Unconscious

If choking is caused by swelling of the airway from an infection, injury or allergic reaction, the Heimlich manoeuvre won't work. Get medical help quickly.

1. Begin ESM; do a scene survey.

2. If the casualty can cough forcefully, speak or breathe, don't touch her. Tell her to try to cough up the object. If a partial blockage lasts for a few minutes, get medical help.

If you think there might be poor or no air exchange, check by asking, "Can you cough?" If the casualty cannot cough forcefully, speak or breathe, use the Heimlich manoeuvre to try to remove the blockage. Go to step 3.

Heimlich Manoeuvre

3. Stand behind the casualty ready to support her if she becomes unconscious. Find the correct hand position and give abdominal thrusts to try to remove the airway blockage.

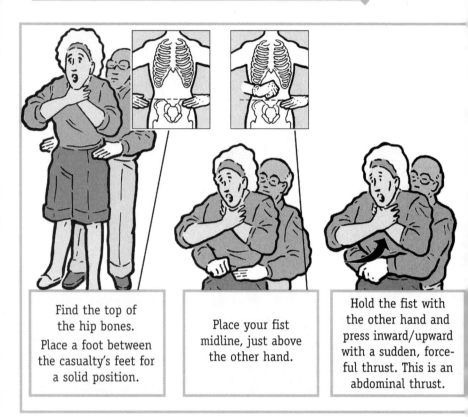

Find the top of the hip bones.
Place a foot between the casualty's feet for a solid position.

Place your fist midline, just above the other hand.

Hold the fist with the other hand and press inward/upward with a sudden, forceful thrust. This is an abdominal thrust.

4. Keep giving the Heimlich manoeuvre until either the object is removed or the casualty becomes unconscious. If the airway is cleared, give ongoing casualty care for choking.

If the casualty becomes unconscious, don't panic. Continue first aid with step 5.

5. As the casualty collapses, lower her to the ground. Send someone to call for medical help.

6. Check the mouth. Open the mouth with the tongue-jaw lift. The forward movement of the tongue may loosen the blockage. Finger sweep to remove any matter.

Protect the head and neck as you lower the casualty.

Call an ambulance. Tell them a woman has choked and is unconscious. Give our location and report back to me once you've called. Do you understand?

Yes, I Do!

Hold the tongue with your thumb. Hold the jaw with your fingers and lift the jaw and tongue upwards.

Hold the jaw in position and slide a hooked finger down the far side of the mouth to the base of the tongue.

Hook any foreign matter and pull it up against the near cheek. Be careful; the object may be sharp or slippery.

Push back on the forehead and lift the jaw.

Seal your mouth around the casualty's mouth.

Pinch the nostrils.

Blow slowly — watch for the chest to rise.

If the chest doesn't rise, reposition the head, check the seals at the nose and mouth and try again.If the chest does rise, give another breath and go to page 312, step 7.

If the chest doesn't rise on your second try, conclude the airway is blocked. Try to clear the airway. Go to step 8.

Kneel astride the casualty.

Find the top of the hips with your hands.

Place the heel of one hand mid-line slightly above the other hand.

Keep the fingers raised, in line with the centre of the body and interlocked if you wish. Give up to five quick, inward and upward thrusts. Give each with the intention of removing the object.

Remove the mask for abdominal thrusts.

7. Try to breathe into the casualty's mouth.

8. Use the Heimlich manoeuvre to clear the airway. Find the right hand position and give up to five abdominal thrusts.

9. Repeat steps 6, 7 and 8 until the chest rises when you blow into the casualty's mouth or medical help takes over. If the chest rises go to step 10.

10. If you remove the blockage, or if the chest rises when you ventilate, give a total of two slow breaths, then, continue the primary survey. Check breathing and pulse. If the casualty is breathing effectively, give ongoing casualty care for choking.

First Aid for Stopped Breathing — Artificial Respiration (AR)

The vital organs of the body such as the brain and heart need a continuous supply of oxygen to stay alive. Artificial respiration (AR) is a way you can supply air to the lungs of a casualty who is breathing ineffectively or not breathing at all.

As you breathe, the air you exhale contains enough oxygen to keep a non-breathing person alive. Artificial respiration involves blowing this air into the casualty's lungs to deliver oxygen to the non-breathing person. The number of times you blow in one minute is called the rate. AR has to be given at the proper rate to make sure the casualty is getting enough oxygen.

Mouth-to-Mouth AR

This is the most commonly used method of AR. The first aider pinches the casualty's nose closed and blows into his mouth.

You arrive at a scene... an unconscious adult (someone eight years old or older) is lying on the floor.

1. Begin emergency scene management. Start the scene survey.

2. Assess responsiveness. If there is no response, go to step 3.

Ask the casualty if she is O.K. Assess any response. Gently tap the shoulders.

3. Send or go for medical help.

Get medical help. Call an ambulance and...

4. Place the casualty face up, protecting the head and neck during any movement. Open the airway by tilting the head.

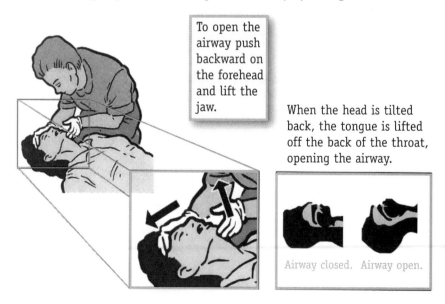

To open the airway push backward on the forehead and lift the jaw.

When the head is tilted back, the tongue is lifted off the back of the throat, opening the airway.

Airway closed.   Airway open.

5. Check for breathing for 3 to 5 seconds.

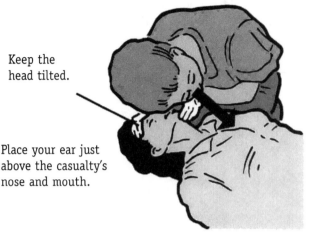

Keep the head tilted.

Place your ear just above the casualty's nose and mouth.

Look... for chest movement.

Listen... for sounds of breathing.

Feel... for breath on your cheek.

6. Breathe into the casualty twice. For an adult casualty, blow for 1 1/2 to 2 seconds. Use enough air to make the chest rise.

Take a deep breath and seal your mouth around the casualty's mouth.

Pinch the nostrils. Blow slowly and watch for the chest to rise.

Move your mouth away and release the nostrils to allow the air to escape.

Look for the chest to fall, listen for air sounds, and feel for air being exhaled against your cheek.

Give another breath and go to step 8.

If the chest doesn't rise when you blow:
▲ Reopen the airway by tilting the head.
▲ Pinch the nose again.
▲ Make a better seal around the mouth. Try blowing again.

If the chest still doesn't rise, give first aid for choking (see step 7).

7. Check for a pulse at the neck. There is a carotid pulse on either side of the neck. Feel for a pulse on the side closest to you. **Do not feel or compress both sides at the same time.**

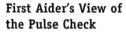

First Aider's View of the Pulse Check

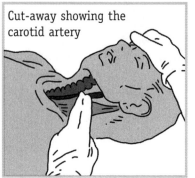

Cut-away showing the carotid artery

> Keep the head tilted.
> Slide two fingers into the groove of the neck just down from the Adam's apple.
> Press gently to detect the pulse, take 5 to 10 seconds.

If there is no pulse, start CPR.

If there is a pulse, continue AR. (See step 8.)

8. Breathe into the casualty once every five seconds (12 times a minute). After one minute of AR, recheck the pulse for five seconds, and at the same time, look, listen and feel for breathing:

▲ If there is no pulse, start CPR.

▲ If there is a pulse and breathing, continue the primary survey.

▲ If there is a pulse and still no breathing, continue AR. Recheck the pulse and breathing every few minutes. Keep giving AR until the casualty starts to breathe on her own, medical help takes over or you are too tired to continue.

Don't blow too hard.
If you blow into a casualty too hard or too fast, the air may go into the stomach instead of the lungs. This can cause a few problems. Only blow hard enough to make the chest rise.

Dressings and Bandages

Dressings and bandages are the basic tools of first aid. They are essential for wound care and for the care of injuries to bones, joints and muscles. You should know how to use commercially prepared dressings and bandages, and also be ready to improvise with materials on hand at the emergency scene. Knowing what makes a good dressing and bandage helps you do this.

Dressings

A dressing is a protective covering put on a wound to help control bleeding, absorb blood from the wound, and prevent further contamination. A dressing should be:

▲ Sterile, or as clean as possible.

▲ Large enough to completely cover the wound.

▲ Highly absorbent to keep the wound dry.

▲ Compressible, thick and soft — especially for severe bleeding so that pressure is applied evenly over the wound.

▲ Non-stick and lint-free to reduce the possibility of sticking to the wound. Gauze, cotton and linen make good dressings; wool or other fluffy materials make poor dressings.

Dressings are available in a variety of sizes and designs. The dressings used most often in first aid are:

▲ *Adhesive dressings:* prepared sterile gauze dressings with their own adhesive strips. They are sealed in a paper or plastic covering and are available in various sizes and shapes, according to their intended use. They are often used for minor wounds with little bleeding.

▲ *Gauze dressings:* in varying sizes, folded and packaged individually or in large numbers. Packaged gauze is usually sterile.

▲ *Pressure dressings:* sterile dressings of gauze and other absorbent material, usually with an attached roller bandage. They are used to apply pressure to a wound with severe bleeding.

▲ *Improvised dressings:* prepared from lint-free sterile or clean material, preferably white. They may be made from a towel, a sheet, a pillow slip or any other clean absorbent material such as a sanitary pad. Plastic wrap or the wrapping from a sterile dressing can be used as an airtight dressing for penetrating wounds of the chest.

Follow the guidelines below for putting on dressings:

▲ Prevent further contamination as much as you can. Use the cleanest material available as dressings, and wear gloves or wash your hands before handling them. See page 299 for more on preventing further contamination.

▲ Extend the dressing beyond the edges of the wound to completely cover it.

▲ If blood soaks through a dressing, leave it in place and cover with more dressings.

▲ Secure a dressing with tape or bandages.

Bandages

A bandage is any material that is used to hold a dressing in place, maintain pressure over a wound, support a limb or joint, immobilize parts of the body, or secure a splint. Bandages may be commercially prepared or improvised.

Handling Dressings

When handling dressings, never touch the surface that will touch the wound. Always handle a dressing from the outer side.

When using bandages, remember to:

▲ Apply them firmly to make sure bleeding is controlled or immobilization is achieved.

▲ Check the circulation beyond the bandage frequently to ensure the bandage is not too tight.

▲ Use your bandages only as bandages, not as padding or dressings, when other materials are available. You may need all your bandages for other injuries.

The Triangular Bandage

One of the most versatile prepared or improvised bandages is the triangular bandage. It is made by cutting a one-metre square of linen or cotton on the diagonal, producing two triangles. Triangular bandages can be improvised from sheets, garbage bags, canvas, etc. The parts of the triangular bandage, identified for ease of instruction, are:

A triangular bandage may be used:

▲ As a **whole cloth:** opened to its fullest extent, as a sling or to hold a large dressing in place.

▲ As a **broad bandage:** to hold splints in place or to apply pressure evenly over a large area.

Fold the point to the centre of the base with the point slightly beyond the base.

Fold in half again from the top to the base.

▲ As a **narrow bandage:** to secure dressings or splints or to immobilize ankles and feet in a figure-8.

Fold a broad bandage in half again from the top to the base.

▲ As a **ring pad:** to control bleeding when pressure cannot be applied directly to the wound, as in the case of a short embedded object. Prepare a ring pad for your first aid kit, ready for use.

Make a narrow bandage.

Form a loop around one hand by wrapping one end of the bandage twice around four fingers.

Pass the loose end through the loop and wrap it around and around until the entire bandage is used up and a firm ring is made — this is a ring pad.

To make a ring pad with a larger loop, tie two narrow bandages together.

Wounds and Bleeding

A wound is any break in the soft tissues of the body. It usually results in bleeding and may allow germs to enter the body. Bleeding is the escape of blood from the blood vessels into surrounding tissues, body cavities or out of the body. The soft tissues of the body are the most susceptible to injury, resulting in wounds and bleeding.

A wound can be either open or closed:

▲ *Open wound:* there is a break in the outer layer of the skin that results in bleeding and may permit germs to enter the body, causing infection.

▲ *Closed wound:* there is no break in the outer layer of skin so there is no external bleeding (but there will be internal bleeding which may be severe) and the risk of infection is low (except in a closed abdominal wound where the risk of infection is high).

The different types of open and closed wounds to soft tissues are given in the table on the next page. When someone is injured, recognizing the type of wound helps to give appropriate first aid.

The aim in the care of wounds is to stop the bleeding and prevent infection. Although some bleeding may help to wash contamination from the wound, excessive blood flow must be stopped quickly to minimize shock.

Bleeding

Bleeding is the escape of blood from the blood vessels. In external bleeding, blood escapes the body through a surface wound. You can see external bleeding. In internal bleeding, blood escapes from tissues inside the body. You don't usually see internal bleeding. Also, bleeding is either arterial, which is bleeding from the arteries, or venous, which is bleeding from the veins.

In **arterial bleeding,** the blood is bright red and spurts with each heartbeat. Arterial bleeding is serious and often hard to control.

In **venous bleeding,** the blood is dark red and flows more steadily. It is easier to stop than arterial bleeding.

Types of Wounds

Contusions or Bruises

Contusions or bruises are closed wounds usually caused by a fall or a blow from something blunt. The tissues under the skin are damaged and bleed into surrounding tissues, causing discolouration. Because there is no break in the skin, there is little chance of infection. A bruise may be a sign of a deeper, more serious injury or illness.

Abrasions or Scrapes

Abrasions or scrapes are open wounds where the outer protective layer of skin and the tiny underlying blood vessels are exposed, but the deeper layer of the skin is still intact. Abrasions are usually due to the skin being scraped across a hard surface (rug burns, road rash). Abrasions do not bleed very much but can be very painful. The risk of infection from dirt and other particles that may be in the wound is high.

Incisions

Incisions are clean cuts in soft tissue caused by something sharp, such as a knife. These wounds may not be as dirty as abrasions, but they may contain fragments of glass or other material.

Lacerations

Lacerations are tears in the skin and underlying tissue. The edges of the wound are jagged and irregular, and dirt is likely to be present, increasing the risk of infection. Lacerations are often caused by machinery, barbed wire or the claws of an animal.

Puncture Wounds

Puncture wounds are open wounds caused by blunt or pointed instruments, such as knives, nails or an animal's teeth. The wound may have a small opening, but often penetrates deep into the tissue. There may be contamination deep in the wound, and internal organs may be damaged.

Avulsions and Amputations

Avulsions are injuries that leave a piece of skin or other tissue either partially or completely torn away from the body. Amputations involve partial or complete loss of a body part, and are usually caused by machinery or cutting tools.

Gunshot wounds are a special type of wound. The entry wound is often small, and may have burns around it. Sometimes there is an exit wound as well, which is usually larger than the entry wound. Because the bullet may bounce around inside the body, the exit wound may not be directly across from the entry wound.

First Aid for Severe External Bleeding

1. Begin emergency scene management. (See start of chapter for more information) Do a scene survey. Assess the mechanism and injury. If you suspect a head or spinal injury, steady, and support the head and neck before continuing.

2. Do a primary survey, and give first aid for life-threatening injuries.

3. To control severe bleeding, apply direct pressure to the wound as quickly as possible. If the wound is large and wide open, you may have to bring the edges of the wound together first.

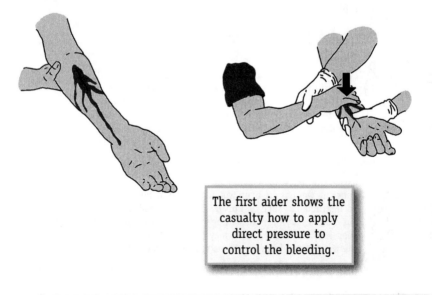

The first aider shows the casualty how to apply direct pressure to control the bleeding.

4. While keeping pressure on the wound, elevate the injury; this will reduce blood flow at the wound.

If injuries permit, elevate the injury above the level of the heart.

5. Place the casualty at rest; this will further reduce blood flow.

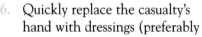

6. Quickly replace the casualty's hand with dressings (preferably sterile) and continue direct pressure over the dressings.

7. Once bleeding is under control, continue the primary survey looking for other life-threatening injuries. Give life-saving first aid as needed.

Blood-Soaked Dressings

If the dressings become blood-soaked... don't remove them. Add more dressings and continue pressure. Removing the blood-soaked dressings may disturb blood clots and expose the wound to further contamination.

8. Before bandaging the wound, check circulation below the injury.

Check the temperature and colour of the fingers, and use the nailbed test.

9. Bandage the dressing in place.

10. Check the circulation below the injury and compare it with the other side. If it is worse than it was before the injury was bandaged, loosen the bandage just enough to improve circulation.

11. Give ongoing casualty care, including first aid to minimize shock.

Nailbed Test

Here's how to do it. Press on a fingernail or toenail until the nailbed turns white, and then release it. Note how long it takes for normal colour to return. If it returns quickly, blood flow is unrestricted. If it stays white, or if the colour returns slowly, circulation may be impaired.

Principles of Controlling Bleeding

The body has natural defences against bleeding. Damaged blood vessels constrict to reduce blood flow, and blood pressure drops as bleeding continues. These factors result in reduced force of blood flow. Blood will clot as it is exposed to air, forming a seal at the wound. Even so, the first aider should try to stop all bleeding as soon as possible, following the ABC priorities.

Steps to Control Bleeding

The following steps will control all but the most severe bleeding. You can often do these all at the same time.

Direct pressure

Apply pressure directly to the wound to stop blood flow and allow clots to form. When bleeding is controlled, keep pressure on the wound with dressings and bandages.

Elevation

Raise the injured limb above the level of the heart to use gravity to reduce blood flow to the wound area. Elevate the limb as high as is comfortable.

Rest

Place the casualty at rest to reduce the pulse rate. Unless the bleeding is from a head wound, the preferred position is lying down with feet and legs elevated.

Minor cuts and scrapes that cause slight bleeding are easily controlled with pressure, elevation and rest. Severe bleeding must be brought under control quickly to prevent further blood loss and to slow the progress of shock.

Preventing Further Contamination

All open wounds are contaminated to some degree. From the moment of injury, there is risk of infection that continues until the wound is completely healed. Stopping bleeding is your priority, but do it using the cleanest materials available.

Minor Wound Care

Follow the principles listed below for cleaning a wound. Tell the casualty to seek medical help if signs of infection appear later.

- ▲ Wash your hands with soap and water and put on gloves if available.

- ▲ Do not cough or breathe directly over the wound.

- ▲ Fully expose the wound but don't touch it.

- ▲ Gently wash loose material from the surface of the wound. Wash and dry the surrounding skin with clean dressings, wiping away from the wound.

- ▲ Cover the wound promptly with a sterile dressing. Tape the dressing in place.

- ▲ Remove and dispose of gloves in an appropriate manner and wash your hands and any other skin area that may have been in contact with the casualty's blood.

Tetanus Infection

Any wound may be contaminated by spores that cause tetanus, a potentially fatal disease characterized by muscle spasms. Tetanus is commonly referred to as "lockjaw."

Deep wounds, especially those caused by animal bites or those that may have been contaminated by soil, dust or animal feces, are at high risk of tetanus infection. Advise a casualty with this type of wound to get medical help.

Wounds to the Eye

Sight depends on one of the most delicate and sensitive organs of the body, the eye. The eye can be injured very easily, and for this reason, extra care must be taken to protect the eyes from hazards. When an eye is injured, proper first aid given right away may prevent partial or complete loss of eyesight.

Particles in the Eye

A particle of sand, grit or a loose eyelash on the eyeball or under the eyelid causes discomfort and inflammation of the tissue around the eye. When this happens, the eye becomes a characteristic pink or reddish colour. Tears may not be enough to loosen and wash away such particles.

First Aid to Remove a Particle from the Upper Eyelid

Begin by using the lashes of the lower eyelid to sweep away the particle from the upper eyelid. Tell the casualty to gently hold the eyelashes of the upper eyelid and pull the lid straight out and then down and over the lower eyelid. Let go of the eyelashes. The lashes of the lower lid may sweep away the particle as the upper lid slides over the lower lid.

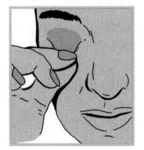

Try this a couple of times. If it doesn't work, expose the inner surface of the eyelid to locate and remove the loose particle.

Pull the upper lid over the lower lid, then let go.

First Aid for Removing a Particle from the Lower Eyelid

1. Gently draw the lower eyelid down and away from the eye ball while the casualty rolls the eye upward.

2. Wipe the particle away with the moist corner of a facial tissue, clean cloth or a cotton-tipped applicator.

Warning

Don't try to remove a particle from the eye if it:

▲ Is embedded in the eyeball or surrounding tissue.

▲ Is sticking to the eyeball.

▲ Cannot be seen — even though the eye is inflamed and painful.

Signs and Symptoms of a Fracture

One or more of the following signs and symptoms will be present when a bone is fractured:

▲ *Pain and tenderness:* it is worse when the injury is touched or moved.

▲ *Loss of function:* the casualty cannot use the injured part.

▲ *A wound:* the bone ends may be sticking out.

▲ *Deformity:* any unnatural shape or unnatural position of a bone or joint.

▲ *Unnatural movement.*

▲ *Shock:* this increases with the severity of the injury.

▲ *Crepitus:* a grating sensation or sound that can often be felt or heard when the broken ends of bone rub together (don't test for this).

▲ *Swelling and bruising:* fluid accumulates in the tissues around the fracture.

Sprains

A **sprain** is an injury to a ligament. A first-degree sprain is a stretched ligament; a second-degree sprain is a partly torn ligament; a third-degree sprain is a completely torn ligament. Without specialized training it is difficult to determine the degree of a sprain. Be cautious and give first aid as if the injury is serious. Sprains of the wrist, ankle, knee and shoulder are most common.

The signs and symptoms of sprains may include:

▲ Pain that may be severe and increase with movement of the joint.

▲ Loss of function.

▲ Swelling and discolouration.

General First Aid for Injuries to Bones and Joints

Below is general first aid for injuries to bones and joints. The methods of immobilizing different bones and joints follow this general approach.

The aims of first aid for bone and joint injuries are to prevent further tissue damage and to reduce pain.

1. Begin emergency scene management and do a scene survey.

2. Assess the mechanism of injury. If you suspect a head or spinal injury, call for medical help, then steady and support the head before continuing.

3. Do a primary survey and give first aid for life-threatening injuries.

4. Steady and support any obvious fractures or dislocations found in the primary survey (during the rapid body check). Dress any obvious wounds to prevent further contamination. Protect any protruding bones.

5. Do a secondary survey to the extent needed. When you find a bone or joint injury, carefully and gently expose the injured area. You may have to cut clothing to do this without moving the injured part. Take a good look at the entire injured area to determine the extent of the injury. Look for a wound indicating an open fracture. Most open fractures have only a small wound, but there is still danger of serious infection.

> **Warning**
>
> Do not give a casualty with a fracture anything to drink; this could complicate medical treatment. If the casualty complains of thirst, moisten his lips with a damp cloth.
>
> Only straighten injured joints as far as you can without causing increased pain or until there is resistance. Splint the limb in the most comfortable position if it won't straighten easily.

Check the circulation below the injury. If circulation is impaired, medical help is needed urgently.

6. Steady and support the injured part; you can do this, a bystander can do this, or the casualty may be able to do this. Maintain support until medical help takes over, or the injury is immobilized.

7. Now decide what action is best. If medical help is on the way and will arrive soon, steady and support the injury with your hands until they arrive. If medical help will be delayed, or if the casualty needs to be transported, immobilize the injury. Consider the following when making your decision:

▲ Are there other risks to the casualty? Are there risks to yourself or others?

▲ If medical help can get to the scene, how long will it take?

▲ Do you have the materials needed to properly immobilize the injury?

▲ How long will it take to immobilize the injury compared to how long it will take for medical help to arrive?

8. Apply cold and compression to the injury, as appropriate, and elevate the injured part.

9. Give ongoing casualty care until medical help arrives. Monitor circulation below the injury site.

Splinting Materials
Definition

A splint is any material used to prevent fractured bones from moving unnecessarily. Fractured arms, hands, fingers, legs, feet and toes can all be splinted. A good splint is:

▲ Rigid enough to support the injured limb.

▲ Well padded for support and comfort.

▲ Long enough, which means:

 ◆ for a fracture between two joints, it extends beyond the joints above and below the fracture,

 ◆ for an injured joint, it's long enough for the limb to be secured so the joint can't move.

There are many commercial splints available. You may have access to one of these if the incident happened at a workplace, sporting event, etc. Be trained in using these splints and follow the manufacturer's directions.

A splint can be improvised from any material, as long as it works to immobilize the injury. The casualty's own body can be used as a splint. One leg can be splinted to the other. Fingers and toes can be splinted to the next finger or toe. This is called a "natural" splint.

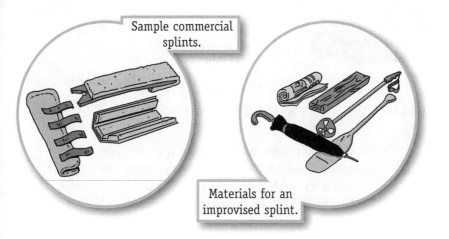

Sample commercial splints.

Materials for an improvised splint.

Other Materials Needed for Splinting

To put the splint on you will need materials for padding and bandages. **Padding** does two things:

▲ It fills in the natural hollows between the body and the splint, ensuring the injured limb is properly supported.

▲ It makes the splint more comfortable.

Always pad between a splint and the injured limb, and between two body parts to be bandaged together.

Bandages are used to secure the splint to the body. If you have triangular bandages, fold and use them as broad bandages. When using bandages:

▲ Make sure they are wide enough to provide firm support without discomfort.

▲ Pass them under the natural hollows of the body — go under the knee, the small of the back, the hollow behind the ankles.

▲ Tie them tightly enough to prevent movement, but not so tight they cut off circulation. Check circulation below any bandages you've tied every 15 minutes.

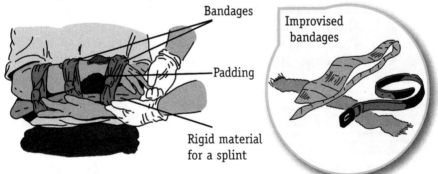

Bandages

Improvised bandages

Padding

Rigid material for a splint

First Aid for an Insect Bite or Sting

1. Begin emergency scene management. (See first part of this chapter for full explanation of emergency scene management.) Do a scene survey. Do a primary survey and give first aid for the ABCs (see page 265). Examine the sting site closely, looking for

the stinger that may still be in the skin. If it is there, remove it by carefully scraping it and the attached poison sac from the skin. Don't use tweezers, fingers or anything that may squeeze more poison into the body.

2. For the irritation at the site of the sting, apply rubbing alcohol, a weak ammonia solution or a paste of baking soda and water. Ice can also be used. Don't use alcohol or ammonia near the eyes.

Scrape the stinger and poison sack from the skin with a sharp edge, like a knife blade or a credit card.

Use a paste of baking soda and water to relieve the irritation.

If the sting is in the mouth, give the person a mouthwash of one teaspoonful of baking soda in a glass of water, or a piece of ice to suck on. If there is swelling in the mouth, or if there is difficulty breathing, monitor the person closely and get medical help.

Ticks

Ticks are found in abundance throughout the forests in some parts of Canada. They drop from the foliage onto animals and humans, biting through the skin and anchoring themselves to the tissue with barbed mouth parts. A tick will suck the host's (the person or animal) blood for many hours and may become quite large. At the end of the meal, the tick detaches itself and drops off.

Poison from the tick may be harmful. They sometimes carry disease that can be transmitted to humans. A tick on the body should be removed. If one tick is found, check your body and clothing thoroughly for others.

Types of Burns

Heat Burns (also called "thermal" burns)

Burns from too much heat applied to the body are the most familiar kind of burns. Common heat sources include open flames (like candles or fire), and hot objects (like stoves or car engines). A scald is a heat burn caused by hot liquid or steam. Heat burns can also be caused by friction.

Radiation Burns

Most people have experienced a radiation burn in the form of a sunburn, where the sun is the source of radiant energy. Other types of radiant energy that can cause burns include X-rays, arc welder's flash and radiation from radioactive material.

Recognizing Burns

Use the signs and symptoms of burns to recognize them and determine the degree of the burn (sometimes this is difficult to do). The mechanism of injury will also give you clues as to the severity of the burn and whether the injury is critical.

First-Degree Burn

▲ Skin colour is pink or red

▲ Slight swelling

▲ Skin is dry

▲ Tenderness to severe pain in the injured area

Second-Degree Burn

▲ Skin looks raw and is mottled red in colour

▲ Skin is moist and ranges in colour from white to cherry red

▲ Blisters that contain clear fluid

▲ Extreme pain

Third-Degree Burn

▲ Skin is pearly-white, tan-cloured or charred black

▲ Skin is dry and leathery

▲ You may see blood vessels and bones under the skin

▲ Little or no pain (nerves are destroyed)

Burn Dressings

A good burn dressing is sterile, lint-free and won't stick to the injury when it is removed. If you don't have something like this, use something clean and lint-free, like a linen sheet.

A new type of burn dressing is the "gelled water" burn dressing. These sterile dressings are coated with a jelly-like substance that is mostly water. As such, the dressings are effective in cooling the burn, keeping it clean and providing pain relief. Use these dressings according to the instructions on the package.

First Aid for Radiation Burns

Radiation burns are caused by radiant energy — energy that radiates from a source. Sunburn and snowblindness are radiation burns caused by sunlight. Sunlamps at tanning parlours can also cause radiation burns to the skin and eyes. Other causes of radiation burns include X-rays and the flash of arc welding.

First Aid for Sunburn

Sunburns can range in severity from those that are mildly uncomfortable to those that are serious, cover a large portion of the body, and are complicated by heatstroke. For minor sunburn, give first aid as follows.

1. Begin emergency scene management and do a scene survey. (See the start of this chapter for more information.) Get out of the sun. Gently sponge the area with cool water or cover with a wet towel, to relieve the pain. Repeat this step as needed to relieve pain.

2. Pat the skin dry and put on a medicated sunburn ointment or lotion (these can cause an allergic reaction in some people). Apply the lotion according to directions on the package.

3. Protect burned areas from further exposure to the sun.

4. Don't break any blisters — doing so may promote infection. If large areas of the skin begin to blister, get medical help.

5. If the casualty begins to vomit, or develops a fever, give first aid for heatstroke and get medical help.

First Aid for Intense Light Burns to the Eye(s)

Burns to the eyes may be caused by intense light such as direct or reflected sunlight and arc welder's flash. Snowblindness is a common injury of this kind. As with a sunburn, the casualty may not feel the tissue damage happening, but will develop symptoms several hours after exposure.

Signs and symptoms include:

▲ Sensitivity to light

▲ Pain

▲ A gritty feeling in the eyes.

Give first aid as follows.

1. Begin emergency scene management; do a scene survey and a primary survey. (See the start of this chapter for more information.) Wash your hands or put gloves on if available.

2. Cover the eyes to cool them, and keep the light out.

The casualty will be temporarily blinded, so you must reassure her often and explain what you are doing. If the casualty doesn't want both eyes covered, even after an explanation and reassurance, then cover only one eye.

3. Get medical help and give ongoing casualty care.

Hypothermia

When hiking, be aware of the danger of hypothermia. This is the lowering of the body's temperature or loss of body heat faster than the body can produce it.

The normal temperature of the body's core is 37°C (98.6°F). If the body core temperature drops more than two degrees, the body's tissues cannot function properly. This state of generalized cooling is called hypothermia. Hypothermia is a condition that can be detected and corrected by a first aider if recognized early.

How the Body Loses Heat

There are five ways the body loses heat. The table below explains each of these. In an outdoor emergency, heat loss by conduction and convection (wet and wind) are often the main contributors to hypothermia. But when trying to prevent heat loss, you must look for all the ways the body is losing heat.

How the Body Loses Heat: Examples and Prevention		
Heat	Explanation	Prevention
1. Radiation	Heat radiates from the body into the air around it.	Wear a warm hat.
2. Breathing	Cold air is inhaled, warmed by the body and exhaled, causing heat loss.	Wear a parka with a "tunnel" hood or "ski-tube." The air you breath will be warmer than the outside air.
3. Evaporation	Body heat is used to evaporate liquid on the skin.	Keep your skin as dry as possible.
4. Conduction	Heat moves directly from the body to a cold object that the body is touching.	Don't get wet. Wear fabric next to your skin that moves the wet away (e.g. polypropylene).
5. Convection (wind chill)	The thin layer of warm air around the body is replaced by cooler air, which the body must now heat.	Wear windproof clothing with snug cuffs and collars to keep the wind out.

How the Body Adapts to Heat Loss

The body has a number of ways to minimize heat loss, and keep the body core warm. One of the first things the body does when it is losing heat is start shivering. The muscle action of shivering generates heat. By shivering, the body is trying to warm itself. If the body keeps getting colder, the blood vessels in the arms, legs and at the skin surface get smaller. This keeps the blood in the core, where it is warmest. By doing this, the body core uses the surface tissues to insulate itself from the cold.

If heat loss continues, the body processes get slower. This includes thinking, muscular action and the senses. Shivering will slow down and then stop. The muscles get stiff and movements become jerky. Thinking is confused, speech difficult and the senses dulled. The heart and breathing rates slow down and the person eventually loses consciousness. At this point, the condition is very serious. The heartbeat becomes unsteady and faint, and finally the heart stops beating.

When the heart stops beating, the person is considered dead. However, when body tissues are cold, they aren't damaged as easily by a lack of oxygen. For this reason, there is often a chance of resuscitating a hypothermic person who doesn't show any signs of life. This means that as long as you aren't putting yourself or others at risk, you should continue your rescue efforts to get a hypothermic casualty to medical help.

Signs of Hypothermia

There are three stages of hypothermia: mild, moderate and severe. The table below lists the signs for each stage, but it may be hard to tell exactly when one stage ends and another begins. Body temperatures are not listed here because the first aider has no practical way to take the temperature of the body's core.

Signs of Hypothermia			
Sign	Mild	Moderate	Severe
pulse	normal	slow and weak	weak, irregular or absent
breathing	normal	slow and shallow	weak, irregular or absent
appearance	shivering, slurred speech	shivering violently or stopped, clumsy, stumbling, pupils dilated, skin bluish	shivering has stopped
mental state	conscious but withdrawn or disinterested	confused, sleepy irrational	unconscious

Recognizing Hypothermia

The key to successful first aid for hypothermia is recognizing the casualty's condition as soon as possible, and then preventing hypothermia from getting worse. Hypothermia is the obvious thing to look for at the end of a cold winter day, but it is less obvious when the temperature is above zero. Be on the lookout for hypothermia whenever the temperature is below 20°C, the weather is windy, wet or both, or the casualty is in one of the groups at risk for hypothermia.

Sometimes hypothermia is mistaken for other conditions. Hypothermia has been mistaken for drunkenness, stroke and drug abuse. This often happens in the city, where a warm environment doesn't seem far away. For example, an elderly person's home may not feel cold to you since you are warmly dressed, but in fact the room temperature is 15°C, the elderly person is under-dressed, and is hypothermic.

And don't forget yourself. As soon as you begin to shiver, think "I've got to prevent further heat loss." If you don't, hypothermia will soon affect your mind, and you won't be able to think clearly enough to take the right actions.

First Aid for Hypothermia

First aid for hypothermia aims to prevent further heat loss and get medical help.

1. Begin emergency scene management and do a scene survey. (See start of chapter for more information.) If the temperature is lower than 15°C, suspect hypothermia either as the casualty's main problem or as a complication of another injury.

2. Take measures to prevent further heat loss:

   ▲ Cover exposed skin with suitable clothing or covers; make sure the head is well insulated.

   ▲ Adjust the casualty's clothing to keep wind or drafts out. Wrap the casualty in something windproof — reflective "space blankets" and plastic garbage bags are good for this.

   ▲ If possible, move the casualty out of the cool or cold environment. If you cannot move indoors, protect the casualty from the wind.

   ▲ Loosen or remove tight clothing.

Cautions in First Aid for Hypothermia

▲ Handle the casualty **very gently** and keep him horizontal if possible. Cold affects the electrical impulses that make the heart beat. As a result, the hypothermic casualty's heart beat is very delicate. The heart can stop with rough handling of the casualty.

▲ When checking for a pulse in a casualty who may be hypothermic, continue checking **for one to two minutes.** The heart may be beating very slowly or very faintly — you have to take longer to find the pulse.

▲ Don't give the casualty any alcohol, coffee, or other drinks with caffeine, or let him smoke. These can increase heat loss.

▲ Don't rub the casualty's body to improve circulation. This will cause cold blood to flow back to the body core and cool the body further.

▲ Wet clothing causes severe heat loss. If you are in a shelter and have a dry change of clothes, gently replace wet clothes with dry ones. If you are not sheltered, put the dry clothes over the wet clothes. If you don't have dry clothes, press as much water out of the wet clothes as possible and wrap the casualty with something windproof.

▲ Insulate the casualty from cold objects. Have him sit on a rolled-up jacket or lie on a blanket.

3. Get medical help. If you have to transport the casualty, transport in the recovery position.

4. Give ongoing casualty care, monitoring the ABCs. If breathing is ineffective, give assisted breathing. (See page 267.) If there is no pulse, give CPR, but don't delay transporting the casualty.

Frostbite

Frostbite refers to the freezing of tissues when exposed to temperatures below zero. It is a progressive injury with two stages: frostnip (superficial frostbite) and deep frostbite.

First Aid for Superficial Frostbite

1. Begin emergency scene management and do a scene survey. (See beginning of chapter for more information.) Gradually rewarm the frostbitten part with body heat.

   ▲ Cover frostbitten toes, ears, etc. with warm hands.

▲ Warm up frostbitten fingers by breathing on them or placing them in a warm area of the body like the armpit, abdomen or groin.

2. Take measures to prevent these areas from freezing again — either stop the activity or dress more appropriately.

Heat Exposure and Illnesses

Prolonged exposure to extreme heat or heavy exertion in a hot environment can cause heat illnesses.

Heat Cramps

Heat cramps are painful muscle cramps, usually in the legs and abdomen, caused by losing too much water and salt through sweating. Heat cramps are usually caused by heavy exercise or physical work in a hot environment. They are not serious and may be reversed by first aid. The casualty will complain of cramps and show signs of excessive sweating.

First Aid for Heat Cramps

1. Place the casualty at rest in a cool place.

2. Give the conscious casualty water to drink. She can have as much as she wants.

3. If the cramps don't go away, get medical help.

> **Cautions in First Aid for Frostbite**
>
> ▲ *Do not* rub the area. Tiny ice crystals in the tissues may cause more tissue damage.
>
> ▲ *Do not* rub snow on the area. This may cause further freezing and tissue damage from the rubbing.
>
> ▲ *Do not* apply direct heat. This may rewarm the area too quickly.

> In a dry environment, the casualty may not seem to be sweating because the sweat evaporates quickly.

Heat Exhaustion

Heat exhaustion is more serious than heat cramps. The casualty has lost fluid through sweating. Circulation is affected because the blood flows away from the major organs and pools in the blood vessels just below the skin.

Signs and Symptoms of Heat Exhaustion

▲ Excessive sweating and dilated pupils.

▲ Casualty may complain of dizziness, blurred vision, headache or cramps.

▲ Signs of shock, including: cold, clammy skin; weak, rapid pulse; rapid, shallow breathing; vomiting and unconsciousness.

First Aid for Heat Exhaustion

First aid for heat exhaustion combines the first aid for heat cramps with the first aid for shock.

1. Begin emergency scene management. Do a scene survey and a primary survey. (See the beginning of this chapter for more information.)

2. Send for medical help.

Shock position, conscious casualty

Recovery position, unconscious casualty

3. If the casualty is **conscious:**

▲ Place her at rest in a cool place with the feet and legs elevated (shock position).

▲ Remove excessive clothing and loosen tight clothing at the neck and waist.

▲ Give her water to drink, as much as she will take. If the casualty vomits, don't give anything by mouth and get medical help right away.

If the casualty is **unconscious:**

▲ Place her in the recovery position.

▲ Get medical help right away.

▲ Monitor breathing and pulse and give life-saving first aid as needed.

4. Give ongoing casualty care until medical help takes over.

Heatstroke (Sunstroke)

Heatstroke is a life-threatening condition where the body's temperature rises far above normal. It is caused by prolonged exposure to a hot, humid, and perhaps poorly ventilated environment. In classic heatstroke, the body's temperature control mechanism fails, sweating stops and the body temperature rises rapidly. In **exertional heatstroke,** the body temperature rises rapidly due to heavy physical exertion in high temperatures, even though sweating continues. Elderly people and those in poor health are more likely to suffer from heatstroke. Without immediate first aid, heatstroke can result in permanent brain damage or death.

Signs and Symptoms of Heatstroke

▲ Body temperature rapidly rises to 40°C or higher. The casualty is hot to the touch.

▲ The pulse is rapid and full but gets weaker in later stages.

▲ Breathing is noisy.

▲ Skin is flushed, hot and dry in classic heatstroke, and flushed, hot and sweaty in exertional heatstroke.

▲ Casualty is restless and may complain of headache, fatigue, dizziness and nausea.

▲ Vomiting, convulsions, unconsciousness.

You can tell the difference between heat exhaustion and heatstroke by the condition of the skin. In heat exhaustion, the skin is moist and cold. In heatstroke, the skin is hot, flushed and may be dry or wet.

Skin is flushed and hot, and may be wet or dry

First Aid for Heatstroke

1. Begin emergency scene management and do a scene survey. Lowering body temperature is the most urgent first aid for heatstroke. The casualty's life depends on how quickly this can be done.

   ▲ Move the casualty to a cool, shaded place.

   ▲ Cool the casualty. Remove outer clothing and either:

Cover her with wet sheets and fan the sheets to increase cooling.

Put the casualty into a cool bath; watch her closely.

Sponge the casualty with cool water, particularly in the armpits, neck and groin areas.

2. When her body feels cool to touch, cover her with a dry sheet. Put the conscious casualty into the shock position, and the unconscious casualty into the recovery position. Monitor the casualty closely. If her temperature begins to rise again, repeat the cooling process.

3. Give ongoing casualty care until hand-over to medical help.

Rescue Carries

Pick-a-Back

This carry is used for a conscious casualty with lower limb injuries, provided he can use his arms. The casualty must be able to help get into position on your back or be already seated at chair or table height.

1. Crouch with your back between the casualty's knees.

2. Have the casualty hold on around your neck.

3. Support the casualty's legs and lift. Use your leg muscles to stand up, keeping your back straight.

Human Crutch

If a leg or foot is injured, help the casualty to walk on his good leg while you give support to the injured side.

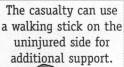

The casualty can use a walking stick on the uninjured side for additional support.

1. Take the weight of the casualty's injured side on your shoulders by placing the casualty's arm on the injured side around your neck and grasp the wrist firmly.

2. Reach around the casualty's back with your free hand, and grasp his clothing at the waist.

3. Tell the casualty to step off with you, each using the inside foot. This lets you, the rescuer, take the casualty's weight on the injured side.

Step off with the inside foot.

Rescuer is on the injured side.

Two-Hand Seat

A casualty who is unable to support his upper body can be carried by two rescuers, using the two-hand seat.

1. The rescuers crouch on either side of the casualty.

2. Each rescuer reaches across the casualty's back to grasp his clothing at the waist on the opposite side.

3. Each rescuer passes his other hand under the thighs, keeping his fingers bent and holding padding to protect against the

fingernails. Hook the bent fingers together to form a rigid seat. Alternatively, the rescuers can hold each other's wrists.

4. The rescuers lift with their legs, keeping their backs straight. Once in the standing position, the rescuers adjust their hands and arms for comfort. When the casualty is securely positioned, the bearers step off together, each using the inside foot.

Four-Hand Seat

A conscious casualty who can use his hands and arms can be carried on a four-hand seat by two rescuers.

1. Each rescuer grasps his own left wrist with his right hand, then grasps the right wrist of the other rescuer with his left hand to form a square.

2. Tell the casualty to put his arms around the rescuers' shoulders and hoist himself up to permit the bearers to pass their hands under the buttocks to position them under the thighs at a point of balance.

3. Instruct the casualty to hold onto the rescuers' shoulders to keep his balance and support his upper body.

4. The bearers step off together, each using the inside foot.

Stretchers

There may be times when medical help cannot be contacted, or for other reasons, cannot come to the scene. When this happens, transport the casualty to medical help. If the casualty can't walk, or if the injury or illness allows only the most gentle movement, a stretcher should be used.

Commercial Stretchers

The most common of the commercial stretchers is the rigid-pole, canvas stretcher. It has hinged bracing bars at right angles between the rigid poles at either end that must be locked in the extended position before the stretcher is used.

Improvised Stretchers

If a commercially prepared stretcher is not available, you can improvise one by using a tabletop, door, or two rigid poles and a blanket, clothing or grain sacks. Don't use non-rigid stretchers like this for casualties with suspected head or spinal injuries.

Improvised Blanket Stretcher

1. Place the blanket flat on the ground and place a pole one-third of the way from one end. Fold the one-third length of blanket over the pole.

2. Place the second pole parallel to the first so that it is on the doubled part of the blanket, about 15 cm (6 in) from the doubled edge.

3. Fold the remaining blanket over the two poles. The casualty's weight on the blanket holds the folds in place.

Improvised Jacket Stretcher

A non-rigid stretcher can also be improvised from two jackets and two or four poles.

> **Warning**
>
> Test an improvised stretcher with someone equal to or heavier than the casualty, to ensure that it will hold.
>
> Check the clearance of an improvised stretcher to ensure that it will pass through hallways, doors and stairways without harm to the casualty.

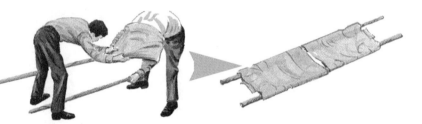

1. Button and zipper the jackets closed and pull the sleeves inside out so that the sleeves are inside. Lay the jackets on the ground so that the top edge of one jacket meets the bottom edge of the other.

2. Pass the poles through the sleeves of the two jackets on either side to complete the stretcher.

3. If the casualty is tall, prepare another jacket as before and add it to the stretcher with the head of the jacket towards the middle.

For more information and/or first aid training in your area, contact the local Red Cross or St. John Ambulance.

CHAPTER 14

▶ Weathering the Outdoors

Weather. It surrounds us everyday, all the time. It affects what we do, and how we do it. It can make life miserable. It can make life pleasurable. We better not take it for granted if we want enjoyable outdoor experiences!

Planning a simple outdoor game during a weekly meeting; going on a week-long winter hike; setting out in a canoe on a deceptively calm and pleasant summer's day; hiking in blistering summer heat. In all these scenarios, weather plays a major role. Most mistakes we make 'reading' the weather amount to little more than inconveniences. Some provide fond, even humorous, memories. However, those who take the weather for granted may find themselves unexpectedly facing a life-threatening situation. Learn to avoid these dangers.

Nature may surprise us occasionally, but by increasing our weather knowledge, we can avoid having a weather hazard turn into a disaster. Be prepared!

All weather starts with the sun. Its rays warm areas at the equator more than the poles; then the warmer air starts moving north or south toward the cold polar air. But the Earth is also spinning constantly, warming up during the day and cooling at night. The seasons, caused by Earth's tilted path through space, add to the complexity of weather patterns. Though it may seem hopelessly confusing, nature has taken care of everything. The result is a planet where water exists, where food can be harvested, and where we can live.

The sun, itself a nuclear furnace, sends energy through space which arrives at the top of the Earth's atmosphere. After many centuries, our atmosphere developed protection systems for life on Earth. For example, X-rays cannot penetrate the atmosphere. Ultraviolet radiation (UV) is selectively filtered out on its way to the surface. Only a small fraction of it reaches the ground.

Water vapour is the atmospheric gas that most affects weather. All life on Earth is based on water, and it exists in all three states: solid (ice), liquid (water) and gaseous (water vapour). Water evaporates from puddles, lakes, rivers and oceans into the atmosphere as vapour, where it is carried along for sometimes thousands of kilometres. Water vapour forms clouds and then eventually returns to the earth in some form of precipitation (snow, rain, hail, sleet).

Water vapour contains energy — billions and billions of heat units which, when released in small quantities, cause changing weather patterns. If released in large quantities, water vapour can cause severe weather.

If you want to understand weather, you need some basic knowledge of its common elements: pressure, wind, temperature, humidity, clouds,

Weather elements: Pressure - Wind - Temperature - Humidity - Cloud - Precipitation - Severe Weather/Weather Extreme

precipitation and severe weather. With these, you'll be able to understand weather forecasts. You may even be able to do some short-term forecasting when out on a hike or canoe trip.

Atmospheric Pressure

Air has weight. Its weight changes as it warms or cools. For example, when air warms up, it expands. As it expands, it gets lighter than the cooler air around it, and rises. (This is how a hot air balloon rises.) On a weather map, the high pressures are normally marked as *High* and the low pressures labeled as *Low*.

Whenever there is uneven pressure, air from the High regions will move toward the Low regions. This moving air is called wind.

Wind

Differences in air pressure cause wind. "Wind" is what we call moving air as it goes from a higher pressure area toward a lower pressure area. But nature is complex; instead of moving in a straight line from High to Low

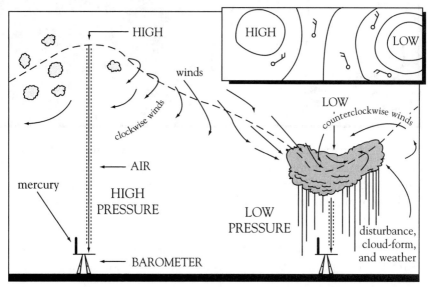

centres, the air currents tend to curve. This produces rotating wind patterns around pressure centres. What's more, depending on pressure differences, the air doesn't always move at the same speed; it can vary from light breezes to hurricane force gales.

This type of wind is associated with large weather systems. But there's another wind phenomenon that can affect a canoeist paddling along a lake shore: the land-sea breeze.

Often, on a calm summer morning, the day looks very promising — a perfect day for a paddle. By noon, a light breeze has started which still poses no problem. By mid-afternoon though, choppy water is building up on all sides of the canoe, causing the paddler to fight through the growing swells. Unskilled paddlers (or sailors) can find themselves exhausted in the breeze. Then, by late afternoon or mid-evening, all is calm again.

A sea breeze (wind that comes from the water towards land) is created during a day when the sun heats up the shoreline, thereby warming the air above it. Since land heats up faster than water, the air over the shore is lighter than its surroundings. It rises and draws air from over the water to fill the void. As the sun stops heating the land later in the day, the air is no longer warmed and therefore no longer rises. The breeze stops.

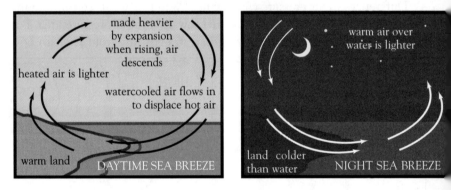

made heavier by expansion when rising, air descends

heated air is lighter

watercooled air flows in to displace hot air

warm land

DAYTIME SEA BREEZE

warm air over water is lighter

land colder than water

NIGHT SEA BREEZE

A land breeze (wind from land heading out over water) is created in the opposite way. It often occurs at night. Since water retains heat better than land, air above the water may be heated more than the air over the shore. The land breeze may become a hazard if you are caught out on open water at night.

Wind Scale (Estimating Wind Velocity)

In 1805, Admiral Beaufort of the British Navy developed a scale to estimate wind speeds. His scale has been modified for use on land and is shown

THE BEAUFORT WIND SCALE

No.	Title	Effect Of Wind		Km/h
0	Calm	Smoke rises vertically		0-1
1	Light air	Smoke drifts		1-5
2	Light breeze	Leaves rustle		6-11
3	Gentle breeze	Flags fly		12-19
4	Moderate breeze	Dust, loose paper raised		20-28
5	Fresh breeze	Small trees sway		29-38
6	Strong breeze	Difficult to use umbrellas		39-49
7	Moderate gale	Difficult to walk		50-61
8	Fresh gale	Twigs break off trees		62-74
9	Strong gale	Slight damage to roofs		75-88
10	Whole gale	Trees uprooted		89-102
11	Storm	Widespread damage		103-117
12	Hurricane	Devastation		Above 117

above. For example, Beaufort number 4, indicates winds of 20-28 km/h (13-18 mph). This would be a moderate breeze which sets small branches in motion.

Temperature

Temperatures in Canada range from - 45°C during winter to 45°C in summer. Occasionally, some days will exceed these limits. Before heading out for a day of vigorous activity, know what temperature to expect; this will affect the type of clothing, food and drinking supplies your group will need.

Heat exhaustion, heat stroke and wind chill are especially important to guard against. (See Chapter 13 for first aid information.) Heat exhaustion is caused by the body's inability to cool itself properly when it gets too warm. The body normally cools by sweating (a process which requires plenty of liquids in the body), and evaporation of that sweat from the skin (which requires both light clothes and air which is dry enough to evaporate the sweat). Some days are so hot and muggy that your body isn't able to evaporate sweat. At these times, stick to light exercise, and drink plenty of liquids in the shade.

Wind chill refers to the temperature which your body "thinks" exists during windy conditions. Your body gauges how much cooling is taking place at the skin level (no matter what the cause) in order to determine how to replace that lost heat. In windy conditions, more heat is lost from the skin than in calm conditions. The "wind chill factor" tells us what temperature the body feels, rather than the temperature which the thermometer measures. Scouts and leaders should always pay attention to wind chill. (You'll find a wind chill table in Chapter 8, page 159.)

Humidity and Precipitation

"Humidity" refers to the amount of water vapour in the air. Meteorologists measure it in two ways:

▲ By determining how many grams of water occur in a cubic meter of air, or

▲ By calculating the percentage of moisture. One hundred percent humidity represents the maximum amount of water vapour air is capable of holding.

A forecast describing 100 percent humidity also probably includes fog, drizzle, rain, sleet, or snow, depending on the outside temperature. Though warm air can hold more water vapour than cold air, when it nears 100 percent humidity, expect precipitation.

What is precipitation?

It is simply water falling out of the sky. Precipitation can come as a liquid (rain), or as a solid (snow). Depending on whether the water vapour has been frozen, then thawed and refrozen, other forms of precipitation include: freezing rain, drizzle, sleet, hail, ice pellets and snow grains.

Clouds

> **Did You Know...?**
>
> Clouds have weight! A typical fair-weather cumulus cloud (the puffy type you see on a sunny summer day) weighs more than a jumbo jet, yet it doesn't fall out of the sky

Clouds are formed when air is cooled below its saturation point (i.e. 100 percent humidity) and the water vapour in the air condenses into tiny droplets or ice crystals. These are so light that they float.

All clouds are created through the same general process, but because of other factors, they appear in different forms. Understanding when the various cloud types form can provide valuable weather clues.

Latin names describe cloud formations. There are three general cloud types: *Cirrus* (feather-like), *Stratus* (in a layer) and *Cumulus* (in big heaps). Furthermore, meteorologists break these down into high clouds, middle clouds and low clouds, based on their typical height above ground. There are a few exceptions; the one most common to us is the *Cumulo Nimbus*, which crosses all levels.

High Clouds

High clouds are made up entirely of tiny ice crystals. The bottoms are about 6,000 meters above the earth. Two types are common:

1. *Cirrus* are thin wispy and feathery. They are frequently blown by high winds into feathery strands called *Mare's Tails*.

2. *Cirro Stratus* form at about 7,500 meters and are thin sheets that look like white veils. Both the sun and the moon shine through them, making rings of hazy light called halos.

Middle Clouds

Middle clouds are usually either layered (i.e. stratus) and puffy (i.e. cumulus) or combinations of these. Their bases are around 3,000 meters above the earth.

1. *Alto Stratus* are dense veils or sheets of grey that often appear fibrous or lightly striped. The sun or the moon does not form a halo, but from the ground appears as if seen through a frosted glass.

2. *Alto Cumulus* are grey or whitish patches, or layers, of puffy or roll-like clouds. Shining through, the sun often appears as a disk.

Low Clouds

Low clouds have bases near the Earth's surface.

1. *Stratus* form as low, uniform grey masses covering the entire sky. These clouds may bring light drizzle, but almost never heavy rain.

2. *Nimbo Stratus* are thicker than stratus clouds, and very grey. They cut off the sun and usually bring continuous rain.

3. *Cumulus* are puffy, white, and often look like cauliflower. The shapes change constantly. Over land, cumulus often form by day and disappear at night. Unless they pile up, they usually mean fair weather.

4. *Strato Cumulus* are irregular masses of clouds spread out in a rolling or puffy layer. They appear as grey with dark shading.

Other Clouds

Cumulo Nimbus are the familiar thunderheads. Bases almost touch the ground, but tops can reach 23,000 meters. Winds shape the tops into flat, anvil-like forms.

Severe Weather and Weather Extremes

Whenever you hear of severe weather and weather extremes, heed the warnings. Too often, people become fascinated with the phenomenon, ignore the danger and place themselves needlessly at great risk. Always be alert for approaching weather dangers, including:

- ▲ Thunderstorms
- ▲ Lightning
- ▲ Strong winds
- ▲ Heavy rains
- ▲ Flash floods
- ▲ Tornadoes
- ▲ Cold temperatures (frostbite, hypothermia)
- ▲ Hot temperatures (heat stroke, hyperthermia)
- ▲ Sunburn
- ▲ Snow blindness
- ▲ Blizzard
- ▲ Drought conditions (extreme dryness, which can mean fire hazards).

Air Masses and Weather Fronts

An air mass is a large body of air that has similar temperature and moisture properties throughout. The characteristics of an air mass usually reflect the region where it originated. Maritime air masses are more humid than continental types. A weather front is the place where two different air masses meet — a zone where active weather usually occurs.

When a warmer air mass is pushing away a colder air mass, we describe it as a "warm front." If the opposite occurs (i.e. cold air is pushing away warm air), it's called a "cold front." As High and Low pressure centres drift across a continent, air masses circulate around them. Knowledge of the pressure changes will help you forecast upcoming weather. Since few people carry a barometer to measure pressure changes, they can study cloud formations over several hours. With a general understanding of air masses and fronts, almost anyone should be able to predict imminent weather fairly accurately. Study the accompanying diagrams. Knowing how to identify cloud types will help you forecast weather.

Weather Forecasting

What is a weather forecast? How is it made? What details appear in a weather forecast? How do you get a forecast?

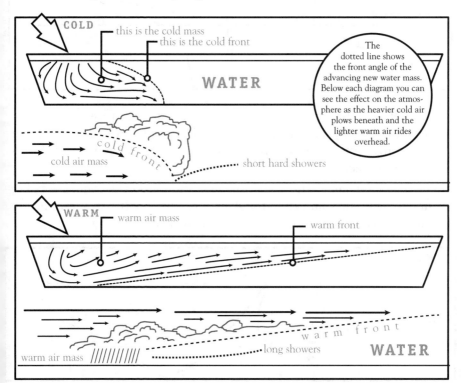

Weather forecasts are predictions of the weather covering several days. Meteorologists conduct forecasts by observing weather patterns all over the world. They feed these observations into supercomputers that make predictions using mathematical formulas. In Canada, Environment Canada is responsible for making weather forecasts.

Most weather forecasts detail predictions of the temperature, sky conditions (e.g. sunny, cloudy), and weather characteristics (e.g. rain, snow, strong winds). If a meteorologist foresees severe conditions, the forecaster will issue a warning of these upcoming events. *Never ignore official weather advisories or warnings.* Use them to make alternate plans, or to prepare yourself. People who ignore weather warnings are making a dangerous mistake.

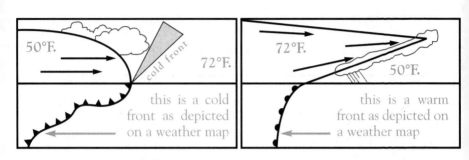

50°F.

cold front

72°F.

this is a cold
front as depicted
on a weather map

72°F.

50°F.

this is a warm
front as depicted on
a weather map

Before setting out on an outdoor adventure, get a weather forecast from local newspapers, televisions or radios. When in the field, rely on radio broadcasts. As well, park rangers often post weather forecasts for all campers to see.

But most importantly, learn to read the signs of upcoming weather fronts. By keeping an eye on the skies, you'll have reasonable lead time to take necessary precautions, winter or summer. Heed the signs!

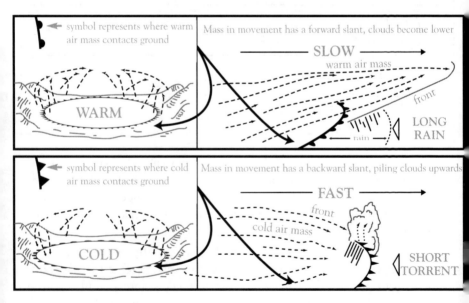

symbol represents where warm
air mass contacts ground

Mass in movement has a forward slant, clouds become lower

SLOW

warm air mass

front

WARM

rain

LONG
RAIN

symbol represents where cold
air mass contacts ground

Mass in movement has a backward slant, piling clouds upwards

FAST

front

cold air mass

COLD

SHORT
TORRENT

Forecasting for Yourself: Some Simple Rules.

David Phillips of Environment Canada has prepared a handy list of practical weather signs (below) that can provide hints for those wanting to forecast the weather. By noting cloud formations, wind direction, sky colour, and temperature and moisture changes, you can often accurately predict sunshine and rain, calms and storms.

Look for Cloudy, Unsettled Weather When:

▲ The barometer falls steadily.

▲ The wind blows strongly in the early morning.

▲ The temperature at night is higher than usual, owing to clouds.

▲ The temperature is far above (or below) normal for the time of year.

▲ Clouds rapidly move in various directions at different levels.

▲ High, thin, wispy clouds begin dominating the sky. They thicken and drop lower to the ground, sometimes producing a ring or halo around the sun or moon.

▲ Clouds darken on a summer afternoon.

▲ High- and/or middle-level clouds darken and move from the south and southwest.

▲ The sunrise is red.

Look for Steady Rain or Snow When:

▲ The barometer falls steadily. (If the pressure falls slowly, rain or snow will come within a day; if it falls rapidly, expect precipitation very soon.)

▲ Winds blow from the southeast to northeast and north.

▲ Clouds are low and uniformly flat and grey.

> ## Did You Know...?
>
> In Canada and the United States, a special radio frequency broadcasts weather information continually, 24 hours a day. A radio equipped to receive this special frequency is available in some stores.
>
> Before going into remote areas, check with either a local Environment Canada office or the U.S. National Weather Service Office to see if you can receive the broadcast from the area.

▲ Leaves show their undersides. Strong south winds, running ahead of the rain, will flip the leaves over.

▲ There is a ring around the sun or moon.

Look for More Bright Weather When:

▲ The barometer is steady or rising slowly.

▲ A gentle breeze blows steadily from the west to north.

▲ Winds swing from south to southwest, or from east or northeast to the northwest.

▲ Cloud (amount and number) decreases in the late afternoon.

▲ Cloud base rises, and humidity decreases.

▲ Evening sky is clear, and the setting sun looks like a ball of fire.

▲ Morning fog breaks within two hours of sunrise.

▲ The night before, heavy dew or frost occurs.

▲ The moon shines brightly, and the wind is light.

▲ A bright blue sky has high, thin wisps of cloud.

Look for Fog When:

▲ Warm winds are blowing humid air across a much colder surface (either land or sea).

▲ The sky is clear, the winds are light, and the air was humid the night before.

▲ Warm rain is falling ahead of the warm air.

▲ Water temperatures are warm, and the air is much colder.

Look for Clearing Skies When:

▲ The barometer rises.

▲ The wind shifts to any westerly direction (especially from east through south to the west).

▲ The temperature falls rapidly, especially in the afternoon.

▲ Increasing breaks appear in the overcast.

▲ Clouds become lumpy.

▲ Dark clouds become lighter and steadily rise in altitude.

▲ Fog lifts before noon.

▲ Frost or dew is on the grass.

Look for Showers (Thundershowers) When:

▲ The barometer falls.

▲ Winds blow from the south or southeast.

▲ The morning temperature is unusually high, air is moist and sticky, and you see cumulus clouds building (rain probably within six hours).

▲ Dark, threatening thunderclouds develop in a westerly wind.

▲ Thick, fluffy clouds develop rapidly upwards during early afternoon.

▲ You hear loud static on your AM radio (thunderstorms within the hour).

Look for Heavy Snow When:

▲ The barometer falls rapidly.

▲ Winds blow from the east or northeast.

▲ The air temperature is between -10°C and -1°C.

▲ A storm lies to the south and east of you.

Look for Temperatures to Rise When:

▲ The wind shifts from the north or west to the south.

▲ The nighttime sky is overcast with a moderate southerly wind.

▲ The sky is clear all day.

Look for Temperatures to Fall When:

▲ The barometer rises steadily (in winter).

▲ The wind shifts into the north or northwest from the south.

▲ The wind is light and the sky is clear at night.

▲ Skies are clearing, especially in the winter.

▲ Snow flurries occur with a west or north wind.

Final Forecast

A "forecast" (as the word implies) foretells upcoming weather you can expect over the next hours or days. Forecasts are not always perfect. Weather conditions can vary considerably even several kilometres away. The effects of valleys, shorelines, altitude and distance can significantly alter local conditions. Speak to people living in the area you plan to visit, learn the region's idiosyncrasies, and always heed severe weather warning signs.

Weather can be wonderful. Weather can be dangerous. Because no one can ever control the weather, a wise Scout is prepared for the unexpected.

CHAPTER ⑮

▶ Natural History

Where We Live: Planet Earth

Earth and eight other planets (together with the sun) make up our solar system. It forms part of the Milky Way Galaxy.

Earth is a planet, a large cold body, with no light of its own except that which reflects from the sun. Between Earth and the sun are the planets Mercury and Venus. Venus is sometimes called the Evening or Morning Star because it appears in the west at dusk and in the east at dawn.

Further away from the sun than the Earth are Mars (sometimes called the "red" planet), Jupiter, Saturn, Uranus, Neptune and Pluto. Between Mars and Jupiter whirl asteroids — two thousand or more 'baby' planets — some of them over several kilometres in diameter. You can sometimes see Mars, Jupiter and Saturn with the naked eye as bright spots in the sky. Occasionally you may also see Mercury in the early morning or evening.

Planets follow their own paths around the sun. Early astronomers noticed that the paths of planets were not straight, but contained loops. After studying the loops, astronomers decided the sun was the centre of our solar system and not the Earth, as people thought at one time.

The Earth is not a smooth, round ball floating in space. Its plains, mountains, oceans and deserts make up the planet's crust. These create different environments. In Canada, we have mountains in British Columbia, plains on the Prairies, valleys in Ontario, and rocky land in Northern Ontario, Quebec and the Maritimes.

The Sun

The sun in our solar system is a star like all the rest. It appears so hot, large and brilliant because it's so much closer to Earth than other stars. The sun is about 150 million kilometres away. The nearest star, Sirius, is 25 times as bright as our sun, but it is much farther away — 80 trillion kilometres away in fact. Here's a way to picture the immense distance. Imagine this dot • is the Earth, and the sun is about 30 meters away. Sirius would still be more than 16,093 kilometres away!

The sun is so large that 109 Earths could be placed in a line side by side across the surface of it. They wouldn't remain there for very long as the terrific heat (5,537°C or 10,000°F) would turn them into vapour in a flash.

Without the sun's heat and light, Earth would be lifeless. Our planet turns on its axis and also revolves around the sun, creating night and day, and the seasons. We tell time by this movement. Using the sun and stars, skilled navigators can determine their exact position anywhere on earth.

Moons

Though some planets have many moons or satellites circling them, Earth has only one moon, which is 386,232 kilometres away.

The moon itself does not give off light; instead it reflects sunlight. Lighter and darker patches on the moon's surface appear like a face — the "man in the moon." Lunar mountains and plains reflecting sunlight create these patches. Besides lighting up the Earth at night, the moon's attraction has an important effect on our oceans. Its gravitational pull causes the rise and fall of oceanic water levels twice each day; these are called "tides."

Life on Earth

Life on earth exists in a delicate balance.

"Each living thing on Earth is a spark of sunlight caught in a vast web of life. And each living thing is connected through the energy and material strands of that web to every other living thing." — **Steven Van Matre**

The Web of Life

"Light, air, water, and soil are the elements of life,

Life is divided into producers, consumers, and decomposers,

Everything is becoming something else;

Everything has a home.

Homes in a defined area form a community;

Inhabitants of these communities live together in competition,

Cooperation, or neutrality.

Man is the chief predator." — **Steven Van Matre**

One way to illustrate how people affect the environment and thus the "web of life," is to look at Van Matre's definition. In particular, let's consider the line, "Everything is becoming something else." Pick anything, and look at what it is made of, what it does and what it will be in 100 years. Left undisturbed, nature will guide it through its life cycle. When people interfere, the cycle is often disrupted, causing irreparable damage.

Van Matre states, "The Earth is in trouble, and we are the problem." Here's a more positive way to look at it. "The Earth is in trouble, and we are the solution."

Before we can reduce our impact ("live more lightly on the Earth") we must first understand how things work.

All living things depend on light, air, water and soil for survival. When these are present and plentiful, plants and animals can survive within an "ecosystem" — a community made up of all animals, plants, and bacteria which co-exist within a given environment. Ecosystems operate through two basic patterns: cycles (water and food), and successions (plant and animal).

Water Cycle

Long ago, people thought water sprang from an ever-flowing source deep in the centre of the Earth. About 350 years ago, an English astronomer (Edmund Halley) discovered the amount of water flowing in streams was about the same as the amount of water falling in areas drained by them. Since then, scientists have learned that water moves in a continuous flow from the sky to the earth, to the sea and back to the sky again. This movement of water is known as the "water cycle," or "hydrologic cycle."

Precipitation is the moisture which falls to Earth as rain, hail, sleet or snow. The total amount of precipitation varies from place to place. For example, 25 centimetres of moisture may fall in the north each year, while Toronto gets an average of 76 cm. Some parts of Vancouver Island get well over 254 cm per year. (One place in India — Sherrapunji — holds the world's record of 2,540 cm of moisture.)

Evaporation

Evaporation is the changing of water, ice or snow into vapour. Water left in a pail gradually disappears; it evaporates into the air. How fast it evaporates depends on how much moisture is already in the air, and whether the air can absorb any more. The diagram of the water cycle shows that evaporation takes place as moisture falls; it occurs from all surfaces on which it lands.

Plants and animals also play a major role in the water cycle. Not only do they consume moisture to survive and grow, they process it and release it once again to the atmosphere through transpiration (plants), and respiration or perspiration (animals). This moisture, together with the moisture evaporated from streams and elsewhere, collects in the form of clouds. Once the cloud reaches a saturation point, moisture falls back to Earth. Then it becomes part of the stream again, or is absorbed by the soil; from the soil it goes to the plant or animals again as the cycle continues.

Chemical Makeup of Water

Water is made from two chemicals: hydrogen and oxygen. The chemical symbol for water is H_2O. This means water is made from two parts hydrogen and one part oxygen. Interestingly, hydrogen alone is very explosive and oxygen alone is highly flammable, but together they form a solution that puts out fires.

Water behaves differently than any other liquid. At 0°C, water becomes a solid — ice. At 100°C, it becomes a gas — steam. Water is unique because it is *lighter as a solid* than it is as a liquid. (That's why ice floats on top of water. If ice didn't float, lakes and other water bodies would freeze from the bottom up, preventing fish and other marine life from surviving winter months.

Uses of Water

Life can't exist without water. It's one of Earth's most important resources. Water makes up 71 percent of the human body. We must drink several litres of water a day to stay healthy. It cycles through our body flushing waste, diluting enzymes, and carrying nutrients. Water is so vital that an average

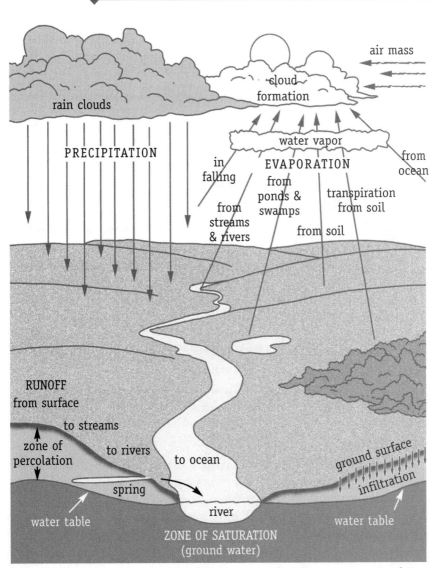

air mass

cloud formation

rain clouds

water vapor

PRECIPITATION

in falling

EVAPORATION

from streams & rivers

from ponds & swamps

from ocean

transpiration from soil

from soil

RUNOFF from surface

to streams

zone of percolation

to rivers

to ocean

ground surface

spring

infiltration

water table

river

water table

ZONE OF SATURATION (ground water)

Canadian home uses more than 450 litres per day! Farms, too, use plenty of water; a cow drinks up to seven litres every day.

Plants need water, too; a big tree may use up to 1,350 litres on a summer's day. Plants also use water for growth, for cooling, and for respiration — the way a plant breathes. It takes in carbon dioxide and gives off oxygen during the day; at night it takes in oxygen and gives off carbon dioxide.

Food Chain Cycle

The path of energy through an ecosystem is called the "food chain." Food chains are very important because they help maintain a very delicate ecological balance. When the food chain is undisturbed it keeps itself in check. For example, where grass is plentiful, mice and rabbits will flourish; where there are lots of mice and rabbits, birds and foxes will flour-

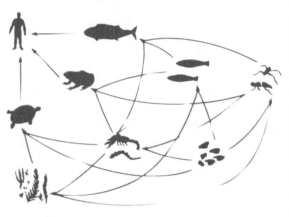

ish, and so on. When the number of fox and rabbits increases because of the abundance of food, they will gradually reach a point where the food supply will not support their numbers. When this happens the fox and rabbits will die from hunger. As their numbers decrease, the grass will come back and the number of mice and rabbits will grow again. Thus, the cycle continues.

This cycle consists of "producers, consumers and decomposers." It begins with plants — "producers" for the ecosystem. The plants pass through the "consumer stage" and end as "decomposers."

Producers

Plants provide most of Earth's food from materials they take from the air, sunlight, water and soil. As plants grow, they also produce oxygen; this helps replenish the atmosphere's supply. Nutrients are stored in the plants until they are consumed by animals or insects.

Consumers

All animals require food to stay alive. Some animals (herbivores, like rabbits, mice and cows) eat plants only; other animals (carnivores, like wolves, bird of prey, and snakes) eat other animals for survival. Herbivores have digestive systems that break down and digest plants only. Carnivores are one step removed from plants in the food chain. They don't consume plants directly, but instead feed on other animals. For example, a worm eats leaves or grass, a bird eats the worm, and a fox eats the bird.

Each plant or animal provides food for animals high above it on the food chain, and each plays a role in controlling the plant or animal population below it on the chain.

Some animals (including humans and bears) are omnivorous — they eat both flesh and plants.

Decomposers

All animals, carnivores, herbivores and omnivores digest their food. Once their bodies have taken the nutrients from the food, they excrete the remnants as feces. This waste, along with dead plants and animals, falls to the ground or to the bottom of a body of water. When other smaller animals and insects pick through it, eating what they can, the rest of the waste will decompose further. Eventually it will break down even more until soil and plants absorb it entirely. Once again it will provide food for animals. Thus the cycle continues.

Other terms applied to animals are predator and prey. Predators are insects or animals that feed on other animals which become the prey. Some animals are both predators and prey. For example, bears are predators when they are fishing and hunting for their food, but they become prey when people hunt them.

Plant Succession

Just like animals, plants must compete for food, water, space and sunlight to survive. As plants grow, they alter their environment, making it suitable for new and different plants to grow. Eventually, these replace the original plants. This process is called "plant succession."

Here's an example. After a forest fire destroys an area or an area is clear-cut, new plant life quickly springs up. Annual seeds, blown by the wind, are often first to grow. They take root, hold the soil in place and prevent erosion. This provides suitable soil for grass to grow. When the grass is in place, conditions may be right for shrubs and other small trees to grow. As these grow, they block the sunlight from the grass, making it difficult for the grass to live. Eventually larger trees grow and take over the forest as the "dominant trees." In turn, these trees block even more sunlight from reaching the forest floor. Eventually, not enough sunlight penetrates the overhead leaf cover to allow smaller trees or plants to survive. At this stage, leaves and a fine bed of needles will carpet the forest floor where little else will grow.

Animal Succession

Animals need food, water and shelter for survival. Several different kinds of animals may eat or prey on the same food, but require different shelters. Others may require similar shelter, but different food. Each animal has its own "place" in its community. As trees and plants move through their succession, they provide habitat for different animals. These animals must be able to find their food within the forest to survive.

As the forest changes around them, the animals will change, too. For example, when there is lots of grass and weeds, small bugs and insects will flourish, as will mice and small animals. Birds and animals that prey on these will also multiply, and so on up the food chain. As the forest grows and the sunlight no longer reaches the forest floor the remaining grass will be eaten or die. The small animals and insects that made this their food or home will no longer survive and so on up the chain. When the forest changes, it may no longer be suitable food or habitat for some animals, but it will be just right for others, and they will eventually move into the area.

Watch for areas near your home where you can see this process. Look for an old abandoned farm. In the old farm field, you'll find certain animals. Where trees have begun to grow and have taken over, you'll find different animals; and where fields border the forest, yet another group of animals will live.

These cycles and successions keep nature in balance. Because each plant and animal is dependant on others, they flourish or founder on the "health" of the overall chain of life.

Natural Resources

Webster's Dictionary describes natural resources as "actual and potential forms of wealth supplied by nature, as coal, oil, water power, arable land, etc." Other natural resources include sunlight, minerals, trees, plants, and animals.

Some resources are "renewable" (e.g. sunlight, water, wind, vegetation, crops, trees and animals); others are not.

Non-renewable resources (those that can be entirely used up) include minerals such as iron, copper, aluminum, coal, natural gas and oil.

Even renewable natural resources, if not used wisely, can disappear forever or at least become endangered. Our dependence on these resources grows as our populations rise. We need more space, clean air, food, and energy.

The world is using up its resources quickly, but equally alarming is the growing evidence that manufacturing and refining by-products are harmful to the environment. In fact, very often they harm the air, land and water that we need for survival.

Conservation

Webster's Dictionary describes conservation as "the act or practice of conserving; protection from loss, waste, preservation, etc. The official care, protection or management of natural resources."

Conservation simply means using our natural resources wisely. It means restoring the resources we have abused, such as worn-out soils, and polluted air and water. It means planning for the best use of our resources for the most people for the longest time. Let's all minimize our impact by recycling and reusing products over and over again.

Scouts Canada actively teaches youth and adults to respect the environment. Scouting programs encourage people to practise sound conservation methods enabling us to lessen or minimize the impact we have in our daily lives.

The World Scout Bureau, together with the World Wildlife Fund (WWF), have produced The World Conservation Code.

The World Conservation Code

Each one of us has both the opportunity and the responsibility to care for nature as if our very life depends on it. In fact, it does.

Consciously and unconsciously, we all follow codes of good behaviour. Some are enforced by law; others are unwritten standards of ethics and morality.

Nature, too, deserves our care and respect. The World Wildlife Fund International has proposed the following conservation code. Read it over and adopt it as yours.

▲ I will respect all living things, for each is a link in the chain that supports life on Earth.

▲ I will take from nature only what can be replaced, so no species will disappear.

▲ I will not pollute the air, soil or water.

▲ I will not buy products of endangered animals, plants or forests.

▲ I will keep my neighbourhood clean and will respect the environment wherever I go.

▲ I will call attention to cases of pollution and any other abuse of nature.

▲ I will not waste fuel or energy supplies.

▲ I will set an example of good conservation conduct and show others why it is important for everyone to do so.

▲ I will rejoice in the beauty and wonder of nature all the days of my life.

Now let's have a closer look at some "natural resources" we're likely to encounter during Scouting activities.

Plants

Plants (from mosses and lichens, towering pines) cover the Canadian landscape from coast to coast. Learning about plant life can be both fascinating and useful; it makes hikes and camps more interesting, and sometimes even more comfortable. How? If you know what poison ivy or poison sumac look like, you can avoid them.

Plants are divided into four main groups (called "phyla") ranging in size from microscopic to enormous. Each group has characteristics unique to itself.

Like animals, plants grow, breathe, reproduce and use food. However, most plants make their own food using energy from the sun through a process called *photosynthesis*. Photosynthesis uses the chlorophyll in plants, removes carbon dioxide from the air, and produces oxygen. Without plants, we would not be able to survive. Not only do plants produce oxygen, they also make moisture to keep the water cycle operating; they produce food for us and other animals; they produce medicines and they supply us with materials to clothe and house ourselves.

Plants have adapted so they can live in almost any habitat: water, icy arctic, scorching desert, and temperate soils. When identifying plants, look where they're growing. This provides valuable clues. Then study their size, shape, manner of growth, leaf types, flower colour, seeds or fruits, and more. A nature guide will be invaluable and will increase your enjoyment.

Forests

Trees are one of Canada's most important natural resources. Wood provides many vital products for everyday life. Though we can't replace some resources like copper and petroleum, if forests are managed carefully they are a valuable renewable resource.

Trees cover nearly half of Canada. The variety is great, ranging from Douglas fir and Sitka spruce of the West Coast forests, to maples, birches, spruce, and balsam firs of the East. One hundred and seventy different kinds of trees grow in Canada. Twenty-three softwoods or conifer species (cone-bearing), and 32 hardwood or deciduous (broad leaved) species are commercially useful.

Trees grow from seeds, and tree seeds come in many shapes and sizes (e.g. nuts, acorns, berries and pods). Birds, insects, animals, and even people eat them. Often the seeds are hidden, enclosed inside hard shells as

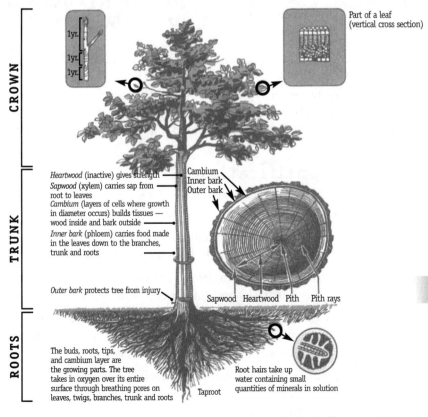

CROWN

Part of a leaf
(vertical cross section)

1yr.
1yr.
1yr.

TRUNK

Heartwood (inactive) gives strength
Sapwood (xylem) carries sap from root to leaves
Cambium (layers of cells where growth in diameter occurs) builds tissues — wood inside and bark outside
Inner bark (phloem) carries food made in the leaves down to the branches, trunk and roots

Outer bark protects tree from injury

Cambium
Inner bark
Outer bark

Sapwood   Heartwood   Pith   Pith rays

ROOTS

The buds, roots, tips, and cambium layer are the growing parts. The tree takes in oxygen over its entire surface through breathing pores on leaves, twigs, branches, trunk and roots

Taproot

Root hairs take up water containing small quantities of minerals in solution in the walnut and beech trees, or between the scale of cones, as in the pine or spruce (evergreens) trees.

Each year, trees produce billions of seeds. Millions of these are gathered, planted, grown into tree seedlings and then transplanted to reforestation areas. Each year, Canadians plant over 55 million trees.

Spring is the best time for tree planting. In past years most planting was by hand; recently machines have taken over the lion's share.

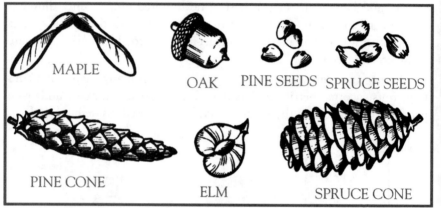

MAPLE

OAK   PINE SEEDS   SPRUCE SEEDS

PINE CONE

ELM

SPRUCE CONE

Why machines?

They're faster than humans. A planting machine can plant about 2,000 trees each day; a human can only plant about 700. Machines, however, can only work where the land is level and free of heavy brush and large stones.

Tree identification
Coniferous (softwoods) Trees

Examples: Spruce, Pine, Cedar

Leaves: Needle-like; remain on the tree for years (except tamarack, which drops its needles each fall).

Buds: Partly or completely surrounded by needles (except tamarack) and cannot be readily seen even in winter.

Wood: Gummy and composed of short fibres. Usually soft and easily worked, although some softwoods may be rather hard and difficult to work.

Fruit: Cone-like with scales; each cone contains many seeds.

Deciduous (Hardwood) Trees

Examples: Maple, Birch, Poplar

Buds: Can be readily seen in winter along the branches when the trees are without leaves.

Wood: Not gummy. Usually hard and difficult to work, although a few are rather soft and easily worked.

Fruit: Various forms; nut-like (acorns), or with wings (maple), or often berry-like. Appears either singly or in small clusters.

Alternate or Opposite?

Hardwood leaves may be alternate (as on a birch), or they may grow opposite each other (as on maple).

Simple or Compound?

Naturalists refer to hardwood leaves as "simple" when only one leaf appears on each stem (as on birch), or as "compound" when several leaflets make up the entire leaf (as on ash). The diagrams at right show a simple leaf and a compound leaf with its many leaflets.

alternate   opposite

simple   compound

How to Use a Tree Key

A "key" helps you easily and quickly identify an unknown object. Tree keys are made showing the similarities and differences between leaves in the summer, and buds or twigs in the winter. To use the key, begin at the word "Start" and proceed through the key following those characteristics which best suit the twig or leaf you are trying to identify. By proceeding step-by-step through the key, you will eventually identify the unknown leaf or twig.

The first time you use this key, take a leaf or twig that you already know, and work your way through the key. If it leads you to the correct name of the tree, then you have used the key properly. The following tree keys only provide definitions for some common trees. For a more complete reference, check your library or local book store for a book on Canadian trees

Summer Key for Hardwood Trees

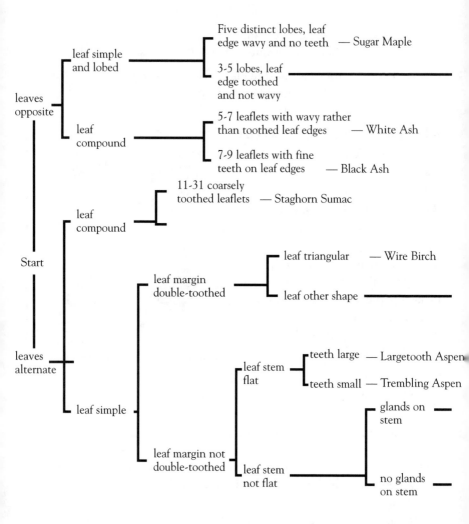

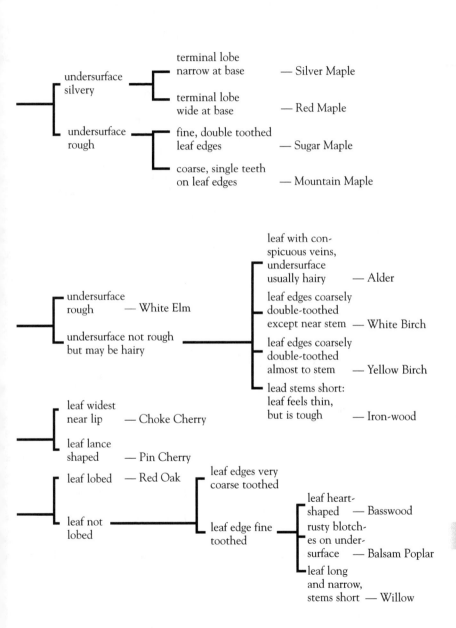

undersurface silvery
- terminal lobe narrow at base — Silver Maple
- terminal lobe wide at base — Red Maple

undersurface rough
- fine, double toothed leaf edges — Sugar Maple
- coarse, single teeth on leaf edges — Mountain Maple

undersurface rough — White Elm

undersurface not rough but may be hairy
- leaf with conspicuous veins, undersurface usually hairy — Alder
- leaf edges coarsely double-toothed except near stem — White Birch
- leaf edges coarsely double-toothed almost to stem — Yellow Birch
- lead stems short: leaf feels thin, but is tough — Iron-wood

leaf widest near lip — Choke Cherry

leaf lance shaped — Pin Cherry

leaf lobed — Red Oak

leaf not lobed
- leaf edges very coarse toothed
- leaf edge fine toothed
  - leaf heart-shaped — Basswood
  - rusty blotches on undersurface — Balsam Poplar
  - leaf long and narrow, stems short — Willow

Summer and Winter Tree Key for Softwoods

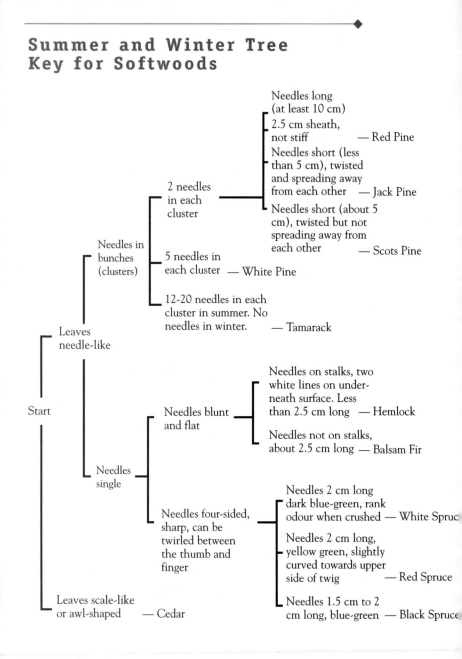

Start

Leaves needle-like

Needles in bunches (clusters)

2 needles in each cluster
- Needles long (at least 10 cm) 2.5 cm sheath, not stiff — Red Pine
- Needles short (less than 5 cm), twisted and spreading away from each other — Jack Pine
- Needles short (about 5 cm), twisted but not spreading away from each other — Scots Pine

5 needles in each cluster — White Pine

12-20 needles in each cluster in summer. No needles in winter. — Tamarack

Needles single

Needles blunt and flat
- Needles on stalks, two white lines on underneath surface. Less than 2.5 cm long — Hemlock
- Needles not on stalks, about 2.5 cm long — Balsam Fir

Needles four-sided, sharp, can be twirled between the thumb and finger
- Needles 2 cm long dark blue-green, rank odour when crushed — White Spruce
- Needles 2 cm long, yellow green, slightly curved towards upper side of twig — Red Spruce
- Needles 1.5 cm to 2 cm long, blue-green — Black Spruce

Leaves scale-like or awl-shaped — Cedar

Wild Flowers

Do you like identifying wild flowers and plants? It's a rewarding and exciting hobby. People today no longer consider wild flowers "just weeds," as they did in the past. Now we understand that they play an important part in the ecological balance and cycle of forests, meadows and woodlands.

Wild flowers and many other plants have four parts to them: roots, leaves, stems, and flowers. Each plays a role when you are identifying the flower.

Wild flowers also have three basic strategies for surviving: annual, biennial and perennial. Annual plants germinate, flower, produce seeds and die, all in one year. Biennial plants germinate and produce leaves one year. The next year they produce a flower and seeds, then die. Perennial plants are different; they germinate, produce flowers and seeds, and grow back the next year. If conditions are right, perennials will grow in the same area for many years.

Identifying wild flowers begins with knowing the flower parts: petals, stamens, pistils and sepals.

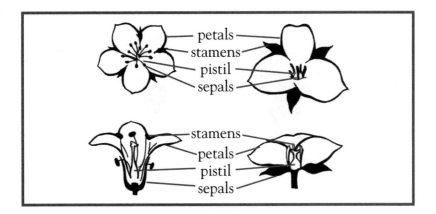

Each province and territory has adopted a special flower that serves as a symbol of that area. The following pictures show the provincial/territorial flowers of Canada.

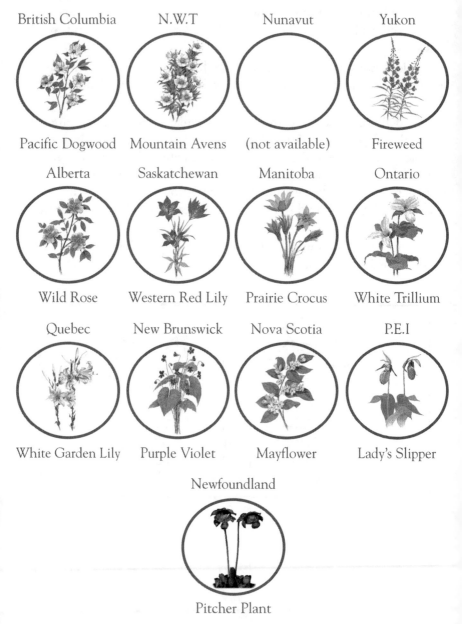

British Columbia — Pacific Dogwood

N.W.T — Mountain Avens

Nunavut — (not available)

Yukon — Fireweed

Alberta — Wild Rose

Saskatchewan — Western Red Lily

Manitoba — Prairie Crocus

Ontario — White Trillium

Quebec — White Garden Lily

New Brunswick — Purple Violet

Nova Scotia — Mayflower

P.E.I — Lady's Slipper

Newfoundland — Pitcher Plant

Mammals

Seeing a mammal, like a deer, bear, otter or fox in its natural habitat, is a rare treat. They just aren't everywhere you look in the outdoors. Mammals use their keen sense of smell, hearing and sight to keep away from human intruders. Some use speed for escape, others use camouflage; some sleep during the day and play only at night.

Mammals have internal skeletons and are warm blooded. Unlike birds, which are covered with feathers, mammals may be covered wholly or in part with hair. Mammals bear their young alive and feed them milk through special glands.

Mammals usually have four limbs with toes that end in claws, nails or hoofs. In some cases, these may take different forms; in dolphins and whales, the front limbs are flippers, while seals have fin-like flippers. Bats are the only mammals that can fly; their front limbs have evolved into wings.

Mammals are placed in groups called "orders" which identify animals with similar characteristics. Some of these similarities include teeth, reproduction and bone structure. There are 19 orders including pouched animals, moles and shrews, bats, flesh eating mammals, seals and sea lions, rodents, hares, rabbits (pikas), hoofed mammals, whales and dolphins.

Whenever you're hiking or camping, always take care of the forest and woodlands. This is home to animals, birds and insects. Your carelessness may destroy it and threaten the continued existence of some living animals.

Little Brown Bat

Body length:	22 cm (including wingspan)
Weight:	8 grams
Food:	Flying insects including moths, beetles, mayflies, mosquitoes (up to 3000 in one night).
Notes:	Primarily nocturnal, bats sleep during the day and hunt during the night. Bats hang upside-down when resting.

Beaver

Body length:	90-130 cm
Weight:	13-34 kg
Food:	Cuts down trees. Eats bark, small branches and pond vegetation.
Notes:	The Beaver is the national emblem of Canada. Its pelt spurred the exploration of Canada. A Beaver's incisors grow continuously. As they grind against each other, they sharpen to a chisel-sharp point.

Black Bear

Body length:	150-180 cm
Weight:	90-125 kg
Food:	Eats almost anything: berries, dead animals, insects, mice, honey, vegetation, acorns and other wild nuts.
Notes:	Bears don't really hibernate in winter; they come out on warm days. Generally they avoid humans unless "conditioned" by easy handouts in national parks.

Coyote

Body height:	110-130 cm
Weight:	10-20 kg
Food:	Small mammals, rodents, birds, eggs, fish, insects. Coyotes will sometimes kill deer and small livestock.
Notes:	Coyotes sometimes howl at night. They will cross-breed with dogs, creating "coy-dogs." The coyote carries its bushy tail low.

White Tailed Deer

Body length: 150-210 cm

Weight: 45-135 kg

Food: It grazes on grass and brush in the summer; gathers in "yards" in winter, eating twigs, sprouts, fruit and crop residues such as corn, wheat or soybeans.

Notes: This deer got its name from the white underside of its tail and buttocks. When startled, it flips its tail over its back and either listens or runs.

Grizzly Bear

Body length: 178-213 cm

Weight: Males 250-350 kg, females 125-175 kg.

Food: Plants and vegetation feature in most of their diet. Grizzlies consume grass, berries, roots, and inner tree bark, as well as some insects and carrion.

Notes: The grizzly is the second largest terrestrial North American carnivore (polar bears are the largest). It has a distinctive hump over the shoulders and extremely long claws.

Moose

Body length: 240-300 cm

Weight: 320-635 kg

Food: In winter, a moose lives on trees and twigs; in summer, it supplements its diet with leaves, plants and water plants.

Notes: Males shed their antlers every winter and grow new ones in the summer. Moose are the largest members of the deer family. An adult male stands taller at the shoulder than the largest saddle horse and eats up to 22 kg of twigs a day in the winter.

Porcupine

Body length:	60-100 cm
Weight:	4-13 kg
Food:	During the winter, porcupines feed on bark and twigs; in summer, they feast on leaves, plants, grasses, and some water plants.
Notes:	Porcupines have thousands of quills which they use as a

defence. More quills grow as they're used. Quills are hollow; this helps the animal to float in water because of the air trapped in its quills.

Racoon

Body length:	60-95 cm
Weight:	5-13 kg
Food:	Racoons will eat almost anything. Their diet ranges from insects, bees, berries, plants, nuts, acorns, to eggs, squirrels, rabbits and freshwater clams.
Notes:	These animals are very distinctive with a black "mask" around

their eyes and rings around their tails. They have dextrous hands. Nocturnal.

Red Fox

Body length:	60-110 cm
Weight:	3-6 kg
Food:	Red foxes eat mice, rabbits, eggs, berries, and carrion.
Notes:	These animals have a thick bushy tail with a

white tip. They are very intelligent and secretive. It's the only fox to range all over Canada. Trappers value its fur which appears in four colours (black, silver, red, white — Arctic).

Red Squirrel

Body length:	25-35 cm
Weight:	140-280 g
Food:	It eats nuts, cones, mushrooms, and berries.
Notes:	Squirrels are tree-dwelling mammals that become very noisy when they spot intruders.

Snowshoe Hare

Body Length:	30-50 cm
Weight:	1-2 kg
Food:	Eats bark, twigs, shrubs
Notes:	Snowshoe hares are usually called rabbits. Their large hind feet act as snowshoes in the winter, allowing them to travel quickly through deep snow. Its fur changes from brown (summer) to white (winter).

Whales

Canada has many different species of whales. They live near Canada's three ocean coasts, as well as in the St. Lawrence River. They vary greatly in size and type, encompassing both threatened and established species.

Wolf

Body length:	15-20 cm
Weight:	26-79 kg
Food:	Wolves prey on large mammals. When these aren't available they eat smaller mammals and birds. Wolves hunt in packs.
Notes:	Wolves often howl at night. They have a highly structured social structure; a dominant male and female wolf act as pack leaders.

Tracks

How to Make a Plaster Cast

It's easy to make plaster casts of animal tracks. All you need is:

▲ Strips of cardboard, 5 or more cm high (to make a collar)

▲ Tape

▲ Plaster of Paris

▲ Container and stir stick

Put the cardboard collar around track. Mix plaster and water together until its texture becomes like thin batter. Pour it at once into the track, 2.5 cm deep. After the plaster hardens, carefully remove the plaster cast from the track. Take off the collar and gently clean the track with a brush and water. Smooth the plaster edges.

This plaster mold creates a "negative cast" and looks just like the animal's actual paw or hoof. Do you want to find interesting tracks? Look near watering holes where animals drink.

Birds

Birds are warm-blooded animals with internal skeletons. Their bodies are wholly or partly covered with feathers. Their young are hatched from eggs; most birds are capable of flying. Hollow or partially hollow bones help lighten the load birds have to carry aloft.

Birds are classified into groups according to similarities in their bills, feet, and wing forms. Before you can identify a bird accurately, you must note its size (e.g. Sparrow, Robin, or Crow size), colouring and habitat.

The following birds are a sampling of those found in Canada. Use a resource book (e.g. *Peterson's Field Guide*) to identify birds in your area.

The following are a few birds you might see:

Land Birds

Black-capped Chickadee

Description: Grey above with a white underside shading to light brownish buff along its flanks. A very distinctive black cap covers its head. Pure white cheek patches and triangular black patch on its throat complete its markings.

Habitat: Chickadees live in flocks in tree-covered areas where they dig their nest holes in soft rotting wood. They don't migrate.

Feeding: As well as being a popular bird at feeding stations, chickadees live on insect eggs, lice, sawflies, spiders and other insects. Their tiny feet allow them to clutch an upright trunk or hang upside down to search for insects. Chickadees are one of the most important pest exterminators of the forest or orchard due to the amount of insects they catch.

Voice: Chickadees make a variety of cheeps and twittering notes. The most familiar call is "chick-a-dee-dee-dee."

Blue Jay

Description: About 30 cm long, it is a vivid blue colour with a crest on its head and a white face. A black band encircles its neck. The bird can raise or lower its crest, indicating the bird's mood.

Habitat: Blue Jays prefer to live in mixed wood forests, especially where it can find nut trees (acorn, beechnuts, hazel nut, etc.). It is comfortable nesting close to buildings. Blue Jays range from the eastern provinces, and across southern parts of Alberta, Saskatchewan, Manitoba and Ontario. They are partial migrators (i.e. they move south from colder regions).

Diet: Blue Jays eat vegetable matter like acorns, nuts, wild fruit, corn and other grains, as well as insects. Blue Jays help control tent caterpillars by feeding hundreds to their young. They also prey on the eggs and young of other birds. Blue Jays will use feeders during winter. Blue Jays will hold a seed or nut between their feet, and hammer on it with their bill to open it and extract the seed. Blue Jays will often hoard food in several places around their territory.

Voice: Blue Jays have an ear splitting screech which signals intruders or predators. They also have a more gentle, musical "kloo-loo-loo" call.

Great Horned Owl

Description: This owl is one of Canada's most common large birds of prey. It has prominent ear tufts or "horns." Enormous yellow eyes are set in a broad face, and it has a curved beak and claws, plus long fluffy feathers.

Habitat: Found throughout Canada, except in far north areas, the Great Horned Owl lives and hunts through all kinds of forests. The bird does not migrate.

Diet: A nocturnal hunter, its night vision and hearing are acute. Its feathers allow it to fly in total silence, and its sharp claws are effective weapons. The bird's large size allow it to hunt a wide range of prey, including shrews, mice, and rabbits, skunks, grouse and geese.

Voice: Listen to its soft hooting ("whoo-hoo-ho-o-o") on silent evenings in the forest.

Downy Woodpecker

Description: The Downy Woodpecker is one of the smallest woodpeckers found in Canada. Measuring only 15-18 cm long, it weighs 22-33 grams. Woodpeckers are able to cling to trees, using their toes to grip, and their long tails as a support against the tree. The Downy Woodpecker is black and white with a broad white stripe down the back from the shoulders to the rump. The breast and thighs are white; cheeks and necks have black and white lines. Their wings have a black and white checkered pattern. The crown of the head is black. Males have a small scarlet spot at the back of their heads. Their bills are long and strong for pecking holes in trees.

Habitat: Downy Woodpeckers live throughout Canada, up to the far north. They stay in Canada year-round but abandon the far north in winter.

Diet: At the start of spring, downy Woodpeckers feed on free-flying and hidden insects found in the bark and hollows of trees. Later in the season, they eat caterpillars, mayflies, moths, and small fruits. The small size of Downy Woodpeckers allow them to hunt insects on small, thin branches in trees.

Voice: This bird uses a variety of calls, including a sharp "tick, tchick, tcherrick." Occasionally, you might hear them drumming with their beaks on dry twigs.

Water Birds

Canada Goose

Description: The Canada Goose has a black head and crown, long black neck, and whitish cheek patches. The rest of the body is elongated, with feathers ranging in colour from pearl grey to dark brown, depending upon the region.

Habitat: The Canada Goose can be found throughout Canada. Most nesting sites are found near water — on islands, lake shores and in marshy areas. This bird's annual migration foretells spring or fall. Canada Geese mate for life.

Diet: Canada Geese thrive on water plants and grasses.

Great Blue Heron

Description: The Great Blue Heron is Canada's largest heron. The birds stand up to one metre high, with long legs, necks and bills. Their heads are white with a black strip on each side that extends from their yellow eyes to slender black plumes off the back of their head. The back is greyish blue, and the breast is white with black streaks.

Habitat: Great Blue Herons populate Canada as far north as Newfoundland and Alaska; however, they fly south in the winter, except for regions in British Columbia. Herons like to nest in tree tops in woodlands that are a few kilometres away from their watery feeding grounds.

Diet: Great Blue Herons feed on small fish, shellfish, reptiles, frogs or amphibians, and sometimes small birds. They have two feeding techniques. One method is for the bird to stand perfectly still in the water, with its neck extended toward the water. When a prey comes close enough, it plunges its head into the water and grasps the prey with its long beak. The other method is to slowly walk through the water, disturbing the prey from its hiding place, and then catching it with its bill. Herons swallow their food out of the water, using a deft movement of their head to flip the catch head first down their gullet. Herons are sociable birds and will share their nesting sites with other smaller herons.

Loons

Description: The Common Loon is quite striking with a black and white checkered back, black head, and white ring around its neck. It has a white belly and wing linings. The bill is quite large and is black. Loons are very streamlined, with their legs set far back on their body, which helps with their diving and swimming. The Loon appears on Canada's $1 coin, affectionately called the "Loonie." Loons have a very well-recognized cry, a wavering call often heard echoing across the water.

Habitat: Loons can be found across Canada and migrate during the winter. Although they nest on land, the nest is close to the water or surrounded by water as on a sedge mat or muskrat house. They generally spend all their time on water.

Diet: Loons are predators, eating fish (suckers, catfish, smelt, minnows), crayfish, snails, salamanders, and leeches. They will sit motionless on the water watching for prey. Once spotted, they dive quickly, frequently chasing their prey through the water. They are excellent swimmers.

Mallard

Description: This duck is one of the most well-known ducks in Canada. The male is distinctive with its head and neck a brilliant green; it has a white collar and dark chestnut on its body. The underparts and sides are a light grey. You might be able to see a light purplish colour in green feathers from some angles. A distinguishing mark seen when flying is a purplish-blue patch at the back of the wing, bordered by faint bars of black and conspicuous ones of white. Female Mallards are brown, with patches and streaks of darker brown. Their legs are more in the centre of their body. This enables them to walk well on land. Mallards sound like barnyard ducks when they quack.

Habitat: Mallards appear throughout Canada, particularly in the Prairies. They prefer fresh water lakes and streams but will nest quite a distance from water. Some Mallards will overwinter in Canada, but most travel to the United States, where they find ice-free water.

Diet: Mallards eat vegetable material, although they will eat small crustaceans, insects and larvae. Mallards eat huge quantities of mosquito larvae. These ducks are "dabblers" — they tip their bottoms up out of the water when they reach down to get food just below the surface. In the water, they feed on weeds and plants that grow in the shallows. They also like to eat barley and wheat.

Fish

Fish are interesting animals. They are cold-blooded, with an internal skeleton. They live in water and breathe through gills, using oxygen dissolved in water. Most fish have two pairs of fins and three single fins. They have eyes on the side of their head and scales on their body. Fish lay eggs in the water.

Fish are classified into four groups:

▲ Those that live in fresh water but spawn in salt water (e.g. eels).

▲ Those that live in salt water only (e.g. blue fish, albacore, or codfish).

▲ Those that live in fresh water (e.g. black bass, pike or channel catfish).

▲ Those that live in brackish water part of the time and fresh water or salt water part of the time (e.g. white perch).

Water temperature, light, the amount of oxygen in the water, differences in chemicals in the water, depth of water, currents, and the amount of silt or other pollution all affect fish. Fish such as trout, need clear, cold water and lots of oxygen. Carp, on the other hand, can live in warm, muddy water with much less oxygen. Most fish have definite temperature requirements for spawning.

Reptiles/Amphibians

Amphibians

Amphibians (e.g. frogs, salamanders, toads and newts) start their life in water or in other moist surroundings in a larval stage. Adult amphibians generally live on land, but some exceptions exist. They generally lay eggs in a jelly-like substance.

Reptiles

Reptiles (e.g. snakes, lizards and turtles) are born or hatched on land. At birth, they appear as tiny copies of their parents. All reptiles have scales, plates or rough shields. They breathe using lungs. Most lay leathery eggs on land, but some give birth to live young.

Both reptiles and amphibians play an important role in the balance of nature and the food chain. Frogs are one of the more valuable amphibians since insects (including black flies and mosquitoes) form the bulk of their diet. Most snakes are harmless, although many are killed needlessly each year because people fear them and don't understand their value. Insects and small rodents make up most of a snake's diet. (Always check with your local wildlife department to see if there are poisonous snakes in your area.)

Amphibians depend on external temperatures for warmth; in Canada, they must hibernate during the winter to escape freezing temperatures. Their skin is moist, even slimy, but toads have dry skin. Because they don't drink water, amphibians absorb moisture through their skin. Their skin also acts as a means of breathing, although they do breathe through nostrils too.

Insects

Insects live and grow everywhere. Scientists have identified more than 600,000 different ones around the world. You can find at least one thousand species in your own area if you look for small insects as well as larger, more obvious ones.

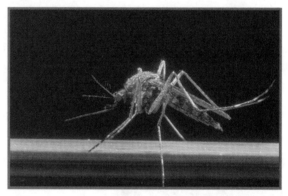

Only a small percentage of insects are harmful to plant life, but these destroy about ten percent of all crops. This costs millions of dollars each year. Other insects (especially those in hot, moist climates) such as mosquitoes, black flies, and ticks can annoy and even infect animals and people.

Insects play an important role in balancing nature. Many songbirds eat nothing but insects; freshwater game fish feed on them, and birds and some mammals make insects a regular part of their diet.

Insects make the rich plant life and wildlife of the world possible. While at times insects can be a nuisance (chemicals are being developed daily to control their populations), insects pollinate flowers which produce the fruits of certain plants. Without insects, we wouldn't have apples, grapes, clover. Without insect pollination, there would be less cotton and fewer oranges and garden vegetables. Some insects help control other insects. They all fit into a balanced ecological system.

An adult insect always has six jointed legs and a jointed body. When not yet an adult, an insect may be a caterpillar, a wood-boring larva, or an underwater creature. When full grown, adult insects have three pairs of legs and three parts to the body: a head, a thorax (or middle section), and an abdomen. Some insects have wings.

All insects begin as eggs, laid by the female in leaves, in the ground or on water. Insects become adults in different ways. Some, such as beetles, butterflies, and moths go through four stages: the egg, the caterpillar (or larva), the cocoon, and adult. In the second stage as a larva, the insect feeds actively and grows. When it reaches a certain size, the larva weaves a cocoon around itself. Within this casing, the larva undergoes tissue changes and finally breaks from the cocoon to emerge as an adult.

Some insects go through three stages only. For example, dragonflies start as eggs laid on water plants. Then they hatch into a nymph which lives underwater and breathes through gills. As the nymph grows, it sheds its skin and grows a new one. When the nymph is full grown, it climbs out of the water, its skin splits open, and the adult insect emerges.

Insects, such as grasshoppers and praying mantis, go through two stages. The eggs hatch into miniature replicas of the adult, and then the insect grows, moults (sheds its skin), grows, and moults until it reaches full growth. Wings appear only on adults, during the last moult. If you see an insect with wings, no matter how small, you will know it is an adult.

Insects have different feeding mechanisms. Butterflies and moths have sucking tubes for taking nectar. Plant lice and squash bugs have sucking beaks with which they get plant sap. Grasshoppers have jaws for chewing leaves, and praying mantises have jaws for eating other insects.

Insects are divided into smaller groups called "orders," using the wings as the marks of distinction. There are eight main orders and a few minor ones. About 90 percent of the insects you will find belong to the eight major orders. These are:

Bees and Wasps

These insects are important for pollination. Bees also produce honey from plant nectar. Other insects in this group include ants, sawflies, and ichneumons. The most highly developed insects are in this category.

Butterflies and Moths

The most often seen butterfly is the Monarch with its distinctive black and yellow markings. The attractive patterns on these insects are produced by the tiny shingle-like scales on their wings that rub off when you handle them.

Flies

These insects are the most common pest of animals and humans. Mosquitoes, houseflies, fruit flies, botflies, midges, and robber flies belong to this group. Maggots are the larvae of flies.

True Bugs

These insects have a sucking beak; their wings fold flat over their backs. True bugs include water striders, giant water bugs, chinch bugs, ambush bugs, squash bugs, stinkbugs and bedbugs.

Grasshoppers and Crickets

These insects have mouth parts formed for chewing plant materials. Mantises (also part of this group) eat other insects.

Dragon Flies

These are strong flying insects that eat other insects captured while on the wing. Some dragon flies may live as long as three years as underwater nymphs before emerging as adults.

Relatives

The following creatures are not true insects but are close relatives.

Millipedes

These are found in damp places and usually in decaying vegetation. They have two pairs of legs on most of their body segments. They range in size from 2 mm to as much as 10 cm.

Centipedes

These non-insects have long antennae and one pair of legs on each segment of their body. They have claws behind their head to kill their prey. They eat insects and spiders.

Spiders

Spiders differ from insects in that they have four pair of legs and two body segments. All spiders can spin webs to protect their eggs or to capture insects as food.

Crayfish

These distant relatives of insects live in damp meadows or water. They may be from 7 cm to 15 cm long, have a hard outer shell with five pairs of legs and claws on the front pair to catch food.

> **Water: It's a Precious Resource**
>
> Water can be stored on or in the ground. Oceans, ponds, rivers, lakes, swamps and marshes can hold water on the surface (called "surface water"). All water below the Earth's surface is called "ground water."

Interesting Trivia

Oceans cover roughly three-quarters of the Earth's surface. This incredible water supply is only useful for limited applications because it is so salty.

Fastest Mammals

Cheetah: Fastest land mammal over a short distance. May run at speeds of 100 km/h per hour for 180-270 metres.

Pronghorn: Fastest land mammal over a long distance. Can run 55-70 km per hour for 6 km, and can reach speeds of 90 km/h for shorter distances.

Killer Whale: Fastest marine mammal over a short distance. Can sometimes swim up to speeds of 55 km per hour for about 450 metres.

Largest Mammals

Blue Whale: Largest animal in the world, also the largest animal that's ever lived. May grow to more than 30 metres long and weigh more than 135 tons.

Giraffe: Tallest land mammal (6 metres high).

African Elephant: Largest land mammal. This elephant may stand more than 3.2 metres tall at the shoulder and weigh more than 6 tons.

Best Jumpers

Red Kangaroo: Can jump more than 12 metres in one bound and can jump more than 3 m high.

Jerboa: Can broad jump up to 3 metres in a single bound. (Jerboa's bodies may be only 12.5 cm long!)

Cougar: Can jump 5 metres high and can broad jump 9 meters.

Best Breath Holders

Sperm Whale: Can hold its breath for one hour and 15 minutes.

Weddell Seal: Can hold its breath up to one hour.

Fastest Fliers

Swifts: Can fly at speeds over 180 km/h.

Fastest Bird that Swims

Penguins: Can swim at over 50 km/h.

Tallest Bird

Ostriches: Can stand over 2.2 metres tall and weigh over 155 kilograms.

Smallest Bird

Bee Hummingbirds: Are only 5 cm long.

Smallest Egg

A Hummingbird's egg: Is smaller than the smallest jelly bean.

Largest Egg

An Ostrich egg: Is up to 15 cm long.

Largest Wingspan

The Wandering Albatross: Has a 3.5 metre wingspan.

CHAPTER ▶ 16
▶ Cycling

A gorgeous sunny day. A gentle breeze in your face. Stirring sounds of nature. And you and your friends zooming up a trail on mountain bikes or pounding out the pavement on a cycling road trip. The adventurous world of cycling beckons to you!

Cycling is one of the most popular activities in Canada. Not only do people ride for fun and leisure, but hundreds of thousands bike to work or school as well. Many city streets include bicycle-only lanes, and some Canadian cities have bike racks on buses to accommodate those wanting a "combined commute."

Road biking, track biking and mountain biking are Olympic sports. In fact, mountain biking is one of the fastest growing sports and leisure activities in the world.

Cycling (of any kind) is a great activity for everyone. It promotes fitness, environmental awareness and safety.

When planning a cycling activity, you need to consider several factors, including equipment, safety, cost and skill.

Buy the Right Bike

Buy a bike in the same way as you would buy new camping equipment. Visit lots of stores. Check out web sites from bike and part manufacturers. Pick up buyer's guides. But… before you research bikes, *research yourself*.

Why do you want a bike? What kind of riding do you plan? On-road? Off-road? Heart-pumping aerobic training? Single-track trail rides? Rocketing down some terrifying downhill run? Busy city commutes?

Many types of bikes are available; each has its own strengths and weaknesses.

Road Bike

Road bikes are generally lightweight — just great for riding on dry pavement. They have curved (down-turn) handle-bars to help put you in an aerodynamic riding position. Most road bikes have 10-16 gears. They are light and fast, but their thin tires are only suitable for very smooth, hard, dry surfaces. Don't plan any off-road adventures with this bike; it's not designed for it. However, it's perfect if you're looking to pound out lots of pavement kilometres for a great aerobic workout.

Touring Bike

These bikes have the same basic shape as road bikes but with a sturdier (heavier) frame and thicker tires. These are good for long trips on pavement. They offer light weight and speed, but the thicker tires will give you better handling and won't go flat as easily. These bikes are excellent for long road tours (hence the name).

Mountain Bike

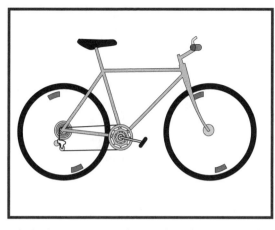

If you're looking for off-pavement riding on dirt roads and trails, you can't beat a good mountain bike. These bikes feature very sturdy frames and a wide range of gears (18-24). Whether you're racing across a level, straight trail or struggling up a steep rocky pathway, you'll always find the right gear. Thick, knobby tires will help keep you on the trail and rarely go flat. (You might want to add a pair of slick tires to turn your mountain bike into a sleek street machine.)

Many mountain bike models include front suspension forks and/or rear suspension for a cushier ride. But, unless you're planning to tackle some tough trails, save your money (and the extra bicycle weight suspension carries) and go with a traditional rigid fork.

Hybrid Bike

Popular in the late '80s and early '90s, hybrid bikes are lighter mountain bike frames with thinner tires. Hybrids are perfect for commuting on city streets, but won't be very manoeuvrable on trails — especially on wet, muddy rides.

Size Is Important!

Whatever type of bike you decide to buy, proper sizing is imperative. People often mistakenly get bikes that are too big for them. Make sure you "try on" a new bike before buying it. You should be able to stand over the top tube with 7-10 cm (3-4 ") clearance. When you're on the saddle (seat), you should be able to comfortably have your hands on the handlebars with your body on a 45-degree angle. The handlebars should be about 5 cm below your saddle.

Don't Forget Accessories

Scores of different accessories are available that will make bike riding safer, easier and more enjoyable. Browse through a local store. Even this is fun!

Lights

In many areas, bikes must have front and/or rear lights. It's the law. If you plan to do any riding in twilight, dark or dusk hours, make sure you use lights. You'll stay visible and be able to see better.

Bell

A working bell (or some other sounding device) will help warn pedestrians or other cyclists about your presence and intentions. Several Canadian cities require a bell on every bicycle. Don't be afraid to use your voice when approaching a pedestrian or cyclist. In fact, a friendly greeting and, "Passing on the left," statement is often more effective than ringing a bell.

Water Bottles

Dehydration can become a serious problem during a long, hot ride. Make sure you take plenty of fluids. A simple water bottle works well, or, if you want easier access to refreshments on long rides, consider a self-hydration system (e.g. Camelback™). This consists of a bladder you wear on your back with a tube running over your shoulder to a spot near your mouth. You fill the bladder with fluid (water, sports drinks, etc.), and when you're thirsty, simply put the tube in your mouth and suck. This system lets you carry more fluids, and drink them much easier — especially important during a long distance race. These are suitable for backpacking as well.

Locks

Bicycle thefts are rampant in North America. If you plan to leave your bike unattended anywhere, bring a good lock along; otherwise, you're tempting fate.

The best lock is a long U-lock. If you have quick-release hubs on your wheels, take your front wheel off, place it beside the rear wheel, then lock the two wheels through the frame onto a bicycle rack or stand. If you have a quick-release seat, take it with you when you leave.

Saddlebags

Are you bringing lots of things with you on a bike ride? If yes, consider buying a set of saddlebags (also called panniers) or some other pack that attaches to your bike. Wearing a backpack while riding is not only uncomfortable but potentially unsafe. Straps hanging down off your pack could get caught in your bike's wheels and/or brakes. A heavy pack may also throw you off balance at a critical moment. If you must strap on a pack during a ride, make it a low-riding fanny pack.

Tool Kit

At any time your bike may require emergency repairs or quick adjustments. Be sure you have a basic tool kit for these unexpected moments.
Your kit should include:

▲ A pump (frame-mounted is best). Make sure you have the right
   valve attachment — Schrader (like a car's tires), or Presta
   (narrower valve).

▲ A spare tube (with the right size and valve).

▲ Three tire levers.

▲ Patch kit.

▲ Allen keys (4 mm, 5 mm, 6 mm). They're useful if you need
   to adjust your brakes, handlebars, or seat.

▲ Six inch crescent wrench.

▲ Universal spoke tool (to tighten spokes).

▲ Screwdriver.

Computer

If you just can't ride without knowing how fast you're going and how far you've gone, get a computer for your bike. Computers range from the basic (speedometer/odometer), to "Cadillac" models (speedometer/odometer, average speed, trip distance, heart-rate monitor, cappuccino maker, stock market ticker, etc.).

Helmet

Wear a CSA-approved helmet when you ride. It's the law in many parts of Canada; it also makes common sense. Wear the helmet low enough that it covers much of your forehead.

Maintenance

A well-maintained bike is the first step toward safe, fun and reliable riding. Three "keys" to outstanding maintenance are: clean, inspect, and lubricate. If you ride your bike regularly, take some time for simple maintenance once a week.

A bicycle repair stand makes maintenance easier and speeds the process. If you don't have one, lean your bike against a wall or railing while you work on it.

Get Clean!

Use a rag to wipe your bike down, or wash it with a brush and mild detergent. Take another rag, spray it with a lubricant, and wipe each component (derailleur, crank set, brakes, etc.). Wipe your tires and rims with a clean, dry rag, then wipe your chain clean.

Inspect

While you're cleaning your bike, keep an eye out for developing trouble spots. Inspect your frame for cracks. Check for loose bolts on components, then inspect your wheels. Watch for loose spokes. Spin the wheel to make sure it's "in true" (no major wobbles). Check for loose bearings by trying to wiggle the rim. (The rim should have no loose play.) Examine your tires to make sure they have no foreign objects embedded in them that could cause a flat. Check also for bulges and cuts. Make sure your tires are inflated to the correct pressure.

Test your brake levers and your shifters, and then check your brake pads to make sure they're hitting the rim properly. You don't want the pads hitting too close to the tire (or the spokes).

Lubricate

A well-oiled chain will deliver a smoother ride. After you've wiped the chain clean, apply a lubricant.

Is your chain really dirty and encrusted with sand or grit? You might need to remove the chain and immerse it in solvent to properly clean it before lubricating.

"Oh No. A Flat!"

Sometime in your cycling life, you'll get a flat at the *worst* possible time — guaranteed! Make sure an unexpected flat doesn't ruin your cycling experience; master the art of quickly repairing flats and changing tubes. It's easy.

Always Carry Your Repair Kit and A Pump

▲   When you get a flat, move a safe distance away from the road or trail, and remove the damaged tire. (A quick-release hub will save you lots of time.)

▲   Insert the flat end of a tire lever between the tire bead and rim, about 5 cm from the valve. Pry off the bead by pulling *down* on the lever and hooking it onto a spoke. Insert a second lever about 5 cm on the other side of the valve. Then using a third lever, pry the beads off the rim at 10 cm intervals. You only need to remove the beads from one side of the tire.

▲   Starting opposite the valve, pull the tube from the tire. Now, remove the valve from the rim.

▲   Find the leak on the tube by inflating it and listening for escaping air. To confirm, rub a bit of saliva on the spot. If there's a leak, the saliva will bubble up.

- ▲ Match the leak in the tube to the corresponding area of the tire. Inspect that area of the tire for damage or embedded foreign objects. Make sure its damage-free before you install a new tube. If you forget, you may just have to repeat your efforts.

- ▲ Inflate a new (or repaired) tube until it begins to take some shape.

- ▲ Insert the valve into the rim.

- ▲ Work the tube back into the tire making sure the tube doesn't twist and develop kinks. This will cause a "pinch flat."

- ▲ Using only your hands, work the tire back onto the rim, starting at the valve. When it becomes too difficult, completely deflate the tube and finish the job.

- ▲ When the tire is back on the rim, inflate the tube. Spin the wheel to make sure there are no bulges or dips. If there are, deflate the tube and rework the tire back onto the rim.

Fixing a Tube

It's usually faster and easier to install a new tube rather than repair an old one. But, on the trail, you might not have a readily-available new tube. Here's how to repair an old one.

- ▲ Rub sandpaper over the area around the leak.

- ▲ Apply a thin coat of glue to the sanded area, and let dry.

- ▲ Peel the backing off the patch and apply it.

- ▲ Inflate and re-install the tube.

Practise repairing tubes and tires before you get on the road so you'll be ready when a flat happens for real. Remember: Flats are inevitable.

Depending on your knowledge and expertise, you might want to perform other maintenance on your bike (truing wheels, changing brake pads, repacking bearings, etc.). If you plan to do the work yourself, pick up a good bike maintenance book or take a course. (Many shops offer good ones.) Before starting work on an expensive new bike, you might want to hone skills on a trashed bike you rescue from a junkyard.

If you're not sure you can handle a job, ask a professional bike mechanic to do it. A safe, reliable bike is important. Never leave it to chance.

Rules of the Road

Whether you're leisurely riding on a neighbourhood street or commuting through crazy downtown traffic, you need to practise safe cycling. Bike accidents can happen quickly and suddenly. (A bike will always lose in a crash with a car!) Did you know that most bike accidents occur near home and on streets with speed limits of 50 kph or less?! Follow these simple rules *every* time you're on the road. They'll make your cycling experience safe and enjoyable.

1. Never ride without a helmet.

2. Ride *with* traffic, not facing it.

3. Ride approximately one metre away from a curb or row of parked cars. This way you won't need to swerve away from obstacles (e.g. sewers, car doors, pedestrians).

4. Be predictable. Don't make unexpected turns or manoeuvres on your bike. Make sure cars and pedestrians around you know what you're going to do.

5. Use hand signals. Hold your left arm out straight pointing left to make a left turn signal. Stick your left arm out but bent up vertically from the elbow to make a right turn signal. Indicate a slowing or stopping signal by holding your left arm straight out, bent down vertically from the elbow.

6. Scan all around before making any turn or lane change.

7. Obey all traffic laws. Some cyclists think that, because they're only riding their bike, they can "run" stop lights and stop signs and break the law. Bicyclists are subject to the same laws (and fines) as other road vehicles.

8. Know what all traffic signs mean.

Rules of the Trail

Here are some mountain biking rules to follow for a safe and enjoyable ride.

1. Watch for others on the trail. Hikers and other mountain bikers may appear anywhere. Be careful when approaching corners and blind spots.

2. Welcome others on the trail with a friendly greeting. Share information with them about the trail you're on (tough parts, great views, obstacles, etc.).

3. Always yield to hikers.

4. Never trespass. Stay off private property.

5. Stay on the trail. Don't veer off into uncharted territory.

6. Leave wildlife alone. Give animals a wide berth. Wait for them to leave the trail.

7. Don't litter. Pack out what you pack in.

8. Stay off trails that are designated "hikers only."

9. Stick to trails you can handle. Don't race off on an "expert" trail if you're a beginner. Gradually develop your skills before you tackle the tough trails.

10. Bike with a friend or group, never alone.

11. Bring a good trail map.

12. Leave word with someone about your route and estimated return time.

13. Don't ride on very wet and muddy trails. Wait for trails to dry out before you start riding. Rocketing through mud may seem like fun, but it's hard on the trail and your bike.

Follow these tips and you'll really enjoy biking adventures.

You can incorporate cycling into almost any Scouting activity. It could be a mountain biking meeting night, or a week-long (or weekend) cycling road trip. (Some groups cycle across Canada to Canadian jamborees!) When participating in a long-term cycling activity, be sure to follow the basic rules around camping, field trips and outdoor activities.

Whether it's a leisurely ride on a paved bike path, a long road tour to a far-off destination, or a wild adventure on mountain trails, you'll find fun, fitness and adventure on your bicycle.

CHAPTER **17**

▶ **The Stars**

For thousands of years, people have looked up into the night sky and been filled with wonder, fear and excitement. Sailing through space, countless stars provided a magnificent spectacle. For many of our ancestors, the night sky became a source of mystery as they searched for answers to questions about where they came from, and where they might be going.

The stars provided ancient societies with religious symbols, and helped travelers find their ways to distant lands. As science developed, its theories offered new insights how Earth and our solar system were possibly created.

Often people grouped stars into figures or "constellations." The name comes from Latin: "con" (meaning: together), and "stella" (meaning: stars). The practice probably goes back to times when shepherds spent many nights under the stars watching sheep or tending cattle. In much the same way that people sometimes see shapes of animals or other figures in clouds, the ancient Greeks and Romans "saw" their mythical heroes, kings and queens, gods and goddesses, and even monsters in stars.

Get Starry-Eyed

When is the best time to study stars?

Any night without clouds or smoke to obscure your vision provides perfect conditions for star-gazing. You can study stars at any time of year;

both summer and winter offer abundant opportunities to watch them course across the sky. Stars usually seem brighter in the country for two reasons: no street lights dim their brilliance, and less pollution covers the heavens with haze.

Stars appear to make a complete turn around the Earth every 24 hours, in the same direction as the sun (east to west). But stars aren't really moving; it's the Earth revolving on its axis. Since the Earth also moves around the sun, star schedules change by about four minutes every night. Stars 'rise' four minutes earlier each night. One year later, they rise again at the same time as the previous year. As the seasons progress, you'll see different stars in the sky overhead. Stars directly to the *North* will be the same, but those above the North Star in one season will be *below* the North Star at the same hour of the evening six months later.

The North Star and Related Constellations

A good starting point for star-gazing, the Big Dipper leads to several other constellations. The Big Dipper (a group of eight stars found in the northern sky) is the best known constellation. Four stars form the bowl of the dipper, and four make up the handle.

Sometimes you'll see only three stars in the handle, but the second star of the handle is really two: a big star and a little one.

Use the pointers of the Big Dipper — the two stars farthest from the handle — to guide you to the North Star (or Pole Star, also called Polaris). The North Star forms the end of the Little Dipper's handle. The Latin name for the constellation that includes the Big Dipper is Ursa Major

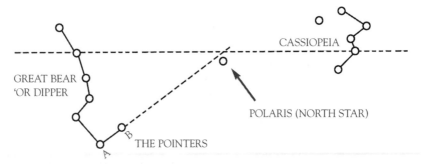

(Big Bear). Ursa Minor (Little Bear) includes the grouping of stars known as the Little Dipper. Between the two dippers dangles the Dragon (or Draco), a long wandering line of not-too-bright stars.

If you go back to the Big Dipper again and move from the pointers through the North Star in a curved line across the sky, you will meet a crooked "W" formed by five stars. This is Cassiopeia, the Queen. Nearby is her husband, King Cepheus, who looks like a square house with a triangular roof.

To find the fifth constellation, imagine a line intersecting the line between the Big Dipper and Cassiopeia, with the midpoint being the North Star. In one direction along this line (the same direction in which the handle of the Big Dipper lies), you will find a bright star which seems to have a rectangle of four smaller stars hanging from it. The bright star is Vega, in the constellation Lyra, or the Lyre.

In the opposite direction of the North Star is another bright star, Capella, with three faint ones nearby. This is the sixth constellation — the she-goat with three kids. This group belongs to a larger constellation, Auriga (or the Charioteer), which appears as a rather vague, five-sided figure.

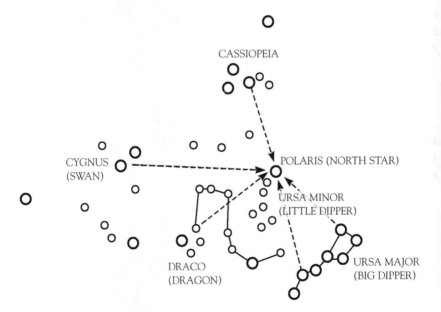

These seven constellations close to the North Star appear in the sky year-round. At times Vega dips under the northern horizon when Capella is high in the sky, and vice versa, because of the stars' courses.

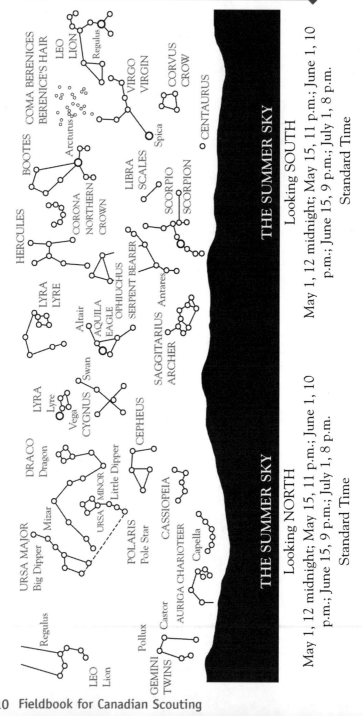

THE SUMMER SKY

Looking NORTH

May 1, 12 midnight; May 15, 11 p.m.; June 1, 10 p.m.; June 15, 9 p.m.; July 1, 8 p.m.

Standard Time

THE SUMMER SKY

Looking SOUTH

May 1, 12 midnight; May 15, 11 p.m.; June 1, 10 p.m.; June 15, 9 p.m.; July 1, 8 p.m.

Standard Time

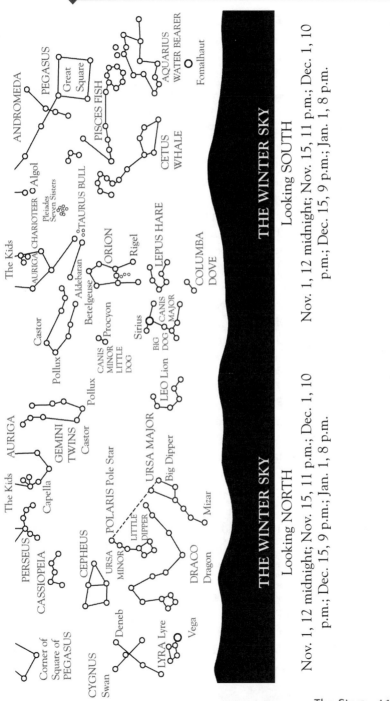

THE WINTER SKY

Looking NORTH

Nov. 1, 12 midnight; Nov. 15, 11 p.m.; Dec. 1, 10 p.m.; Dec. 15, 9 p.m.; Jan. 1, 8 p.m.

THE WINTER SKY

Looking SOUTH

Nov. 1, 12 midnight; Nov. 15, 11 p.m.; Dec. 1, 10 p.m.; Dec. 15, 9 p.m.; Jan. 1, 8 p.m.

Summer Stars

On a summer's evening, locate the stars which swing around the North Star: the Dippers, Cassiopeia, Vega and Capella. This time follow the North Star until you locate the sickle-shaped Lion (Leo) with the star Regulus. Between the Lion and Capella are the two twins, Castor and Pollux, also known as Gemini. Between Capella and Cassiopeia lies the three-angled figure of Perseus. Between Cassiopeia and Vega, five stars form a wide cross: the Swan (Cygnus) or the Northern Cross.

Starting again from the Big Dipper, follow the curved line of the handle until you reach Arcturus, the brightest star in a constellation which looks like a big kite. This is called Bootes, the Herdsman. Next to the Herdsman, you can make out a half-circle of dim stars; this is the Corona, or Northern Crown. Continuing, you will see Hercules (shaped like a lop-sided "H"), and then find yourself at Vega.

Looking south, right in front of you hovers Scorpius, the Scorpion. Its tail swings toward the horizon while its head points toward Spica — the bright star of the "Y"-shaped Virgo, the Virgin. Behind the Scorpion, you'll find Sagmartus, the Archer, almost buried in the Milky Way. Above him flies Aquila, the Eagle. This constellation does actually look like a bird with its wings spread. The brightest star of the Eagle is Altair which, with Vega and Deneb in the Northern Cross, form a brilliant triangle.

Winter Stars

On a winter's evening, start again from the Big Dipper and follow the pointers through the North Star and Cassiopeia until you strike a line of three stars: Andromeda. The star at one end of the line, with three more, forms the famed Pegasus square. The other end of Andromeda points toward Perseus (almost overhead).

The finest group of stars in the winter sky is Orion to the south. Two bright stars make up his shoulders, three small ones form his triangular head, and two more his legs. Three stars are his belt, and three more his sword. After drawing a line through Orion's belt, you come to the red star, Aldebaran, the "eye" in the "V"-shaped head of Taurus, or the Bull. Continuing further, you will find the Pleiades or Seven Sisters. If you have good eyesight, you can count six. With a telescope, you can see more than two hundred! Starting again with Orion, follow the line through his belt in the opposite direction until you hit Sirius, which, next to the sun, is the brightest star in the sky.

Other Phenomena

Meteors or "shooting stars," as some people call them, are not stars at all but bodies of minerals and metals flying through the universe. When the Earth gets close to their paths, it attracts them. As they fall through Earth's atmosphere, they heat up to such a point that they appear as bright streaks, and the high friction temperature almost entirely consumes them. Pieces of meteors which land on Earth are called meteorites; these usually contain large amounts of iron.

Comets are large balls of ice, rocks, and other space debris which travel through space in very large orbits around a sun. As a comet get closer to our sun, it forms a tail, creating a streak in the sky. Most comets have very long orbits and appear infrequently. Halley's Comet is a very famous one; it appears every 76 years. Another, Comet Kohoutek, which appeared in 1974, will not be seen again because its orbit takes it far out into deep space.

Many other interesting discoveries await our exploration of the sky and space. Astronauts have landed on the moon, have built laboratories to orbit the Earth and have used space shuttles to repair satellites. The universe holds many unsolved puzzles that the ancients (as well as our own minds) couldn't even begin to grasp. Space forms a vast frontier beckoning us onward.

INDEX

PHOTO CREDITS

Scouts Canada would like to thank the following photographers for their pictures:

Wayne Barrett	400
Jim Dicker	348
Ross Francis	v
Len Godwin	iv, 149, 157, 158, 168, 169, 170, 172, 177, 184, 186
Allen Macartney	i, 5, 21, 22, 24, 25, 26, 27, 28, 29, 34, 36, 37, 46, 47, 51, 54, 56, 63, 74, 76, 81, 82, 83, 85, 87, 88, 89, 91, 92, 106, 115, 117, 119, 121, 141, 153, 182, 197, 217, 226, 271,407
Anne MacKay	243
Anthony Scullion	ii, 1, 2, 3, 4, 6, 7, 17, 27, 48, 50, 61, 78, 95, 96, 103, 123, 124, 128, 146, 251, 276, 280, 281, 282, 285, 292, 293

NOTES